ACCLAIM

"This beautiful collection showcases the weight and glory of those who wear, protect, or even create the crown. From traditional royals to sci-fi nobles, and fantasy princesses to world-jumping lovers, *Crowns* will no doubt sweep you off your feet. With striking prose, humor, depth, and vivid landscapes, I found myself immersed in each unique world and the characters that lived and breathed within them."
—EMILY BARNETT, award-winning author of the short story *Sky Rays* and the upcoming novel *Thread of Dreams*

"*Crowns* is a delightful collection with a sharp edge. It perfectly balances the beauty of royalty with the danger of power."
—NATHANIEL LUSCOMBE, author of *Moon Soul*

"For fans of happily ever afters and true love, *Crowns* is a heart-throbbing, swoon-worthy collection of beautiful stories. From far-off lands to modern day settings and futuristic worlds, the adventures in this anthology will leave your heart full and a smile on your face."
—V. ROMAS BURTON, award-winning author of the Heartmaker trilogy and The Legacy Chapters series

"Nobility, courage, self-sacrifice...these are the themes explored in Brigitte Cromey's precious, deep-hearted novella. When two characters are so determined to do what is right and good, can they make room in their lives to allow a childhood affection to blossom into romance? We live in dark times, and desperately need stories like these to help us find the light of hope. This is a tale after my own heart, and I will read it again and again in the days to come."
—AMBER KIRKPATRICK, author of *Until the Rising* and *Unleashed*

"Such an amazing page-turner filled with absolutely everything I love—political intrigue, princess/bodyguard romance, and swoony moments that keep drawing me back to read them again and again. This story [*Guardian's Oath*] is sure to please fans of Tara Grayce and K.M. Shea."
—BRYN SHUTT, author of *Illuminare*

"*Guardian's Oath* is a delicious blend of adventure, magic, and heart. Brigitte Cromey crafted a lovely story perfect for fans of childhood friends-to-more, forbidden love, and royal romance. Readers will find themselves rooting for the characters as they evade danger within their own borders, as well as their feelings for one another. This novella is a shining jewel in the *Crowns* anthology."
—CRYSTAL D. GRANT, author of *Shadowcast*

CROWNS

A Heartbooks Anthology

Crowns

Quill & Flame
PUBLISHING HOUSE

Edited by
Brittany Eden & Brigitte Cromey

Quill & Flame
PUBLISHING HOUSE

Crowns

Published by Quill & Flame Publishing House, an imprint of Book Bash Media, LLC.

www.quillandflame.com

DEDICATION

Something softer in her petals
Something brighter in her colors
Something sweeter in her scent
Something stronger in her stem
Something lighter in her carriage
Something heavier in her depth
Something wiser in her veins
Something deeper in her roots
Something different, something similar
Something lovely
Daughters of the King,
you are flowers of beauty

TABLE OF CONTENTS

Guardian's Oath by Brigitte Cromey.......1
Flight or Fight by Kaitlyn Carter Brown.......138
A Marriage of Inconvenience: Part One by Robin Rakkeby.......148
All in Jest by Annee Clark.......165
A Marriage of Inconvenience: Part Two by Robin Rakkeby.......171
Green Gloves by Katie Fitzgerald.......186
The Cottage Court Charlatan by Hannah Carter.......193
Callisto Falls by C. Ash.......205
The Queens Under Glass by Danielle Robertson.......216
The Disheveled King, a poem by Anne J. Hill.......229
Lessons of Kingship by Amber Kirkpatrick.......233
There Was a King, a poem by Amelia E. Clawford.......238
Runaway Princess, a photo from Marie Lynch.......241
Oasis by Kristen Bazen.......243
Thirst, a poem by Brittany Eden.......255
The Light We Need by Liz Koetsier.......259
Danish Crown, a photo from Sarah Harmon.......270
Crown Jewels by Hope Bolinger.......272

Queening by Hailey Huntington.......275
Checkmate by Megan Miles.......281
The Princess is Buying Stabby Things by Yakira Goldsberry.......286
Elven Princess, art by Ruth Lumpkin.......301
Royally Imperfect by J.M. Hackman.......303
Once and Future by Abigail Falanga.......328
A Collision of Fate, a poem by Sara Anderson.......334
Mosaic by Ava Lauren Grayson.......336
The Weight of Worlds by Abby Johansen.......340
Through The Looking Glass, a photo from Shannon Alldredge.......362
Heavy is the Head by AJ Skelly.......364
Knots and Tangles by S.M. Jake.......369
The Crownmaker's Curse: Part One by Cassandra Hamm.......377
Crowns of Consequence, a poem by Brooke J. Katz.......395
The Crownmaker's Curse: Part Two by Cassandra Hamm.......399
New Life in Old Places, a photo from Benjamin Cromey.......419
Author biographies.......422

CROWNS

GUARDIAN'S OATH

Brigitte Cromey

In this fantasy romance novella, Princess Talianna and Sir Gavin of Andel are bound to their oaths, but fulfilling them may cause their own hearts to break.

BEFORE

THE PRINCESS'S FIRST UNDERSTANDING OF THE MATTER came after a playfellow's innocent question. "Why don't you have any cousins?"

Her nurse, upon the repetition of the question that evening, cupped her charge's face in her soft hand and stared into the princess's eyes for a long moment. It was difficult, explaining the weight of it to a girl who was barely old enough to understand. "Come with me, Tali." Her other hand stayed around the girl's as they went to the study, where she pointed to an embroidered wall hanging beside the fireplace. "You see?" Her wrinkled finger caressed the stitching, tracing down the names of Talianna's forebears until she came to a long, unbroken line—a tree with no branches, ending in a single name.

Talianna Victoria Marie. Princess of the house of Emrys.

"You, little one, are the only daughter of an only son." The nurse knelt beside Talianna and hugged her shoulders. "The only child of your line. And one day, sweet"—she raised the child's hand to her lips, little realizing how well her charge was listening—"you'll be queen."

That night, after her nursemaid had put her to bed, Talianna lay awake for hours, the burden of expectations and responsibility settling on her eight-year-old shoulders.

She finally whispered her promise into the darkness, the creaking trees beyond her windows the only witnesses to the vow. *If this is to be my life, I will study hard and listen well to become the queen they all expect me to be.*

"So do I swear."

Ten years later, Talianna stood atop the dais on a darkened spring evening. By then, the lonely years had acquainted her with the particulars of the matter—with no siblings and a mother long bereft of strength, the weight of the crown would fall upon her head, and hers alone. It was a fact not lost on the enemies of the realm, and the last few years had seen increasing threats to her safety. On this night, a week after an assassination attempt had claimed the lives of both her history tutor and guard captain, the faces of the few advisors around the dais were drawn with worry.

The young man who now knelt before the king had been the subject of much discussion by the court, the ink of his appointment not even dry before the gossips began whispering.

A knight, recently reassigned from a border posting.

Second son of a baron—barely nobility at all.

Hardly worthy of the position, but not many would accept a role that equated to well-paid servitude and a constant threat of death.

Young. Too young, this 'Gavin of Andel'.

Once Talianna had heard the name, memory sketched in the remainder with painful clarity. She'd once known Gavin's laugh, green eyes, and companionable nature as well as she knew her own reflection, before duty and study had driven them both from childhood games. His hair had once been the color of sunlight, but the years had tarnished it to a dull blond, made darker by the shadows creeping through the edges of the hall as he swore his oath.

"I, Sir Gavin of Andel, do solemnly swear to guard the princess Talianna to the fullest of my ability. May the blows of those who seek to cause her harm fall upon my head. May her enemies be my enemies, her danger my danger, and her life my life." The knight raised his head to look her in the eye, and a flicker of a smile crossed his face before retreating behind solemnity. "This do I swear, until my king releases me from my oath or I perish in the fulfillment of my duty."

Talianna extended her hand for her new protector to kiss, the last words of his oath settling around them in the stillness of the hall.

Both of us are bound to our oaths of duty, me as surely as him. The dreams of childhood will have to stay where I left them.

CHAPTER ONE

MIDWINTER

WINTER WEATHER POUNDED against the windows of Talianna's sitting room as Gavin stood before the fire. A storm had been threatening them all week and had finally broken in fury on the eve of the midwinter festivities. Fine grains of snow sifted against the small-paned windows as the wind whistled down the chimney. Even with the cold outside, the room was bright and warm. The fire danced merrily against hardwood logs, its cheerful crackle mixing with the giggling coming from behind the door to Talianna's dressing room.

"Sir?" A spare man clad in crimson velvet approached the fireplace; a chamberlain, no doubt come to take him to task about the princess's lateness to the ballroom. "Sir, the High Steward begs me to inquire..."

"Yes, yes." Gavin straightened his dress clothes as he went to the door connecting Talianna's private rooms with the rest of the suite. Animated conversation could still be heard beyond, and he rapped hard on the polished wood. "Your Royal Highness? Your father's becoming irritated at you."

"He can wait," Talianna replied from behind the door, her words punctuated by an amused laugh. "I'm almost ready."

"I'm sorry." Gavin turned to the servant with an apologetic smile. "She has a mind of her own. It shouldn't be too much longer."

As the door closed behind the chamberlain, Gavin resumed his place in front of the hearth. Within a few minutes, the dressing room door clicked open, and Talianna appeared, trailed by a handful of maids and ladies-in-waiting. In the two and a half years since he'd assumed command of her personal guard, the bright eyes and rounded cheeks of his childhood friend had melted into the sophisticated lines of a young woman with dark hair and sharp wit. Her burgundy and gold skirts rustled as she walked to stand beside him, a gleam in her eye as she measured her height in high-heeled slippers against his.

Gavin smiled. He was still taller. "Your shoes won't avail you much," he said with a grin. There had been a time in their childhood when the girl, two years younger than him but propelled by genetics, had been taller than he was. He turned his foot so she could see. "I'm wearing boots."

"Ah well," she sighed. "I still had to check." She glanced at the door. "Is my father very upset?"

Gavin crossed his arms and raised an eyebrow. "No. Unless you count the *three* chamberlains he's sent to ask if you're ready to be announced yet."

"It would be unforgivably rude to keep them waiting any longer." She gave him a mischievous grin, deep brown eyes flashing against her glowing skin. "He must've noticed I was postponing my entrance as long as I could." Her voice dropped low enough for only those nearby to hear her. "Between us, I can't stand the Treluthian ambassador."

Gavin snorted as the rest of the girls tittered. With a sigh, Talianna crossed the room to where yet another chamberlain hovered anxiously. "Thank you for your patience. Will you tell the High Steward that I am on my way?"

The man bobbed a quick bow and scurried away as Talianna swept into the receiving room, trailed by her ladies-in-waiting. Gavin followed, keeping a few paces behind Talianna as they proceeded from her rooms in the direction of the public areas of the palace.

The corridors gleamed with holiday decorations, and the scent of pine and holly filled the air from the garlands lavishly decking the tops of floor-to-ceiling windows. The figures of the girls ahead of him were almost dwarfed by the height of the hallway, the bright colors of their gowns an excellent foil against the darkness of the winter storm outside.

From this vantage point, Gavin could see the exact moment that Talianna assumed her public personality. In the amount of time it took to pass from one corridor to another, her back straightened and she seemed to grow taller. The laughter in her voice changed, as if each note in her voice was being carefully tuned to perfection. He sighed, wishing he hadn't first noticed the change several years ago. The Talianna he knew of old was bubbly, warmhearted, and practically sparkled from within. The version of herself she always presented to the court was more subdued—shimmeringly beautiful, perfectly composed, gracious, imposing—the image of the perfect royal heiress.

No matter how often he witnessed it, the change never failed to sadden him.

The ladies-in-waiting stopped ahead of Gavin as they approached the gilded ballroom doors. They fluttered around and adjusted each other's appearances before the chamberlains ushered them inside. Talianna stood to one side, her face utterly composed. She reached up to adjust her gold and pearl tiara as the last of her ladies passed through the doors. "How do I look?"

Gavin smiled. She unfailingly asked this question before every state event. After two and a half years of being in close proximity to her, he recognized it as her way of assuring herself that at least one person could still see the girl behind the public façade.

"You look terrible." He raised an eyebrow as he stepped into his usual position a few feet behind her. "I'm not even sure why anyone would bother coming to this dinner, knowing you'd be there to spoil it."

She laughed, the public persona settling over her features with a sigh as she stepped up to the double door. A wash of light and color filled Gavin's senses as the heralds pushed open both doors, gold and crystal shining from the walls and ceiling of the grand ballroom.

"Her Royal Highness, Princess Talianna." A hush spread over the ballroom as the crowd of lords, ladies, diplomats, and honored guests sank into low curtsies and bows, their formal attire making the assembly appear as rich and vibrant as the contents of a jewel box. Talianna swept across the threshold, acknowledging the crowd before regally crossing the floor to greet her father and the Treluthian ambassador.

Gavin frowned as he slipped through the doors, taking in the assembly with one keen-eyed sweep. The queen was not appearing tonight, it seemed. Although Her Majesty was much beloved by her people, her appearances in such formal settings as the Midwinter Ball were few and far between. Talianna had once confided in him that her mother's illness was progressing rapidly, to the dismay of those who knew her best. Whatever the manner of the queen's failing health, it meant Gavin's dealings with Talianna's parents were relegated mostly to her father—a strong man and good ruler, and one determined to see his line continue at all costs. *Though so far, not by pressuring his daughter to marry.*

Gavin shook the relieved thought from his mind. His feelings for Talianna had long since crossed the border from friendship to something deeper, but any slip would mean the end of their friendship *and* his role of guardian. The reminder prompted him to check the dagger at his side—its decorative hilt made it less sturdy than he would have liked, but it was nevertheless the only weapon *anyone* was allowed to carry into the ballroom.

A foolish idea, but at least it means no one's tripping over a sword they can barely use. Gavin eyed one of the courtiers as the man escorted a lady to her seat at one of the long tables surrounding the perimeter of the hall, stifling a smile at the fellow's pompous gait. *Better to leave the swords to those who can use them.*

He flicked his eyes toward the ballroom doors, where crimson-uniformed guardsmen could be seen beyond the threshold. Other members of Talianna's personal guard were interspersed among them, their dark blue uniforms less conspicuous but their gazes sharper as they surveyed the hall. He gave a small nod to himself, satisfied that—at the very least—reinforcements were close at hand, should they be needed.

As servants began appearing from the kitchen entrances to place dishes of lavish food on the tables, Gavin skirted the edge of the hall to take his place with his back to the wall a few yards from Talianna's chair. The other guardians—those of the king and foreign delegates—greeted him with stilted nods before returning to their examination of the crowd of revelers. Gavin settled into parade rest, allowing his mind to sink into the routine of scanning the crowd and observing the patterns of servants as they served the guests by rank. He could still feel the wind vibrating past the roof, an occasional gust making a howling sound as it swirled past the edge of the hall. Talianna glanced back at him, and he gave her a reassuring smile.

Don't worry. I'm here if you need me.

Talianna fidgeted in her chair as one of the servants placed a steaming dish of soup in front of her. She waited for her father to take his first bite before dipping her spoon into the creamy liquid. With her mother's growing frailty, she'd had to steadily take on more and more responsibilities in the years since Gavin had become her guard commander. By this time, it was second nature to slip in and out of the version of herself that everyone needed to see: strong and flawless, the very embodiment of hope in the future.

The storm could still be heard whistling beyond the roof of the hall, and she wished she could be enjoying this meal in her room with her friends. Even though she'd long resigned herself to the demands of public life, she couldn't deny the pleasure of quiet nights spent in good company.

"It's a beautiful evening," her father said as he leaned closer. On his other side, the Treluthian ambassador was deep in conversation with his companions; no doubt comparing the styles of their balls to the ones in his homeland. "Isn't it, my dear?"

Talianna didn't have to manufacture a smile for her father. "It's glorious. I always love seeing all the pretty dresses and jewels the ladies put on display for the evening."

"Some more than others," her father said, a hint of a chuckle running through his voice as he nodded in the direction of the lower tables.

She looked where he'd indicated and raised an eyebrow at the sight of several noblewomen's dresses: obviously expensive, but in colors and cut that made her think of the sordid tales whispered by those of her ladies with older brothers. "That is..." She searched her imagination for the appropriate word. "That is spectacular." One of the foreign delegates laughed on the king's other side, his voice somewhat louder than manners dictated, and she leaned closer to her father. "Though, this year things seem a bit—oh, I'm not certain. It's like everyone is trying too hard to make things bright and beautiful. It feels forced, I suppose."

Her father nodded almost imperceptibly. "Things are tense," he admitted in an undertone. "It was never in the plan for the emissaries to remain here over the winter holidays, but the storms along the coast—" He stopped talking as the servants arrived to collect their soup bowls and lay the next course before them. "Well, it wasn't something I had anticipated, but we must always be courteous to our neighbors. I only wish they weren't so perceptive; some of them are starting to ask questions about you. I suppose they must've heard rumors."

She set her fork down with a deep breath. "Rumors regarding?"

The king gave a quiet shake of his head. "Just the usual. Mostly wondering why I haven't announced my heir's betrothal yet, now that you're so close to coming of age. I won't lie to you and say that I'm not concerned myself, but—"

Talianna cast a glance at the tabletop, aware that her stiffening shoulders would spell the tension clearly for anyone who happened to be watching. It took true effort to raise her head and speak as lightly as if they were merely discussing idle gossip. "If you're concerned, you know that you have every right to make the decision on my behalf."

Even as the words emerged, she wished she could take them back. *Don't be foolish,* she chided herself. *The choice of a husband is the one thing this role allows you for yourself. Don't throw it away.*

"Tali," Her father set down his knife and squeezed her hand—a gesture tantamount to a full hug. "Don't worry. I'm not so anxious as to take your choice from you. It's a pressing matter, to be sure, but"—he withdrew his hand and sat back as the Treluthians at the other end of the table laughed again—"I'm certain whomever you select will be entirely worthy of both your hand *and* your responsibilities."

Talianna sighed, her appetite gone as her father turned his attention to their guests. It was this ongoing conversation that, with each iteration, made the weight of her impending marriage press further and further onto her shoulders.

Worthy. A word that, on the surface, meant the usual things—of good character, an acceptable rank, well-educated and better spoken. Over the years, it had taken on a meaning of its own; one that now felt as mythical as a dragon, and unfair as a fight against one.

It's your choice, but remember...

It's your choice, but make it count.

Without meaning to, she found herself turning her head to catch a glimpse of Gavin, his presence like a warm fire behind her. It was a habit she'd fallen into once she'd realized he was one of the few who saw through the persona she donned for each public event. Longing struck unexpectedly, and she had to quickly drag her eyes back to the colorful assembly. With no older brothers to take the crown, and Gavin the son of lesser nobility, she'd long resigned herself that the romantic dreams of childhood would have to remain buried.

Talianna did her best to smooth the furrow of worry from her brow, smile, and look like she was enjoying the festivities. *Stay focused, Tali.*

Once dinner was over, the tables were cleared away and the dancing began. Gavin moved from the edge of the dais to a place near the wall as servants began circulating through the hall with platters of sweets and trays of hot and cold drinks. He ignored the buzz of conversations around him, keeping his eyes on Talianna as she made her way up and down the dance floor with one partner after another. After one rather rigorous reel, she cast an imploring glance in his direction. He ignored it, turning instead to examine the guard at the door. While they'd danced together at smaller events, it wouldn't be proper for him to take up a dance while other higher-ranked noblemen were present.

A woman's voice startled him from his contemplation. "Good evening, Milord."

He looked up in surprise. The speaker was one of the Treluthian ladies who had come with the ambassador and been stranded in the storm. Her auburn curls were piled high on her head in the courtly style, and her emerald-colored dress revealed far too much bosom for someone of her advancing age and apparent status.

"Good evening," he answered politely, keeping an eye out for Talianna as she proceeded down the line of dancers.

"Not dancing tonight?"

"Not I, no." He smiled. "I'm not much of a dancer."

"Oh!" She pressed a hand to her chest, surprise unconvincingly painting her heavily adorned features. "But you're so light on your feet, so alert!"

A nagging feeling pinged in the back of Gavin's head. "I'm all left feet on a dance floor. I'm afraid I'd bring you little enjoyment as a partner." He gave a slight bow in her direction before stepping away. "Enjoy the party."

The lady called an insult his way as he left, the shrillness in her words a counterpoint to the alarm coursing through his blood as he scanned the dance floor. The ballroom was still crowded with revelers, but Talianna and her partner had disappeared.

Where is she?

Cursing his own inattention, he stopped and searched the crowd for a glimpse of Talianna's burgundy dress. Finally, he spotted her sitting on a couch at the side of the hall, rubbing an ankle and laughing with her dance partner.

Relief flooded through him with a huffed laugh. "Those heels will never stop causing trouble."

Only now aware that his hand had gone to its bejeweled hilt, Gavin released his dagger. Conscious of a few curious stares, he resumed position against the wall to watch Talianna's interactions with the other nobleman. Based on the steady tightening of her jaw, he assumed the conversation was beginning to take a frustrating turn. It was no surprise when she reached up to fiddle with her tiara—their private signal for him to rescue her from whatever uncomfortable conversation she'd been trapped in.

His boots clicked against the floor as he walked over. "Your Royal Highness, I was told that your father wished to speak with you."

She looked up from her conversation with a radiant smile. "Oh! Gavin, thank you. Lord Baldric, may I present Sir Gavin of Andel."

Gavin bowed courteously to the man, whose chin seemed in danger of disappearing into his neck. The lord returned the bow with barely enough courtesy to honor the princess's introduction. His nose wrinkled as he said, "Andel? I've never heard of it."

Gavin chuckled. "Few have. It's a small barony, which is why I choose to stay at court."

"Don't you find it difficult to split your responsibilities?"

He shrugged. "My father still lives, and my older brother oversees our holdings at his side. Besides, my duty is here." He bowed to the lord again before returning his attention to Talianna. "My lady? Your father?"

With a practiced sigh, Talianna accepted his offered hand. Her fingers were warm in his as she took a moment to balance evenly in the high-heeled shoes. "Yes, my own duty calls. Lord Baldric, thank you for your courtesy."

The man bowed genteelly. "The pleasure was mine, Your Highness."

They walked away, Talianna looking up gratefully after a few steps. "Thank you for saving me. He was very irritating." A tinge of sarcasm crept through her voice, unusual for a court event. "He seems not to understand why the heir to the throne would rather spend her days studying diplomacy than having more maidenly pursuits."

"The pleasure is mine." He glanced away to see the nobleman already making for one of the beverage tables. "Though, you might consider speaking with your father, to keep up appearances."

"Yes, of course." She stopped and flexed her ankle gingerly. "I need a break before dancing more, anyway."

They joined the king and ambassador on the dais as the music began for another dance. Talianna sank into her chair with a relieved smile. Gavin excused himself, slipping to the rear of the platform and away from the monarch's direct gaze. In matters regarding Talianna's father, he preferred not to be seen as anything other than a dutiful servant. Kind to Talianna the man might be, but Gavin knew him to be so determined to do the right thing by his people that he wouldn't hesitate to remove anyone who might run the risk of distracting her from her responsibilities.

Like he did thirteen years ago. I wonder if he even remembers that day?

The royals and Treluthian ambassador exchanged pleasantries as the dancers moved through the formations of a gavotte. As the music ended, a servant approached with a tray of cups and offered them to the king.

"Ah, thank you." Talianna's father smiled at the man and lifted a cup from the tray. "Anyone else?"

Talianna nodded, also taking a glass. "Some of these pieces are quite fast. It's tiring!"

The servant excused himself with a nod and turned away. Out of the corner of his eye, Gavin noticed the man directing his steps toward the doors leading to the courtyard—not the kitchens. He took a half step backwards, keeping his eye on the servant. There was something suspicious about the man's manner as he crossed the dance floor. A tightness in his shoulders, perhaps, or a sharpness in his gaze as he looked back at the dais.

Sudden fear clenched in Gavin's gut. Grabbing the sleeve of the guard next to him, he ordered, "Stop that servant going out the doors."

The man's eyes widened as he obeyed, running toward the exit. Gavin looked back at the group on the dais. The king was still laughing over some joke with the ambassador and hadn't noticed the commotion behind him. Talianna's laugh fell on Gavin's ears like a warning bell as she lifted her goblet.

"Milady." Gavin lunged toward her, his voice building to a shout as Talianna sipped from her drink. "Milady, stop!"

Talianna had no time to respond before Gavin knocked the goblet away from her lips. It shattered on the dais floor, sending shards of crystal and a splatter of crimson across the polished stone. "Gavin, what..."

"Majesty, don't touch yours!" Gavin exclaimed, throwing an urgent hand in her father's direction.

Guards were breaking from their positions all around the ballroom, running out the doors with alarm stamped across their faces. The dancers closest to the dais faltered, stopping to look up with concern and confusion as her father demanded, "What is the meaning of this?"

Gavin grabbed her hands and pulled her to her feet, away from the table and away from the spilled drink. His green eyes found hers, as serious as the day he'd sworn his oath. "Princess, how much of your drink did you have?"

"Only a few sips, why?" Worry spiraled in her stomach.

He cast a dangerous glance at the door. "It might be nothing. I—I hope it's nothing. Don't drink anything else, all right?"

"All right."

Gavin squeezed her hands before letting go, his dark blue tunic remaining in the corner of her eye as he stepped to the back of the dais. Others of the king's guard were clustering around, their voices low and urgent as the sounds of the party swelled once more in the rest of the ballroom. The Treluthian ambassador had begun arguing with one of his men at the opposite end of the dais, their words too lost in the background noise for her to make out.

Talianna straightened her shoulders and smoothed her expression as her father turned from reassuring one of the other dignitaries and came to rest a hand upon her arm.

"Your captain may have overreacted. At least, I hope he has." He shot a concerned glance in Gavin's direction before asking, "Are you all right?"

"Yes, I think so." She smiled up at him, blinking as the gold embroidery on his tunic threw spots of light into her eyes. "Don't worry, Father, I'm fine."

"You're sure?"

Talianna nodded, but the movement slowed and changed to a frown as the faint spots kept dancing in her vision. She shook her head slightly, but the sparkling spots didn't dissipate. "Papa, something feels odd."

A tremor sped up her legs, building to a shudder as it ran through her body. Her father's voice blurred and fuzzed through her mind as his hand moved to her shoulder.

What's he saying? What's happening?

"Papa? Something is wrong." Her mouth felt heavy, her tongue tingly. "Something..." Talianna's words trailed into oblivion as a blue tunic flashed through her periphery and strong arms surrounded her. Above and around her, people were shouting, Gavin's voice strongest over all of them. She fought to answer him, or cry out, but her voice dissolved into incomprehensible sound. Darkness closed in.

Pandemonium spread through the palace at the speed of lightning, leaving all within dazed and confused as rumors began flying. Outside, the winter storm raged as alarm bells rang, gates swung closed, and hands flew to weapons. Inside, the tall windows peered down upon a handful of blue-uniformed men traveling in tight ranks through side halls, one of them carrying an unconscious woman clad in burgundy and gold.

Had the windows been able to tell their tale to the winter winds, they would have spoken of a hand brushing wisps of raven hair away from a still face and of a whisper barely heard amid the commotion.

"Tali. Don't go, please. I'll never forgive myself if you die."

Several hours later, Gavin paced back and forth before the hearth in Talianna's sitting room. It was long after midnight, and he'd been roaming restlessly around the room ever since the doctor had arrived and barred him from Talianna's bedchamber. A few of the other men from the personal guard also ranged through the sitting room and the antechamber beyond, the tension in their bodies declaring how frustrating they, too, found the situation.

After an hour, Gavin stopped pacing and turned to his men. "It's no use for all of us to be rattling around in here." He gestured outside, where alarm bells could still be heard beyond the howling wind. "Go join the others in the search. You can report to Lord Kelmar, and he'll direct you." His men looked up, their eyes brightening with the suggestion as he added, "Keep your eyes and ears open and report anything you find to me or to the duke. I'll send someone to find you if anything happens here."

The other guards nodded their assent, a few of them clapping him on the shoulder as they left Talianna's suite. Gavin's second-in-command Tristan shook his head sympathetically as the anteroom door closed on the men's heels. "I had more peaceful nights at the Treluthian border."

Gavin nodded, the tension in his shoulders longing to be released in a fight of some kind. While peace with Treluthia had been declared long before he'd gained his knighthood, there had been enough skirmishes along the long, shared border between the two countries to test both nations' resolve—and their fighting forces' mettle. "The border was easy. At least there, we knew who we were fighting and why. This—" He shook his head. Peace was a more difficult battle than war, especially with unknown enemies sowing chaos at every turn. "Even fighting the wind would be better than this."

A creak from behind interrupted them as the doctor stepped through the door to Talianna's bedroom. Both Gavin and Tristan spun to face him, Gavin's voice overriding his subordinates'. "How is she?"

The doctor gave him a weary smile. "She's had a difficult few hours, but she'll be all right. Is there any word yet on who did this?"

"Not yet." Tristan gave a grim look toward the door. "Though, I expect that'll change soon. The whole guard's been roused, not that it does our lady any good."

"At least she'll recover." The doctor nodded to Gavin. "Your quick thinking saved her." Gavin frowned and looked away as the man added, "I know you're worried; would you like to come sit with her?"

"I would. Thank you."

With the doctor's hand at his elbow, Gavin stepped into the bedchamber. Several assistants in white aprons stood near Talianna's four-poster bed, shifting pillows and tucking the covers around her. The princess laid as still as a statue, her face almost as pale as the neckline of her shift. Seeing her so vulnerable made his footsteps falter in a way that no deadly threat ever had.

One of Talianna's ladies-in-waiting stopped brushing the gown the princess had worn at the Midwinter Ball. She crossed the room to pull a chair to the bedside. "I realize it looks bad, but she's only sleeping," the woman murmured. Like most of the other courtiers waiting outside, she was still wearing her festive attire. "She was asking where you were, earlier." The woman gave him an encouraging smile. "Talk to her. Even if she can't respond, she'll know you're here."

"Thank you." Taking the seat, Gavin wrapped one of Talianna's hands in both of his. Her eyes flickered, face ghastly pale against her pillow. "Will anyone mind that I'm here? Propriety—the king—"

The doctor smiled, wrinkles making his skin pouch around his eyes. "Don't worry. All I know is that the princess's guardian refused to abandon his charge, even in her sickroom." He returned to his work, leaving Gavin holding Talianna's hand.

Hours later, Gavin stretched and stood up. Talianna still slept, more peaceful now that the doctor's medicines had taken effect. Morning light filtered past the curtains of the sitting room as he re-emerged from the bedchamber. Most of the hangers-on had left when they heard the princess would recover, and only a few of his men remained in the antechamber. "Any news?" he asked Tristan.

A twist at the corner of his comrade's mouth heralded the news. "They got him—*and* he talked." Worry lines creased at the edges of his eyes as he looked past Gavin toward Talianna's room. "You're not going to believe this, but the princess wasn't the intended target. His Majesty was."

Gavin swore under his breath. "It was an accident?"

Tristan nodded grimly. "Collateral damage, they're saying."

Gavin's hand tensed, about to go to where his sword normally sat against his hip. "Whomever 'they' are, they need to watch their tongues. That's their future queen they're talking about." He gave a shake of his head. "I came out here to ask if you could stay with her for a bit so I could go change. Maybe now I need to go hit someone while I'm at it."

Tristan clapped a hand on his shoulder. "Go do what you need to."

Gavin ducked through the servants' door with a few words of thanks and hurried down a single flight of stairs to his own quarters. Hastily changing out of his fancy clothes, he dressed according to comfort. He retrieved his sword from the armor rack and fastened it securely at his waist. The sheath of a wrist knife tightened around his right arm, and his hunting knife balanced his sword on the opposite hip. Armed, he collected a book and ink bottle from his bedside table and left the room. He was about to return to Talianna's room when his footsteps slowed.

Collateral damage? Her? He shook his head. *I can't go back in there until I calm down.*

The wind had begun abating outside as Gavin directed his steps to a lesser-known chapel on the ground floor of the palace. Today, with priests gathered in the main chapel praying for Talianna's safety, the place was deserted. His boots made quiet echoes in the vaulted space, candles flickering behind the altar as he sat on one of the front benches.

He sat in silence for several minutes, contemplating the altar and what it symbolized. Eventually, his senses calmed enough for him to open the book he'd brought from his room. A handful of pages in the back listed every time Talianna had been in mortal danger since he had taken over command of the men in charge of her protection.

The hunting accident, when her horse almost threw her. The riot in barony Eland. Even with the gravity of the situation, he had to smirk at one entry. *That poisoned perfume someone gave her...too bad for them that she hates the smell of lilies of the valley.* The levity left his thoughts as he uncapped the ink. Dipping a pen, he wrote in careful script the details of this most recent incident. *Even when she's not the target, she's still in danger.*

Setting the journal aside for the ink to dry, he got up from the pew and knelt at the prayer rail in front of the altar. The words of his oath fell into the silence. "I, Gavin of Andel, do solemnly swear to guard the princess Talianna to the fullest of my ability. May the blows of those who seek to cause her harm fall upon my head. May her enemies be my enemies, her danger my danger, and her life my life. This do I swear, until my king releases me from my oath or I perish in the fulfillment of my duty."

It's not a light promise. He shivered as the words sent a ripple of conviction through his heart. *I almost failed her last night. I can't afford to let that happen again.*

CHAPTER TWO

FLIGHT

TALIANNA RECOVERED QUICKLY from her illness, though the incident left her with even more determination to excel in her duties as heir. She'd already spent most of her time each week in study, but that occupation now grew to encompass every free moment. As spring budded into summer, she spent hours poring over books on history and politics, talking with her advisors, and researching the countries surrounding her realm.

"Father's health isn't the best," she confided in Gavin one afternoon as he walked with her from the council room to the library. "He doesn't say much, but I know he's worried that there won't be much time before all of this lands on my shoulders." Her shoulders slumped, and she reminded herself to straighten them. "I want so badly to rule well and to live up to everyone's expectations, and, and—oh, just to do this *right*."

"You'll do things right," he reassured her. "You're certainly studying enough."

Gavin's presence was a constant amid the study and meetings, broken only when she met with her father in private each week. The weekly audience had been something she dearly looked forward to as a child, when they could speak at length about games, playfellows, and Talianna's most recent interests; things she supposed ordinary fathers and daughters discussed every day. As her responsibilities as heir to his throne had increased, so too did the seriousness of the weekly conversations, until they now resembled more councils of strategy than the easy companionship she'd once enjoyed. And since Midwinter, the topic of conversation now drifted further and further toward the subject of her betrothal; a subject she could only answer with the bitter-tasting platitude: "I'm contemplating it."

In truth, each time the subject turned to marriage, the pressure in her mind increased. There were several men whose bloodlines were aristocratic enough and who possessed the academic and personal qualities necessary, yet the choice never settled in her heart.

You're being sentimental, she chided herself one afternoon while on a rare walk in the rose gardens. The audience with her father that morning had seen him reminding her yet again of his wishes, and this time with a deadline attached. *Father wants this matter settled before my twenty-first birthday, and there are plenty of candidates he would deem worthy. I ought to simply select someone who'll do his best for our people and leave it at that.*

She huffed a sigh into the fragrant air. *I don't want it to end like that, though.* Memories passed through the edge of her mind; of the sound of her parents' laughter as they'd played with her in this very garden. *They had something special with each other, before Mother's illness took her mind.* Talianna trailed her fingers down the velvet petals of a blush rose. *If I could have my wish, I'd be able to choose someone who wasn't only good for our people, but who made me laugh the way Mother made Father laugh.*

Gavin stayed at Talianna's side as much as he could over the months of recovery and study. Although the kingdom had been quiet since the events of Midwinter, he could feel the growing tension as her birthday drew closer. Peace still held sway, but a diplomatic iciness had descended over the court as relations with Treluthia grew more and more strained. As the first days of summer broke over the land, Gavin received a summons to the king's council room.

Leaving Talianna in the library with trusted men to keep watch, he hurried to the council chamber. The interior corridors of the palace were dark and quiet, far from the gold-touched gardens where Talianna occasionally spent an afternoon with her ladies-in-waiting. He stopped outside the room and took a moment to adjust his uniform and compose himself before nodding to the guards outside the door.

"I'm ready."

One of them pounded twice on the door before opening it. "Good luck, Sir."

It was evident from first glance that this meeting would be of a serious nature. The king sat at one end of the table. His face was in a composed expression very much like the royal persona Talianna donned for public events. The Duke of Kelmar, Gavin's commander and overseer of the personal guards for king and queen, sat at the monarch's right. Others of the king's advisors occupied chairs around the table and swelled the room almost beyond its capacity. That number alone would have indicated the gravity of this meeting, but the expressions on the men's faces confirmed his growing suspicions. *This isn't a regular security briefing. It's a council of war.*

"Sir Gavin, thank you for taking time out of your duties to attend us," the king said from the head of the room. "I trust the princess is well?"

Gavin came to attention, one hand going to his sword hilt in salute. "The princess is in excellent health and spirits, Majesty."

"I am glad to hear it." There was something akin to a smile about the monarch's face for a moment as he gestured to a seat at the foot of the table. "Please, sit. Our discussion may be of some length."

Gavin quietly took his seat and did his best to calm his quaking nerves. Most of the other nobles gave him dismissive looks, but Lord Kelmar gave him a reassuring half-smile as Talianna's father addressed the room. "Thank you all for being here today. I know it's difficult to assemble this many of us, so I won't waste your time." The king paused before continuing, his words those of a man who intended his audience to give him their full attention. "With the events of Midwinter, and the growing unrest elsewhere in the country, it's becoming apparent that our enemies are becoming more and more brazen in their attempts to undermine our security."

Heads nodded around the room, Gavin's among them. They'd traced the would-be kingslayer to a malcontent son of a provincial duke, whose perceived claim on the throne had to be traced through several branches of the family tree. Gavin hadn't known for certain if the man's decision to strike the king had been influenced by any specific enemy, but the sheer audacity, combined with the reports of chaos brewing in other corners of the land, made for convincing evidence of outside interference.

Chaos, his old battle master had once said. *Sow chaos behind your opponent's lines, and they'll be powerless against you.*

"The most recent strike against me endangered my daughter's life," the king continued. "I'd hoped that with increased precautions, she'd be able to remain at my side until her coming of age later this year. But with each new threat comes the possibility of her simply being in the wrong place at the wrong moment, like she was at Midwinter. Threats against my life are one thing, but now my daughter's life is in danger." The king frowned, his composed demeanor cracking enough for Gavin to recognize the same heart-stopping fear that filled him with each new threat against Talianna. "She needs to leave."

The words left Gavin's mouth numb with fear. "H-how long have you been planning this?" Everyone turned to look at him with varying degrees of surprise as he stammered, "Why hasn't any mention been made until now?"

"We'd been discussing moving the princess to a safer location for several months, but the events surrounding and following Midwinter have made it clear." Lord Kelmar steepled his fingers over a pile of notes at the other end of the table. "The longer she stays here, the more danger she's in."

Gavin sat in stunned silence as the rest of the council carried on. Now that the urgency of their circumstances had been driven home, the room hummed with discussion—ranging from how to cover Talianna's absence at court to laying plans to isolate and address the sources of unrest elsewhere in the kingdom.

Finally, Gavin felt his mind clear enough to venture a question. "Has there been a decision on where Talianna will go for this period? I mean," he addressed the king. "Your Majesty, my men and I will go anywhere to ensure Her Highness's safety. Is there already a destination in mind?"

The king nodded at a framed map on the wall. "Fife Corbel."

Gavin turned to look as well, though he knew the layout of the country almost as well as he knew his own rooms. The palace lay in the top left corner, a great forest cutting a swath between it and the sunlit coastal regions to the southeast. From his remembrance, Fife Corbel lay on the coast, beyond the forest. "It's far enough, Milord, but why there?"

"The queen's brother, the Earl of Corbel, is Talianna's closest relative." Lord Kelmar ran his thumb down the edge of his stack of notes. "The princess spent summers there with Her Majesty, before the queen's illness became too severe to permit travel." He tilted his head at the map, the lamplight catching in a scar that marked his eyebrow. "It's far away, and not in a heavily traveled area. If we're careful in our secrecy, no one will know where she's gone until months later. By then, hopefully, we'll have contained the unrest enough for her to return home."

Gavin nodded, his mind churning with logistics, concerns, and burning worry. In the end, only one question floated to the top of his mind. "How soon?"

"Next week?" Talianna hadn't had to remind herself to keep her composure in years, but Gavin's news was enough to make her jaw drop. She looked around to make sure no one had overheard her outburst. Fortunately, her ladies had wandered across the grass to take shelter from the sun under the rose arbors and were certainly out of earshot. "So soon? With not even a word of warning?"

He tilted his head, and a spark flared in his green eyes; a brief concession that told her how frustrating the news had most likely been to him as well. "Lord Kelmar has a point. This entire plan is based in secrecy, and every day spent here only increases the chance of someone reaching you." He crossed his arms and leaned against the edge of the fountain they were sitting beside, sunlight throwing a gleam from his sword hilt into her eyes. In the direct sun, his hair looked almost the same gold color as it had been when they were children. "I wanted to leave right away, but your father wants you here for the Flower Bridge Festival."

"I understand why," Talianna said after a moment of thought. "It would be immediately suspicious if I didn't appear with him at the celebrations. If we leave afterwards, it'll take days or even weeks before anyone notices I'm gone. Ordinarily, Mother would be the one to open the festival with him, but—" She looked across the garden, ashamed at the sudden prickling of tears. "Mother doesn't remember what day of the week it is, let alone when holidays are."

Gavin pulled a handkerchief from his tunic pocket and offered it to her. "I'm sorry. I didn't realize..." His voice trailed off as she wiped her eyes.

"It's all right. I don't even think about it most of the time; it just catches me unexpectedly." Talianna cleared her throat. Gavin had accompanied her on her last visit but had waited outside the private sitting room where her mother spent most of her days. "She remembers my name, but time isn't the same for her anymore. When she saw me last, she wanted to know where my nursie was."

He gave a low whistle. "I didn't realize it'd become so bad. That does explain why your father doesn't want us to leave until after the festival."

"Yes." The word stuck in her throat. "It makes sense. Did they say how we're getting to my uncle's holding?"

Gavin frowned. His eyes hadn't stopped roving the gardens since he'd given her the handkerchief. "The most direct and secret way possible: right through the woods."

Talianna followed his line of sight toward the edge of the garden, where the gardens were divided from tended parkland by a wrought-iron gate. Far beyond, the woods swelled in undulating waves of deep green and brown. "Stories say those woods are alive." She grinned. "And that banshees and witches walk between the trees." She tore her gaze away from the distant trees to look directly at Gavin. "Is it really dangerous? I mean, I've heard some of the girls talk..."

He snorted. "All girls talk, but some of your ladies have made it an art form." One of his eyebrows quirked as he added, "They'll hear a hunter's tale that he got from his cousin's father, and between embroidery circles and hawking parties turn it into a tale for the ages."

"I suppose that's true," she admitted. One or two of the younger girls among her ladies-in-waiting weren't the most well-read or burdened with much common sense, but their silliness was refreshing—soothing, even—after hours spent in the company of diplomats and scholars. "But really?" she asked as they got up and began walking under the arch that separated the rose garden from the rest of the grounds. "Is it dangerous?"

"Some parts of the forest are thick enough that we don't always know what passes unnoticed." Gavin raised an eyebrow, conceding, "I did hear a story when I was on the border, about how the trees moved of their own accord to block a raiding party." He shrugged. "The stories might not be too far off with the tales of old magic. But the security council was right: it is the fastest way to get to Fife Corbel, and we'll be able to make good time if we travel with a smaller group."

"If that's what they agreed on..." Talianna stopped to breathe in the perfume of the pink roses that tumbled over the archway. They'd played in this same garden as children, before duty had taken her to her studies and Gavin to training for knighthood.

Say goodbye, Talianna. Her nursie's voice floated through her ears as the sunlight gilded the edges of the rose leaves.

"I'll miss this place." She reached up to break the stem of one of the roses, tucking it into the laces on her bodice. "Even if it's only for a short while, I'll miss it."

Five nights later, a knock sounded on Gavin's door. Jerked from a sound sleep, he stumbled out of bed with a knife in hand and yanked open his bedroom door. "What's going on?"

Lord Kelmar leapt away from the threshold, the light from a lantern flaring and casting eerie shadows against the narrow corridor walls. "Shh! Stand down, it's only me."

Gavin warily relaxed his stance, lowering the knife. "What's happening?" The Flower Bridge Festival had only just concluded, and he and Talianna weren't due to leave for Fife Corbel for another several days. For that matter, he'd barely briefed the men who were to make up the remainder of the escort through the forest. "Is something wrong? The princess—"

"Is asleep. For now," the duke reassured him. "Though, you need to wake her at once." He passed a document to Gavin, the raised crimson and gold of the king's seal imprinted beneath its words. The shadows seemed to thicken around them as the man said grimly, "There's been a change of plans."

In the pale morning light, a back gate of the stables opened onto mist. Talianna drew her hood farther around her face and buried her free hand in the folds of her mantle as she urged her horse into a trot. Ahead, Gavin guided his own horse deeper into the fog that cloaked the gate and shrouded the road leading to the forest.

"Your time and manner of leaving has become compromised," her father's advisor had warned them in the darkest hours preceding dawn. "His Majesty issued me new orders. You're to proceed at once to the eastern road and go as fast as you can to Fife Corbel. We'll send your possessions by caravan along a different route." The man's face had been drawn with worry, matched only by the tension in Gavin's face as the duke clasped his hand and commanded, "Guard her well. The fate of us all rests on your shoulders."

They'd dressed quickly in commoners' clothes, loaded plain saddlebags onto nondescript horses, and made their course for the eastern road. As the sun crested the edge of the trees and set every dewdrop aflame, Talianna reined her horse down to a walk alongside Gavin's. "What happened?"

He raked a hand through his blond hair before letting his hand drop to the hilt of a plain sword. "I briefed the men who were going to accompany us yesterday. They must've decided to bid the capital farewell in fine fashion, because the city guard arrested one of them overnight for causing a drunken disturbance. We're not sure who he might have spoken with over the course of the evening, and it could have been enough to compromise our plans." His jaw tensed. "And your father wanted absolute secrecy."

Talianna shook the hood of her cloak away from her forehead. "So they decided it was best we leave immediately?" She stared into the depths of the forest, sunbeams slicing through the trees as the sun climbed higher into the sky.

"Yes." He tightened his hands around his reins. "I don't like it either, but the orders came directly from your father. I have *some* amount of liberty to question my superiors, but not an order with the royal seal on it."

Talianna nodded. Her father's seal was practically an extension of himself; its appearance tantamount to hearing his voice directly. "Whatever happened must have disrupted more than just our departure," she said, half to herself and half to Gavin.

"I think so as well," he agreed, "I can't think of another reason they'd panic the way they did." His face flushed, and he half turned in the saddle to face her. "I mean—not panic. I don't think they panicked, it's just—"

She found herself laughing, letting go of the tension brought on by their hurried departure. "It's all right. I won't say anything." The surprised relief in Gavin's expression loosened more tightness from her shoulders as she asked, "It's how long of a journey? Three weeks?"

"It *was* three weeks the way we'd planned on traveling," Gavin corrected. "With only two of us, it'll be closer to a fortnight."

"Two weeks," she repeated. "Two weeks before I have to be the princess again."

He chuckled. "Be careful; you might forget how to wear the royal persona."

"Well, I doubt it'll go *that* far." She sighed. "I've had years to perfect it, after all." She shot him a piercing glance. "How long did it take you to realize it was a façade?"

Gavin shrugged, the set of his body in the saddle reminding her how much time he'd spent on different military campaigns prior to swearing his oath. "A few months. I walk behind you all the time, so it was easy to notice when you were getting ready for battle."

"Some days it feels like one," she admitted. "At least for right now, I don't have to worry about being the heir to the throne. I can just be...me. Just Tali." She flicked a hand in his direction. "You can use my old nickname, if you want. There's no one here to overhear, and I won't tell."

A grin caught the corner of Gavin's mouth. "I've never stopped calling you that in my head." He tipped his head back as sunlight filtered through the trees overhead, examining the canopy with eyes that reflected its green and gold hues. "We'd better speed up. Childhood nicknames aside, this adventure could still end in a way that neither of us would've imagined."

Gavin had never thought that a tension-filled departure could lead to such peace. Away from the palace, Talianna's royal persona steadily dissolved, until she seemed more like the girl she had once been. The bubbly side of her personality had returned by the end of the second day, and by the third evening, she was as talkative and cheerful as he remembered her being during childhood.

Keep your wits about you, he reminded himself on the third night, as they set up camp in a clearing beneath a spreading oak tree. *This may be a reprieve from the usual, but nothing has changed between you.* He cast a glance at Talianna as she collected fuel for their campfire. They'd donned simple clothes for traveling, but she made even a plain brown dress and wool cloak beautiful. *Once we're among nobles again, she'll be back to being the princess—and you have a duty to keep your heart from getting tangled into your common sense. There's too much at stake to get lazy now.*

He forced himself to look away and focus on their surroundings. This clearing was a little way away from the road, and he hoped the distance and obscurity would hide them from anyone who happened to be passing during the night. Previous travelers had thought similarly, and a blackened ring of rocks showed where someone had once lit a fire like the one he was now coaxing to life.

"Here." Talianna set a bundle of twigs and dry leaves beside him, brushing dirt from her hands as she knelt on the other side of the tiny circle. Her brow furrowed as she looked at the sky, visible in gaps where the treetops had not deigned to touch each other. "Is there a reason we stopped so early?"

Gavin sat back on his heels. Their interactions had grown much more familiar the farther into the woods they'd gotten, but he hadn't realized she'd learned his patterns for travel so quickly. "We're getting closer to the center of the forest." He glanced at the brambles that screened them from the path. This close, their thorns looked sharp as daggers. "I don't want to spend the night in the deepest part, so we'll get an early start tomorrow and push through the middle of the woods in one day."

He bent over the fire and carefully blew into the growing embers, then added a handful of dry leaves. They caught immediately, the sudden flare of light illuminating Talianna's face with a glow like the sun. She sat down, pulling in her legs and tucking her feet under her worn skirts. "Are you expecting something to happen?"

Gavin snapped a stick and tossed it into the fire. "I don't know, Tali," he admitted. Even if he'd have to eventually resume calling her by her full name, Talianna's childhood nickname warmed his heart each time he said it. "It's still another several days to the edge of the forest, and I don't know what we might encounter as we go. I said I didn't care about the stories they tell about these woods, but that doesn't change the fact that there *are* stories." He looked down, glad that the fire was warm enough to cover the flush spreading across his face. "It was easier to ignore them when I thought we'd have more men with us."

Talianna's thoughtful hum was loud enough to be heard over the soft crackling of the fire. "Then, what will we do?"

"Keep going." He snapped another stick and stabbed the ground with it. "Whatever reservations I had about our departure, your father's order still needs to be carried out. I'll deliver you safely to your uncle's fife; make no mistake about that. As to what we might encounter—" Gavin cut himself off. "I swore to protect you at the expense of myself, and I'll hold true to that oath even if there's no one to witness it. But if we *do* run into trouble, I need you to make me a promise."

"What promise?" Talianna looked up from the fire, and his heart beat faster at how its light turned her eyes amber and gold; the colors of the sun contained in a woman with all of its brilliance.

"Whatever happens, you need to get out of this forest. If you can, stay hidden. If you can't, run." He crossed the campfire circle to take her hand like he had at Midwinter. "Please, Tali. Promise."

"I promise, of course." She smiled. "I'm certain you underestimate yourself, though."

That night, Gavin scaled the oak to discover a mossy hollow where several branches had grown together at the trunk. He laid Talianna's bedding in the depression, telling her, "It might be uncomfortable, but I'll feel better knowing you're above ground." He laid his blanket next to the dying fire, staring into the night sky long after Talianna had fallen asleep in her nest. Finally, Gavin fell into a restless sleep.

A creak woke him—not of a tree or animal, but of boots over rocks. Eyes open, staring into the darkness, Gavin wondered how long it was until dawn. The fire had burned down to coals, but he could make out several dark shapes creeping up on him through the undergrowth. Lying still, he closed his eyes to slits. *Better to make them think I'm alone and unaware than lose the element of surprise.* Inside, his mind was spinning with possibilities and plans. Were they highwaymen, or something worse? Who could have learned about their departure?

"Shh." The deep, unfamiliar voice came from above him. "Check his gear."

Gavin gritted his teeth as his scabbard—laid with the hilt resting near his arm—slid away. Another voice, rough with whispering, muttered, "Army issue. You sure this is the knight?"

"They said he was." It was a different voice than the first. One of the horses nickered, and Gavin opened his eyes to barest slits as one of the dark figures moved to rummage through a saddlebag. "No livery on the horses, either. Doesn't matter; I still think this is our man."

"He's alone, though," another voice whispered. "If this is him, where is *she*?"

A chill that had nothing to do with the unyielding ground sped through his limbs. *They know.*

"Don't know," the first voice replied. "Not that it matters who dies first." Gavin sensed movement close, and his muscles tensed at the sound of steel sliding free of a sheath. "'Sides, she won't last long without him protectin' her."

Panic flashed through his mind as someone loomed over him. In an instant, Gavin rolled to his feet and freed his hunting knife. He stabbed upwards into the jaw of the man who had been about to kick him awake, then yanked down. Shouts rang out, and the man collapsed with a gurgle as Gavin stumbled to get his back to the oak. *Stay quiet, Tali.*

Someone else grabbed his arm, and he blindly swiped with his knife. It caught, and the man backed up with a curse. Yanking another blade from his boot, Gavin settled into a crouch, his eyes adjusting to the darkness as the bandits circled him. The man he had stabbed writhed on the ground for a few seconds before lying still with a rattling breath.

"Guess I underestimated you," the first man said. "That won't happen again. Grab him, lads."

Gavin heard the noise behind his left shoulder too late, as another bandit leapt at him from behind the oak. Others piled on, and he found himself immobile under the sheer weight. His knives twisted out of his hands before something heavy hit the back of his head. The blow dizzied him, and he was only dimly aware as the bandits bound his limbs before loading him onto the horse. Someone thrust a sack over his head, and the horse began moving. His only thought as they began making their way deeper into the forest was that Talianna had remained undiscovered. *Run, Talianna. Do as I said and run!*

CHAPTER THREE

DEFIANCE

STICKS CRACKED AND FABRIC RUSTLED as Talianna slid down from the oak. *They didn't see me. Why didn't they see me?* She leaned against the tree as her limbs shook with adrenaline and fear. After a moment, the pressure of the bark against her skin had settled her tremors enough for understanding to come to mind.

"They never looked up," she whispered. She twisted to press her forehead against the oak's craggy bark. "They never looked up!"

Something at once calm and fierce stirred inside her chest. *I can't leave Gavin.* The memory of his tear-filled eyes stirred unexpectedly at the back of her mind. Her nursemaid's voice had been sympathetic but unmoving that day, when Talianna's childhood had ended. *I've left him before, and look where it got us.*

Talianna pulled the edges of her cloak tightly around herself and set off toward the distant sounds of men talking and laughing, praying every step of the way that this was courage speaking, and not foolishness.

Light stung Gavin's eyes as someone pulled the sack off his head. He looked around dizzily as the men pulled him off the horse and pushed him to the ground near the center of a ring of massive old trees. The ground here was trodden hard and bare, and a fire burned brightly in the center of the ring. Other men like the ones who'd captured him could be seen around the circle. Their clothes were plain, serviceable, and worn, but all bore weapons with the familiarity of those accustomed to using them. Even at this late hour, many were awake; checking gear, playing dice, or talking with their fellows. A man with broad shoulders and an old army-issue sword crossed the circle to demand, "What's going on here?"

One of the bandits prodded Gavin with the toe of his boot. "Sir, we found this one in the oak clearing. He fits the description and there were two horses, but he was alone."

The man made a frustrated noise. "I don't recall saying anything about bringing them back here. How clear did I need to be?"

The outlaw shook his head, a whine creeping through his voice. "We were going to take care of things, but he turned out to have a way wi' a knife."

"Sir, he got Devin," another man said. "He's dead."

"Now that *is* a surprise. I can't let that go unpunished." The outlaw leader looked more appraisingly at Gavin. "Where are you from? Who are you?"

Just protect Talianna. "Treluthian border," Gavin lied. "And I'm only passing through. I didn't mean to cause trouble."

"Hmmm." The man turned away, and for a moment, Gavin thought his ruse had worked. Then, the outlaw spun to slam a boot into Gavin's stomach. "Don't lie to me! Who are you!?"

Gavin caught his breath with a shudder and shook his head. "I'm just a traveler!"

The outlaw leader's hand went to his sword hilt. "I said—"

"Sir?" One of the bandits held out the wrist knife he'd taken when binding Gavin's hands. "He did have this on him."

The leader snatched the small knife from his subordinate, his irritated expression swiftly changing to interest at the sight of the coat of arms stamped on the underside of the sheath. "The White Falcon," he breathed, turning a triumphant look at Gavin. "Barony Andel?"

Gavin's heart sank.

The bandit leader crouched to look Gavin in the eye, a misshapen grin spreading across his face. "Then you must be *Sir Gavin* of Andel, guard commander to Princess Talianna. Do you know how many people are after your skin, and how much they're willing to pay?"

"Not nearly as many as are after my lady's," Gavin answered. "You don't seem surprised to have met us."

"Well, not 'us' just yet." The man stood up and shook the closest man by his tunic front before releasing him with a shove. "Didn't you bastards search the campsite?"

The bandit stumbled backwards as one of the others said, "We did, Sir! There was no one else there!"

"Aye, that's likely. They warned that he might do something like this. You! And you!" The outlaw stabbed a hand in the direction of several of the men. "Get back to that campsite. Search it *properly* this time." The outlaw leader bent down to Gavin once more. "Where did you hide her? Tell us how to find her, and you'll live. The ones that hired us needn't find out, and I'll even overlook you killing one of my men." His voice grated an octave lower. "Refuse, and you die."

Gavin choked back fear and glared silently at the bandit leader. The quiet strained at the edges of the clearing before the outlaw's stare broke with a grim sigh. "Going to be stubborn? So be it." The man stood up and snapped his fingers. Before Gavin had the chance to react or pull away, two of the others had hauled him to his feet and were yanking him to where a set of sturdy posts and shackles stood anchored in the ground.

Pure terror shot through Gavin's veins. He dug his heels into the ground, wrenching his shoulder free for a moment before his captors' grips tightened on his arms. The ropes binding his wrists loosened, and his shirt tangled around his head before being ripped away. Every instinct he possessed screamed for him to fight back, escape, run, as cold iron snapped shut around his wrists.

I'm sorry, Tali. At least I can buy you some time. He set his jaw and focused on the darkness beyond the circle of trees, his oath reverberating in his mind. *May the blows of those who seek to cause her harm fall upon my head. This do I swear, until my king releases me—or I perish.*

Talianna crouched in the shadows on the far side of the clearing as the guards dragged Gavin to the posts. Her breath caught as he stared, wide-eyed and fearful, into the darkness that surrounded her. *Surely, he doesn't know I'm here. He can't.*

Her fingers clutched at the dirt as another bandit walked up holding a coiled whip. *He told me to run. I promised.* Fear froze her hands into fists and her knees to the ground. *I can't.*

The bandit leader walked around to face Gavin and said something she couldn't hear. A spark of defiance flared, thawing her limbs as her friend spat in the outlaw's face. The man reeled back in surprise before backhanding him viciously. Gavin's head snapped to the side, his face contorting in pain. *He's doing this for me. I'm not worthy of that.*

Worthy.

The word went through her heart faster than any assassin's arrow; every connotation of noble birth, good social standing, and courtly manners disappearing into shocking clarity. *The most worthy man I know has been standing at my back this whole time.*

Talianna clapped her hands over her mouth as the man with the whip brought it hissing through the air toward his victim. She closed her eyes before the blow fell, dirt-covered fingers stifling her own scream.

Gavin was not a stranger to pain—no one who'd earned a knighthood was. Still, he fought hard to stop himself from shrieking as the lash cracked across his back. He gritted his teeth and tried not to bite his tongue as another blow came. And another. Another. A ribbon of blood trickled down his spine, warm against his skin as he tried not to scream. The seconds stretched, broken only by shuddering pain and the cracking of the lash before the outlaw leader demanded, "Where is she? Tell me!"

He focused his breathing, calmed his shaking limbs, and said nothing. The man sneered and answered, "It's your life. Be stubborn if you wish." He waved his hand and another blow slammed into Gavin's back.

Talianna hadn't closed her eyes for long. The sound that the lash made as it curled through the air forced her to stay riveted to the scene unfolding in the clearing. Gavin slumped between the posts, his back bloodied and crossed with lash marks. The bandit leader hadn't stopped his attempts at convincing his prisoner to give up her whereabouts—a fact confirmed with a shouted demand that sent a white-hot bolt of terror through her chest. Each time, her friend rallied to challenge his captor, but even Talianna could see it was fast becoming a losing battle.

Can't I stop this? The thought sent a burst of heat through her heart, terror combining with the urge to throw herself from the bushes and into the circle of light. Even as her muscles tensed to obey, sudden cold arrested her movement. A chilly voice echoed at the back of her head, the same painfully correct void that greeted her each time she hesitated in carrying out her royal duties. *You have your own oath to fulfill. If you surrender, your people are lost.*

Talianna forced her eyes shut on the tears as the cold closed over her breaking heart.

I can't. Forgive me.

Her eyelids snapped open as the sounds from the clearing paused. The other bandits' faces had grown drawn and uncertain as their leader once again addressed Gavin's swaying form. This time, the questions were met with silence, and Talianna knew that silence was the only form of rebellion he could muster.

Suddenly, the outlaw's countenance changed from contempt to rage. He wheeled around, and Talianna could hear the order even from across the clearing. "Kill him!"

No. NO!

The lashes redoubled through the air, and for the first time, Gavin screamed.

CHAPTER FOUR

FAILURE

IT DIDN'T TAKE LONG.

Not even a few minutes after the bandit leader had given his merciless order, a hush fell over the clearing. Talianna took a shaky breath, her jaw aching from holding in her own distress as the man with the whip stepped closer to Gavin. He'd stopped screaming a heartbreaking minute before, and his head hung limply between bloodstained shoulders.

The bandit straightened, the quiet in the clearing so profound that his words to his commander could be heard even from the darkness beyond. "I think he's finished, Sir. What are your orders?"

Keys flashed in the firelight. "Dump him in the woods. Then get back here as fast as you can." The outlaw leader glared into the darkness, the set of his shoulders betraying no remorse at what he'd just witnessed. "We've got a princess to catch."

The sound of keys jangling against the shackles was enough to send her heartbeat skyrocketing with urgency. *He's dead.* Talianna caught her breath with a muffled sob. *He's dead, and it's my fault. It doesn't matter what happens now; I'm never going to forgive myself for this.*

She shrank away from the clearing as two other men came to help their comrade unlock the shackles around Gavin's wrists. He remained totally limp as they grabbed his arms and pulled him into the darkness less than fifty feet from where she crouched in the shelter of the bushes.

I have to know for certain. Swallowing her tears, she inched from beyond the bushes and slipped between the trees after them. Behind her, the noise from the bandit camp gradually increased, until it was the same constant rumble of voices that it had been before the harrowing events of the last hour.

The forest beyond the firelight shifted and settled in a thousand shadows, moonglow spilling through gaps in the trees to paint clearings with occasional patches of silvery light. A cluster of birch trees surrounded one such open patch of sky, the undergrowth broken where an old tree had fallen and decayed. Talianna halted as soon as the bandits did. The adrenaline from earlier was wearing off in the dark, quiet depths of the forest, and she could feel tears once more threatening to burst out and reveal her presence. She pressed herself against the smooth bark of one of the trees and peered past its trunk as the man in the lead said, "This ought to be far enough."

The others dropped Gavin's arms, the moonlight casting their shadows in jagged black shapes along the trampled grass. One of them shook his head. "It's a shame. He had spirit."

"Shut up," one of the others said. "He killed one of ours."

"I'm just saying—" He stopped. "Cor. Look."

Talianna's eyes widened as the first man dropped to a knee beside Gavin. The pale moonlight was barely enough to illuminate his bloody, motionless form as the bandit turned him over, but after a moment, Talianna realized what the bandit had noticed. Gavin's chest spasmed once, twice, then subsided into shallow breaths.

Sudden, sharp hope streaked through Talianna's chest. She wrapped her hands around the tree trunk in an effort to stay upright as the bandits took a startled step back.

"Holy Mother," one exclaimed. "He's stronger than I thought!"

"He's alive?"

"Not for long." Steel rasped from its sheath as the second bandit drew a dagger.

Just as he was about to bring the blade across Gavin's throat, one of the others grabbed his arm. "Leave him," he commanded. "He's finished anyway. Whether he stopped breathing at camp or stops breathing here, it's all the same thing."

"But he killed—"

Don't touch him. Talianna's hands tightened on the tree trunk, everything within her building in a silent scream as tears streamed down her face. *Leave him alone!*

The bark beneath her hands flexed, and everything around her seemed to shake. A deep groan reverberated through the ground as the birch leaves rustled menacingly overhead.

All three men cursed and dropped into startled crouches. "Sorcery," the one with the dagger whispered.

Talianna snatched her hands from the tree as if the bark had burned her. *Did I do that?*

The man who'd expressed pity for Gavin bolted first, the dingy white of his shirt disappearing the way they'd come. The other two straightened, the one with the dagger replacing it in his belt as his comrade whispered, "No one says anything about this."

"Right." He took a slow step away, and Talianna caught a glimpse of the whites of his eyes as he turned toward the path. "Not a word."

The rustling of ferns marked the bandits' retreat, and within a few moments the clearing was still once more. Talianna waited with her heartbeat thundering in her ears, until she was certain no one was returning. With a frightful glance split evenly between trees and path, she stepped into the patch of moonlight and hurried to Gavin, lying in the shelter of one of the birch trees. She sank to her knees, feeling under his chin for a heartbeat. After long moments, a weak, rapid pulse thumped against her fingers.

"You're alive." Whatever other words she'd meant to say dissolved into tears. "You stupid fool; why did you do it? Oath or no oath, no one in their right mind would say I'm worth something like this!"

Worth protecting. Worth dying for. Talianna swallowed her tears and took a deep breath. The moonlight shifted over Gavin's face as she looked at him with new understanding.

"I got you into this," she told him. "Now I'm going to get you out." Talianna peered at the sky. Even in the short amount of time they'd been in this grove, the darkness had shifted into the thin light of false dawn. The mental image of this corner of the country—memorized over hours of studying maps and trade routes—leaped to the forefront of her mind. From what she could remember, their destination lay east of the woods—opposite of where the moon was fast sinking.

Talianna's hands flew to the clasp of her cloak. Laying it on the ground, she managed to roll Gavin to his stomach and onto the fabric. The sight of the damage done to his back and shoulders—dirt and blood creating dark shadows across ruined skin—was enough to send a fresh rush of tears to her eyes. She forced down the emotion with a fierce shake of her head, the cold of her royal nature closing over her. *Preparing for battle, he called it. Perhaps it's exactly what I need.*

Wrapping the ends of the cloak around her hands, Talianna began hauling the improvised stretcher in the direction opposite the sinking moon. It didn't take long before dawn began to lighten the woods with a misty grey glow, and the first birds began trilling in the treetops. Gavin barely stirred beyond the occasional moan, but Talianna could see that the movement was taking its toll on his unconscious body. Fresh blood was beginning to spread in dark patches across the fabric of the cloak, and his breathing had changed cadence from barely perceptible to labored and pained.

I can't keep moving him like this.

The forest had opened out onto the bank of a tiny stream, and Talianna halted their progress to rip a band of cloth from the hem of her underskirt. She knelt beside Gavin, her stomach churning with guilt at the sight of injuries now revealed in daylight. "I'm sorry," she whispered as she pressed the cloth into one of the worst gashes. "I'm not a healer; I don't know what else to do."

She glanced over her shoulder in the direction they'd come. There hadn't been any sight or sound of pursuit, and she could only hope that the bandits had gone searching for her in the wrong direction. "This is all my fault. I'm so sorry."

The noise of flowing water was the first thing to fall on Gavin's senses. He opened his eyes to the sight of a stream only a short distance away, its cheerful gurgling harmonizing with the steady drone of bees somewhere nearby. The golden light of true dawn illuminated everything, rapidly blurring as pain overwhelmed his vision. *How did I get here?*

Suddenly, he realized there was fabric under his face—torn, bloodstained fabric the same dark grey as Talianna's cloak. No sooner had the thought crossed his mind when a shadow fell across his face, and Talianna herself appeared.

"You're awake!" She dropped to her knees next to him, one hand going out to touch his shoulder—then stopping. In a heartbreaking moment, he understood what had happened.

"What are you doing here?"

Her eyes darted away from his. "I couldn't leave you alone. I followed you."

"You should have run!" He tried to get an arm underneath himself to sit up, but the motion sent a tearing sensation across his back and shoulders, and he collapsed with a groan. "They're looking for you."

"I know," Talianna said. "I'm not sure how far away we are, but I think they're looking for me at the campsite." Tears started pooling in her eyes. "I'm sorry—I tried to get us as far away as I could, but you're still bleeding, and I don't know what else to do."

He caught his breath as clarity struck. "You saw, didn't you?"

Talianna's voice cracked. "I saw everything."

Fabric rustled as she retreated to the edge of the stream, returning to offer him a dripping handkerchief. "Here. Rinse your mouth out."

This time, his limbs obeyed him. He struggled to an elbow and took the handkerchief, wincing as a metallic taste coated his tongue. It dissipated in the first drops of water, though nothing could erase the memory of blood filling his mouth. "Thank you," he whispered.

"Can I clean your face off?"

Gavin shook his head. "Let me."

She sat back on her heels as he carefully wiped his face. Even that slow movement was enough to send his hand shaking, and the cloth fell to the ground with a dull splat. "Sorry."

"It's—it's all right." She got up and went to soak the handkerchief again. His limbs kept tremoring until he was forced to resume lying on his stomach, face resting on a bent arm. Talianna set a hand to his forehead upon her return, a frown crossing her face as her fingers touched his skin. "You need a doctor."

"*You* need to leave," he insisted. "They're going to figure out soon enough that you're not at the campsite, and if they find you, they'll kill you." He caught his breath on the heels of a spurt of pain. "You have to leave me here and go on by yourself."

Talianna scowled at him. "Absolutely not."

"Tali—"

"No!" She dropped the cloth on the cloak next to him. "If they find you here, they'll finish what they started!"

"Started—finished—it's all the same thing." He forced himself to meet her eyes, hoping beyond all hope that none of the pain was showing through. "Trust me, Tali. You'll only waste time moving me, and it's not going to change the outcome."

"You don't understand," she insisted, her hands tensing in her lap. "I can't leave you here to die!"

"You have to! I'm replaceable—you aren't!" He struggled to sit, getting as far as an elbow before stopping with a pained gasp. Something warm ran down his shoulder as he said, "If you die, this country will tear itself apart. Forget whatever brought us together in the past; what matters now is the people who'll suffer if you're lost. We're on the verge of war as it is, and this could push us over the brink." His heartbeat pounded in his ears, breath growing ragged as he put as much adamance into his voice as he could. "You're meant to lead our people, but you can't do that if you're lying dead next to me!"

Talianna inhaled sharply as if something had stung her. The edge of her skirt brushed his skin as she got to her feet, that barest touch sending a red wash of pain across his vision. The logical part of his mind warned him with a certain solemnity that he was in shock; that soon his injuries would rob him of the ability to think clearly or take action to protect himself or anyone else. *She has to leave.*

Gavin raised his head as much as he could. Talianna was standing at the edge of the river, wisps of dark hair stirring in the breeze as the water rippled past. "Please, Tali," he whispered. "I wouldn't be able to bear it if you died too."

Talianna's shoulders bowed for a long moment. Then, as gradually as twilight snuffing the light from the sky, her posture changed. Her chin lifted, her spine straightened, and her hands closed into fists at her sides. When she finally turned to face him, the childhood friend he'd spent the last few days with was gone, replaced by the woman he'd sworn to protect with his life.

"All—all right," Talianna said, her voice wavering but growing stronger with each word. "I'll do as you say." Her eyes—all business, now—roved the landscape before settling on something behind him. “Can you hide under that bush?”

He turned his head gingerly. A cluster of elder bushes stretched almost to the water’s edge, the space beneath their frothy blossoms clear of grass and shaded from the sun. Gavin gave a brief nod. “It won’t hide me if anyone comes looking, but at least it’s sheltered.”

He gritted his teeth against a wave of pain as Talianna dragged him under the bushes before pulling the cloak from beneath him. The ground pressed cold against his stomach, shivers going up and down his spine before his body grew used to the difference.

Talianna swooped the tattered cloak around her shoulders, her hands pausing as she fastened it at her neck. “Are you certain you don’t want me to leave this? It’d keep you warm.”

“No,” he insisted. “You’ll need it more than I will.”

A shadow crossed her face, cracking the perfect mask over her expression. “Are you sure? I could—”

“Don’t.” The skin across his shoulders burned and stung as he pushed himself to his elbows. “Don’t try to convince me. I can’t give in on this any more than you can.” He nodded in the direction of the rising sun. “Follow the stream; it’ll take you to the coast. When you get to your uncle, tell him what happened and ask your father to send Tristan and the others to protect you.” His voice cracked. “And when you become queen, remember me.”

Talianna’s eyes widened, her own voice breaking behind its regal cadence. “I—I will.” Before he could stop her or pull away, she dropped to a knee and kissed his forehead, the feel of her lips warm even against his burning face. Her own face was flushed as she backed up, pressing a hand to her mouth before gathering it into a fist. “I’ll remember. I promise.”

Gavin watched as she walked away, her footsteps gaining speed as she made her way along the riverbank. After a moment, he let his head fall to his arms with a broken gasp of relief that turned quickly into a sob. The fragrance of the flowers overhead filled his senses, forest sounds a soothing cadence of peace as another shiver wracked his body. *There could be worse places to die. I just never expected I'd be alone.*

CHAPTER FIVE

WOODWIFE

TALIANNA HURRIED ALONG THE RIVERBANK as fast as she could, focusing on getting as far away from Gavin as she could before her breaking heart could have the chance to betray her. His forehead had been warm, so warm as she'd kissed him, her royal nature deserting her for a moment of weakness before she'd forced herself to walk away.

I'm leaving him to die.

As she squirmed past a towering elm, her foot slipped, and she fell heavily into the mud. The shock and surprise combined in a heartbeat with exhaustion and grief, and a sob burst from her chest. *He was crying, too, as you left,* her treacherous heart warned her as she picked herself up. *You heard him.*

Yes, she had. Less than a hundred feet into her flight, a quiet sound had reached her ears—a cry, muffled, most likely, by Gavin in an effort to keep her from turning around.

I've heard that sound from him before. She clutched her cloak tighter and slid down the tree trunk to sit huddled at its base. *And it was my fault then, too.*

The past rushed in.

"You'll need to say goodbye, Tali."

Talianna frowned as she stood up. "Are you sure?" She gently laid her croquet mallet to the side. "Will there be time after lessons tomorrow?"

"I'm afraid not, sweet." Nursie squeezed her hand with something that felt like an apology. "Besides, your father says you must only play with children of your own rank from now on."

"Oh..." Talianna's face grew hot, and she blinked hard against the prickling of unshed tears. Across the pile of mallets, Gavin stared wide-eyed between her and her caregiver. "Are you sure?"

"Say goodbye, my love."

Talianna didn't wait for permission but yanked her hand free from the woman's grasp and dove toward Gavin. His arms met hers, and they clung to each other for a long moment.

"I'm sorry," she said into his shoulder. "I didn't—"

"I know," he said. "I knew it would happen eventually." Gavin's brow was pinched as they drew back from each other, his lips pressed into a thin line. "Just"—he scuffed a hand across his eyes—"don't forget me, all right?"

She took a deep breath. "I won't forget you." Nursie's hand was on her shoulder, already turning her away. "I promise."

Talianna risked a glance backwards as they walked toward the garden gate. The pieces of the game lay scattered in the grass, Gavin standing amid them with his head bowed and shoulders stooped. Perhaps it was her imagination, but she could've sworn she heard a sob as the tangled rose arbor cut off her last glimpse of her best friend.

Talianna pressed a hand to her mouth, but a pained gasp still crept past her fingers at the memory of what she'd done. *I left him.* After a few days of being escorted to and from tutoring sessions, she'd slipped past her nurse and made her way to the garden. There'd been no sign of Gavin. Further questions, answered unwillingly by her servants, revealed that he, too, had been sent away—gone until the moment he'd knelt before her to swear his oath.

We'd been reunited, and I still left him. A rush of tears came to her eyes, as burningly unwelcome as they had been on that afternoon so many years before. This time, she gave them full rein, pulling her knees to her chest and pouring out the years of loneliness into the silent woods.

After a while, her sobbing slowed. Then, from out of nowhere, a voice. "Why so sad?"

Talianna jerked upright, stifling a cry. "Who's there?"

The voice chuckled as a woman came into view from behind a clump of hazel bushes. "Don't be afraid, 'tis only I." She leaned against the elm and ran a loving hand over its bark as she asked, "Why are you crying?"

Talianna wiped her eyes and took a deep breath. Even though she looked young, there was something about the woman that reminded Talianna of her mother. Perhaps it was her beech-brown hair, twisted carelessly into a braid and dangling over one shoulder. Perhaps it was the way she leaned against the tree trunk—as if she was slowly merging with the forest itself—or perhaps it was her stillness; as if time moved differently to her.

"I'm in love with my dearest friend, and I've just left him to die." Having begun, Talianna found herself unable to stop. The woman listened to the story without interruption, only shaking her head as Talianna explained Gavin's insistence on her deserting him.

By the time Talianna's words slowed into silence, the woman's gaze had sharpened. Her hand tightened on the bark of the elm tree. "You say you left him upstream?"

"Yes." Talianna twisted her hands in the edges of her cloak. "He's badly hurt. I tried to help him, but I don't know anything about injuries." Tears welled up again as she added, "And some of the bandits know he's alive. They'll be looking for him."

The woman nodded as if this was a foregone conclusion. "Yes, they're on both of your trails. You won't escape them on your own, and he certainly won't." She lifted her hand from the tree trunk with a sharp look at the canopy. "We don't have much time. Follow me. Quickly!"

Gavin drifted in and out of sleep for over an hour after Talianna's departure. At first, the shade of the elder bushes and cool earth were unbearably cold, every breeze sending uncontrollable shivers across his skin. As the sun rose higher into the heavens, the chill turned to fiery warmth, magnifying the pain in his back and shoulders a hundred times over. His attempts to inch further into the shade only succeeded in reopening a few of the worst gashes, and the dirt beneath him eventually grew sticky with blood.

Worst of all, it became harder and harder to stay awake. Fever settled around him in a heavy, choking blanket, foggy blackness giving way to the sunlit rose garden where he and Talianna had said goodbye so many years before. Like then, she was walking away from him, her shoulders straight with what he now recognized as the first time she'd assumed her royal persona. Unlike that day, her beautiful face was filled with nothing but scorn as she looked over her shoulder.

"Father says I must only associate with those of my status. Surely you know I'm far too good for someone like you. You!" She laughed. "The *younger son* of a baron! Forget friendship; you're only worth anything as a servant."

Gavin clenched his fists, temper boiling over at the unfair accusation even as part of his mind insisted that this was merely a dream. "That's not true!" he yelled, digging his feet into the grass and sprinting in her direction. The rose bushes surrounding the garden reached out and caught him, biting into his skin as Talianna's haughty laughter turned to screaming. A stone corridor opened out in front of him, flaring torches casting pools of light among oppressive darkness.

"Gavin! Help!" Talianna screamed as a masked man dragged her around a corner. "Gavin!"

He startled awake. "Tali!"

Coherence came with the fragrance of elder blossoms and the humming of bees. He was still lying on the blood-soaked dirt, Talianna's and another woman's faces framed above him by sunlight. Somehow, he'd rolled to his side in his sleep, and Talianna was holding one of his arms. "Gavin, breathe. It's only me."

Gasping for air, he tried to sit up and collapsed in agony onto his side as the other woman reached to stop him. Full memory returned then, and he laid still. "Why are you here? I told you to leave!"

"I did leave!" she protested; her voice shot through with urgency. "I didn't get far before Melina found me. She's a healer, and she can hide both of us until you're better."

"Hide us?" he gasped. "She's one woman. What can she do against all of them? We're outmatched, Tali. You need to run!"

"Look, boy." The woodwife—Melina—looked like she was only thirty, but her voice carried the same authority as any training officer's. "I don't have to tell you that you *will* die if you remain here. Trust me, no one will find you *or* your lady." Her sun-browned face was secretive as she added, "There are protections around my home that none can pass."

"Please, Gavin," Talianna pleaded. He wasn't sure he'd ever heard such a tone in her voice as she said, "She can help us. Please."

Gavin closed his eyes against the glare of the sun, which had now slanted far enough to shine fully under the elder thicket. "I—" A ragged sigh escaped his lips. "I'm in no position to argue. Just please," he let his eyes open enough to glare at Melina. "Talianna is worth more to me than anything else, including my own life. You have to keep her safe at all costs."

"Yes, yes." The woman's voice was impatient and brisk. "I swear it, Sir Knight." There was a swish of fabric and a clatter of wood. "Now, be still and let me help you."

"Where are we?"

Talianna jumped as Gavin spoke. Hearing his voice, roughened and pained as it was, sent a wash of relief over her limbs. "You're awake!"

Melina spoke from beside a small hearth as she ladled steaming water into a bowl. Beside her, herbs hung on the whitewashed earthen wall above a polished wood sideboard. "This is my home. I tend to the people who live in these woods and who know where to find me."

"But the bandits don't?" Talianna asked, her voice catching in her throat with sudden fear. "If they find us—"

"They won't. You're safe here, but your knight is still badly hurt." Melina came to crouch and look Gavin in the face. "Sir Knight, if you are going to survive this, I need to clean your wounds." She held a finger in front of his face. "It will hurt."

Gavin gave an exhausted blink. "I understand." A flash of fire went through his eyes. "Does Talianna need to be here?"

Talianna crossed her arms as the woodwife gave her a questioning look. "I'm *not* leaving."

"So be it." Melina tossed her a drying cloth. "Go wash."

Over the next hour, Talianna came to respect the older woman immensely as she painstakingly cleaned and dressed the wounds that the bandits had left on Gavin's back and shoulders. Talianna's heart cracked a little more with each flinch, each gasp of pain from him as dirt and blood were sponged away and dying skin cleared.

All this time, I'd been measuring men by their social status and education, when all along the worthiest man I knew was standing a few feet behind me. She renewed her grasp on Gavin's hand as Melina went to switch dirtied water for fresh. *I can't believe I was so blind all those years.*

After what seemed like ages, the many cuts and swellings were clean, covered in healing balm, and wrapped in layers of light bandages. Talianna fell asleep leaning against the whitewashed wall beside Gavin, his hand still clasped in hers. She woke to find darkness outside the shuttered window, and a smell of food coming from the other room. Gavin still slept, his blond hair damp and darkened with sweat when Talianna laid her hand on his head.

Careful not to disturb him, Talianna poked her head into the other room. Melina stood at a solid table near the hearth, mixing greens in a wooden bowl. "Ah, you're awake. I just came back from checking my traps."

Talianna wrapped her arms around herself. Even with summer's warmth, the earthen house was chilly. "Don't the bandits bother you?"

The woodwife shook her head, and something feral stirred in the depths of her eyes. "They won't try me. Not if they don't want the trees to swallow them alive."

Talianna's breath caught in her throat. When she could speak, her voice had gone thin and squeaky. "Are you a witch?"

"I am not." Melina said firmly. "But you're forgiven for thinking it. My grandmother was a guardian of the forest—a dryad, I suppose." She flicked her gaze toward the ceiling, where the ridges of tree roots crisscrossed the whitewashed ceiling. "They respect me, and no one comes near me or my home unless they allow it. That's how I knew you and your knight were being hunted."

"The...trees." Talianna pressed a hand to her mouth. "When the bandits were about to kill Gavin, something shook the ground and scared them. Did—" She let her hand drop. "Were the trees watching?"

"Mmm-hmm." Melina stood on tiptoes to retrieve a basket from a shelf above the table. "The old blood still runs in the deeper parts of your kingdom, Princess. You'd do well to remember that."

Talianna glanced out the door of the kitchen. Gavin still slept, his bandaged back gently rising and falling under the thin blanket. *She's helped us so far. I have to trust her.* "Will we be all right here?" She nodded at the door. "Will *he* be all right?"

Melina took a handful of mushrooms from the basket, her movements slowing along with her words. "I've done what I can, and my skill is good. But you felt it as well as I did—he's gone feverish, and there's not much I can do if infection sets in. You've known each other for many years?"

"Yes." The simple admission didn't seem adequate, so she added, "Since childhood." *When duty pulled us apart.* "And this isn't the first time he's saved me. I don't know what I would do without him."

"Well, do all of us a favor and pray that he pulls through this." Melina swung a kettle over the fire. "There's only so much that my medicine can do."

That night, Talianna slept on a blanket next to Gavin's cot. She woke a few times to hear him sob in his sleep. In her dreams, the trees whispered secrets through the ground, their creaky voices murmuring, *No one else has been worthy. No one until now.*

Gavin didn't know how long he drifted between waking and sleeping before finally waking to find Talianna holding his hand.

"You've been asleep for three days," she told him, relief lightening her expression. "Well, mostly asleep. Do you remember anything?"

"Only nightmares," he said. "And I think I heard your voice a few times."

She smiled at that. "Melina says your fever's gone. You should be on the mend faster, now that you're not burning up from the inside."

While Talianna's words proved true, it was still another day before Gavin was able to sit unaided. After that, his strength returned quickly. There was something in Melina's care that brought restoration faster than he'd thought possible, until he could walk around the tiny house without his muscles shaking. As the week passed, it became achingly apparent that something had shifted in Talianna's attitude toward him. She rarely met his eyes, and their conversations were marked by tension; as if she was remembering something he had forgotten.

One afternoon, the tension finally broke. They were sitting outside Melina's home, shielded from the setting sun by the leaves of the trees over the house. The woodwife was nowhere to be found, gone on one of her many expeditions through the forest to collect food and check on her traps. Gavin hadn't been certain what he thought about her relationship with the trees, but the proof of her loyalty could easily be felt in his rapidly healing injuries. Besides, there had always been stories told about these woods.

Talianna made a frustrated noise beside him as she examined the rip she was mending in her cloak. The sound was so unlike her usual way of approaching difficulty, and her face so preoccupied with something beyond the simple task, that Gavin couldn't keep silent any longer. "Tali? What's the matter?"

She shook her head. "Nothing."

Gavin reached over and put a hand on her knee, moving carefully to keep the healing skin under his bandages from ripping open. "It's not nothing. You're acting different."

Talianna sighed. "I know. I'm sorry." She set the sewing down and, after a moment's hesitation, put her hand over his. "With everything that happened to you and what you said when I left, I don't know how I should act anymore."

"With what I said... What did I say?" Gavin pulled his hand away, his mind spinning with terrifying possibilities. *I was so feverish, I don't remember. I think she kissed me, but that* has *to be a dream. Did I say something foolish? What's she going to think? What's her father going to think?* He pressed his lips together. "I don't remember what I said. It's all a blurry mess. Tali, what did I say?"

Talianna looked down at the sewing in her lap. "You said you were replaceable." A tear rolled down her nose. "You had no idea you'd survive, but you did everything you could to keep me safe even at the risk of your own life." Her shoulders shook under a shuddering breath. "You sacrificed for me, bled for me, and you *still* called yourself replaceable." Her head flew up, brown eyes turned to gold in the setting sun. "Don't you understand? How can my life mean that much and yours so little?"

"No, Tali," Gavin stammered. *How is she getting this so wrong? Can't she see how precious she is?* "I'd sworn to protect you years ago, even before giving my oath to your father. Together or apart, you've *always* been the one I'd choose above all else!"

Her eyes widened. "What are you talking about?"

"Just after that day when you had to say goodbye," he hastened to explain. "My father sent me away as well; to page training." The memory of those days thrummed through his mind.

"Every family commits at least one of their sons to service. And I need your brother here."

Gavin took the letter as his father passed it across the desk. He fought to keep the quiver out of his voice, the paper crumpling in his fist as he stood as tall as he could. "Yes, Father."

"Don't worry; it won't be all bad. You'll train with the realm's best, and when you're through, you'll be a knight." Lord Andel stepped from behind the desk to hold Gavin by the shoulders and look him squarely in the eye. "I'm proud of you, son. It's a great honor to be able to serve."

Gavin nodded, ducking his head as his father released him. Riding away from the palace the next day, the memory of Talianna's straight shoulders and fierce expression caught his mind. She'd looked so small as she walked away, like the weight of the nation already pressed against her.

"She'll become queen someday," he whispered to himself, drawing his own shoulders straight. "And when she does, she'll need someone to watch out for her. I can do that, even if it means we won't ever be together again."

"I swore that day that I'd protect you with everything I had," he finished. "You're brilliant, Talianna, and not just the way everyone likes to think." His voice caught as fierce longing flooded her eyes, bright and beautiful as the warmth speeding through his chest. "You're as brilliant as the sun, Tali," he whispered. "And I've never been able to keep you out of my heart."

Before he could stop her, she hugged him. Gavin squeezed his eyes shut at the sudden pain in his back and concentrated instead on how soft her hair was against his face.

"You've hidden it all this time," she said as she sat back. The expression on her face was a perfect picture of contentment, so far removed from the perfect mask of court life that Gavin wondered for a moment if he were still feverish. "Did you ever wonder if I might feel the same way?"

"I never dared to hope," he confessed, nerves making his stomach tense. "There's such a gap between our stations, and I'm leagues below the type of man you need at your side."

"Father's only stipulation was that I choose someone worthy." Talianna flushed pink. "The rest I added because I assumed everyone expected it of me." She shook her head, the color deepening in her cheeks. "I can't believe it took something like this to break me of the thought that worthiness was only measured in status and power. I'm so sorry."

"It's all anyone's told you since you were eight," Gavin said. Warmth stirred in his chest, relief dissolving his nerves as he added, "I think I forgive you."

He'd dreamed of kissing her for years, but this was not how he had imagined it would happen. Leaning forward, careful of bandaging, he gently kissed her on the lips. Talianna froze for a moment before leaning into him, gold-touched eyes fluttering closed as her hand found his. Their interlaced fingers tightened for one, two heartbeats before she drew away with a dazzling smile. The sunlight turned the leaves golden, and for a few minutes, he was able to forget the danger.

CHAPTER SIX

SEASIDE

AFTER THE GREEN AND GOLD dimness within the forest, the sunlight glimmering off the sea was almost too bright for Talianna's eyes. Yet there the sea was, stretching out before her in depths as uncharted and hostile as the forest had seemed only a short while before.

"I've spoken with them," Melina had told her and Gavin almost ten days previous, one hand on the trunk of an oak tree as if she were merely translating the words of her timber kindred. "They'll ensure your path is swift and secure as you make your way to safety. Though, I think they may have done that even without being asked. They like you, Your Highness." The woodwife's eyes had shimmered green for a moment as she added thoughtfully, "Perhaps the old blood runs closer to your family line than you thought. If you ever have need, they'll answer to your call."

As nerve-wracking as the journey through the remainder of the forest had been, it was still strange to leave its green depths for the sunlit plains between it and the sea. Fife Corbel sprawled along the edge of the ocean, its coastal grasslands patchworked with hay meadows and livestock grazing fields. While not extremely wealthy, Talianna's uncle had nonetheless managed to build his fife's economy up enough to support a small harbor town some miles away from his castle's walls.

Almost four weeks after leaving the palace, Talianna and Gavin presented themselves in the courtyard outside the manor house of Fife Corbel. Neither had been able to bathe since leaving the woods, Gavin was unshaven, and their clothes were dirty from the road. However, the man at the gate went to fetch his master with only a few backward glances as they stood wearily on the threshold.

"I think they may not have known we'd look like—" Talianna paused, wondering exactly what her uncle's staff might have been told.

"Like peasants?" Gavin finished with a mischievous look in her direction.

"Yes!" she laughed. "You barely look like a knight, and I *certainly* don't look like a princess."

He laughed as well, but the amusement died in his face almost as quickly as it had begun. "Whoever is in charge didn't communicate well. We're later than expected; enough that the caravan with our things probably beat us here. They ought to have been watching for us."

Talianna clasped her hands nervously and looked up at the castle as it rose above the walls. It was built more for comfort than defense, with high, arched windows along the main building's upper levels. The courtyard beyond the gate housed a sprawling garden, where summertime flowers brightened the stone outbuildings, fountains, and practice court. Despite the concern and worry shaking her stomach, Talianna had to smile at the memories of summers spent within these very walls, before studies and her mother's illness had forced travel to cease. "I spent a lot of summers here."

Gavin nodded. "Your father mentioned that." His eyes narrowed as he looked first at the building, then the grassy slopes surrounding the walls. "I know this is far enough that anyone who wants to harm you will have difficulty finding you, but I'll still feel safer once you're *inside* the walls."

"Talianna! Holy Lord of Light, my dear girl; we've been worried sick about you!" Talianna's smile froze on her face as her aunt's unmistakable voice resounded across the courtyard. Trailed by the guardsman who'd gone to fetch her, the lady of the fife bustled across the space between manor house and gate to seize Talianna in a bosomy hug. Half-smothered in perfume and taffeta, Talianna only half noticed as Gavin slipped from her side to resume his traditional position several feet behind her. *That's right. No matter what happened in the woods, our situation hasn't changed.*

The thought barely sank in as her aunt released her and kept talking. "Your things arrived a few days ago, and we've put them in the tower rooms. I didn't even know when to expect you; the letter from your father said there were complicating factors surrounding your departure." She stopped and looked appraisingly at Talianna. "You're a mess, darling. What on earth happened?"

"We had some difficulties on the road, Your Grace," Gavin interrupted from behind Talianna. She had to hide a relieved smile as he took a firm step forward to come between her and her aunt. "I have reason to believe that the princess's situation here could already have been compromised. Her Highness requires a bath and clean clothing, and I need to speak with Lord Corbel at once to make preparations for her safety."

Lady Corbel practically jumped. "Oh, of course. Silly me." She grabbed Talianna's hand and waved them both forward, exclaiming, "This way, both of you. Milord isn't here now; he and the boys are finishing up some business at the port, but he'll be back the day after tomorrow." She led them into the main house before catching the attention of several servants. "You there, fetch hot water to Her Royal Highness's rooms at once."

They were shown to a suite of rooms on one of the upper floors of the main building. Gavin was pleased to see that his and Talianna's accommodations were on the same floor, his room adjoining her sitting room by a hidden door. Sure enough, their belongings had arrived already, and his single chest stood in the corner of his room. He quickly shaved and washed up in the basin near the door and put on a set of his own clothes. Digging in his chest, he retrieved his second-best wrist knife—the unmarked one he'd meant to take with them before their hectic departure from the palace. Tightening the straps around his forearm, he shook his head at his own foolishness. *That's another time one of your failures put her in danger.*

A more rational part of his mind chimed in as he folded a scarf to cushion the small of his back, where new scars crisscrossed healing skin. *The bandit leader made things very clear; someone hired them to ambush us. The odds were against us from the moment we left the palace.* He carefully belted his own sword over his tunic and checked that it was still in good condition. It felt so good, so right, to have the weapon he was most familiar with riding at his hip where it belonged.

Talianna was still in her room when he came out, admiring the way the door closed seamlessly behind him. He paced the floor of the small sitting room, examining the windows and doors. The windows were small, not matching the large-paned arches that graced the side of the building facing the courtyard. He tried the catch on one, and it swung open to allow air and light but not much else. The doors, likewise, were sturdy and banded with metal to stop even the most determined intruder. Whatever his reservations about their situation, their host did know something about ensuring Talianna's rooms were secure.

He wandered over to the writing desk and selected a pen and paper. Writing carefully to avoid smudging the ink, he started penning a letter to the king's council to request a squad of men to be sent to Fife Corbel. Halfway through his description of their journey, however, he stopped.

I'm not sure who leaked news of our departure. Gavin rested his chin in his hand, frowning at the paper as if it could provide him the answers he needed. *Only a handful of people knew Talianna was leaving the palace, and most of them hold high positions within the guard, the council, or both.* He swept the half-written letter from the desk and into the newly laid fire before starting on another, this one addressed directly to Lord Kelmar. *I have to make sure she's not left vulnerable here, and of anyone, he's the one I trust the most.*

He was sealing the envelope shut when Talianna's door opened and she came out, wearing one of her own dresses and with her hair gleaming in a long braid.

"It feels so good to be clean again, and in my own clothes." She tipped her head toward him, a frown creasing the space between her eyes. "Didn't you bathe?"

"I will later," he said. "I wanted to get a head start on some things first." He slipped the letter into his belt. "Did your aunt say the Earl was gone?"

"Him and my cousins both. I think they'll be back soon. Why?"

"I have a letter to send, and I prefer to send it secretly." He gave her a sheepish smile. "After what happened, I'm suspicious of everyone."

Talianna's expression sobered. "I understand. Now more than I ever did." Her gaze flickered between him and the door as one of the maids went out into the hallway with an armful of laundry. When she next spoke, her voice had dropped to a plaintive whisper. "Gavin, what are we going to tell them? About"—she raised a hand helplessly between them—"about this?"

"I'm not sure." Gavin paused, wishing more sunlight could make its way into this small-windowed space. The forest hadn't been kind to them, but it *had* filled Talianna with liveliness unlike anything he'd seen inside a stone building. "I know you'd been wanting to write to your father as soon as you could, but Tali, I'm afraid that whoever paid the bandits is someone very, very close to your father's confidence." He frowned and ran through the very short list of possibilities in his head. "There are only a few people who knew we were taking the forest road, but I'm not sure who hired the bandits to kill us."

Talianna glanced at the door before stepping closer to him and gently wrapping her arms around his torso. Her hair smelled of rosemary, braid still damp as she laid her head against his shoulder. "I'd hoped this would be a safer place."

"It will be, if I have anything to say about it." He held her close for a brief moment before letting her go. *Keep your wits about you. If you let down your guard now, it could spell disaster for both of you.* "I'd just sleep better if I knew who it was that wanted you dead."

Several days later, Gavin followed Talianna down the stairs to the dining room for a formal family dinner. True to Lady Corbel's predictions, Talianna's uncle had returned from business a day or two previous, and had wasted no time in ensuring his niece was made comfortable. Even with his prompt attention to Talianna, Gavin was unimpressed. He'd met the earl at court several times and was irritated to find that his previous assessment of the queen's brother as 'snobbish and condescending' was still the case. *I think I understand why the king never offered him a position at court. At least he's always been kind to Talianna.*

The sounds of cheerful talk and laughter filled Gavin's ears as he and Talianna stepped into the comfortably appointed dining room. Taking his customary place by the wall alongside the other family servants, he watched and listened with amusement as Talianna greeted her aunt, uncle, and her cousins. *You'd think they'd been apart for decades,* he thought as Lady Corbel kissed Talianna's cheek enthusiastically, *and not just for the afternoon.*

His amusement quickly died as Talianna's older cousin Roderick helped her into her seat with a practiced bow. He'd forgotten until Talianna's reminder that the children of the household spanned two decades—two older sons that Lady Corbel had borne to her first husband, and a pair of much younger daughters from her union with Talianna's uncle.

"Roderick and Brendan aren't really my cousins," Talianna had explained earlier that week. "Aunt Adeline's first husband died a few years ago, and she remarried. It's just easier to call them that, after my uncle adopted Roderick as his heir."

Well bred, well spoken, accomplished and *wealthy. Son—or at least heir—of an earl.* Gavin assessed the dark-haired older brother with a practiced eye before turning his gaze to the younger of the two men. They were even within a few years of the princess's age. *If it weren't for the familial ties, either would have been an acceptable marriage match.*

He pushed the thoughts away as dinner began, Talianna's laugh sending a shimmer through his heart and bringing to mind recollections of their time together at Melina's home. Freed from royal constraints of public life and cheered by the discovery of love, their conversations had been long, sweet, and deep as he recovered his strength.

But it can't be like that here, he reminded himself as Lord Corbel impatiently snapped his fingers at one of the menservants. *Not around other nobles. Not around anyone who won't understand. And certainly not until I make sure that she'll be safe.*

After dinner, the family retired to a library adjoining the dining room to talk and catch up. Gavin followed, taking an unobtrusive seat at Talianna's insistence. While the family chatted, he let his thoughts turn once more to the problem of reinforcements. The letter to Lord Kelmar had left via courier the day prior to Lord Corbel's return, but he knew better than to expect a response of any kind in less than a few weeks. *Assuming they decide it's worth the risk of breaking secrecy.*

Deep in thought, he hadn't noticed the drift in conversation from court gossip to the circumstances surrounding his and Talianna's departure from the palace until Roderick commented, "It was quite the ordeal for both of you to get here, I understand." Talianna's older cousin had gotten up from his seat and was leaning against one of the bookshelves, his eyes hardly leaving Talianna as he said, "Mother mentioned that you met with some trouble, but she didn't say what kind."

Gavin couldn't stop his posture from stiffening. He'd told Lord Corbel the whole story in their meeting but hadn't considered what the rest of the family had heard.

Talianna answered for him. "There were complications, yes. Though, I can't speak of all of them." She gave Roderick a dazzling smile that Gavin suspected was calculated to distract more than charm. "Security, you know. We were planning on leaving soon after the festival, but then one night—" In short sentences that left more unsaid that said, Talianna summarized their harrowing journey through the forest. The rest of the family listened with rapt attention, Roderick giving Gavin a cursory approving glance as Talianna explained that he'd been injured in protecting her from the bandits. Even with Talianna handling the tale, Gavin couldn't help a quiet exhale of relief as she finished with, "Had Sir Gavin not acted as he did, neither of us would be enjoying your hospitality now."

"I'm glad he was able to ensure your safety." Lord Corbel said. He cast a more than halfway dismissive glance at Gavin. "I'm certain that you won't have any more difficulties now that you've arrived, dear niece. My men are very dedicated to our family, and any intruders will be hard pressed to reach you with their expertise surrounding you."

Talianna nodded serenely, but Gavin noticed her jaw tightening. "I'm looking forward to the summer activities, though I'll rest a bit easier once Sir Gavin has had the opportunity to strategize." She tipped her head to the side, a flicker of cunning sliding through her cheerful mask. "Can we determine a time for him to meet the men he'll be commanding?"

Gavin had to hide a smile. *He might not see me as an equal, but he'll be hard pressed to refuse his niece.*

He'd gauged Lord Corbel's reaction appropriately. With a few more minutes of conversation, plans were laid for Talianna and Gavin to meet the men-at-arms who'd be assigned to Talianna's personal guard for the duration of her stay in Fife Corbel.

"Perhaps you'd also like to meet on the practice grounds?" Roderick suggested. "It's been a while since I was able to spar with a new opponent." He thumped his younger brother's shoulder gently, earning a grey-eyed glare. "Brendan here is good, but it's not often we get the chance to face off against another knight."

Gavin smiled, ignoring the worried look Talianna flashed him. "I'd welcome it. It's been a while for me as well." *I need to get back into practice.* He frowned slightly as the conversation moved to other topics. *We got out of the woods alive, but there's no telling what will happen once our enemies find out where we are.*

CHAPTER SEVEN

CONTEMPT

THE NEXT MORNING, Gavin met with the men chosen to protect Talianna and assigned them a schedule of guard duty. He wasn't extremely impressed with them, but he reasoned this was a symptom of having worked with the best men the kingdom could offer. More concerning was Lord Corbel's attitude. Talianna's uncle had insisted on attending the security briefing, and what ought to have been a focused planning session devolved into a struggle to maintain his authority over the men-at-arms. Gavin left the meeting fuming and uncertain if any of the plans he'd laid would even be followed in the event of an emergency.

Later that afternoon, Talianna and her maids joined him on his walk to the practice courts at the edge of the castle grounds. The two women weren't anywhere close to the nobility that had marked her previous companions, but Gavin couldn't deny that they knew a thing or two about taking care of their royal mistress. Someone—either the maids or Talianna herself—had selected a blue dress with gold accents for her to wear today, and he wondered if she knew how pretty it made her look as they walked across the grounds.

"Are you certain about this?" she asked, the levity in her voice not completely hiding her worry.

"I'm not worried. I'll be careful." He flexed his shoulders under his shirt, new scar tissue pulling as it stretched. "Besides, I need to hit *something,* and if your uncle overrides my orders one more time, it's going to be him."

Talianna's mouth pressed into a straight, stern line. "I'm sorry."

"It's all right." The words came out a little more harshly than he meant them to. "I'm used to it."

He and the brothers saluted each other as they met in the practice courts, Talianna and her maids taking seats in the shade of a nearby grape arbor. A few of the other men-at-arms were already practicing, and the clatter of practice swords soothed his frustration faster than any kind words would have.

"I know we're nobility and all, but don't go easy on us, all right?" Roderick said as they squared up for their first match. "We could use the practice."

"If you insist." Gavin hefted his practice sword. Its balance wasn't quite what he preferred, but the weighted wood still felt good in his hand. "So long as you promise you won't go easy on me."

Three matches in, Gavin was beginning to wish he'd exaggerated his confidence less. His muscles were getting shaky, and his ribs hurt from where Brendan had gotten a lucky hit against him. Worse, the confidence lent by sparring—and winning—had waned as Talianna's aunt and uncle came to join her in the shade. They'd kept to alternately chatting with Talianna and cheering for their sons, but Gavin couldn't shake the feeling that he was being assessed and found lacking by Lord Corbel. *Does he suspect something about Talianna and I? Is that why he's been so difficult?*

Roderick wiped sweat off his forehead. "One more?"

Gavin glanced over his shoulder at the group under the grape arbor. Talianna's maids had left, and she was happily talking with her aunt, but Lord Corbel gave him a measuring, condescending glance. A chill ran up Gavin's spine. "I think we'd better make this one the last."

"All right." Roderick raised an eyebrow, challenge filling his voice as he assumed a 'ready' position. "Nothing left behind for this one?"

Gavin settled his shoulders. *Remember, he's not his father. Don't hit him too hard.* "Nothing. Give me your best."

Their matches had started slowly up to this point, each combatant testing the defenses of his opponent before attacking. This time, there was no preamble. Gavin circled away from Roderick, pausing only a heartbeat before lunging. Roderick swore and jumped back a pace as Gavin's sword crashed against his.

"Careful!" Brendan shouted from the sideline.

The group under the grape arbor seemed to have noticed that this bout was fiercer than the previous one. As his and Roderick's swords met once more, Gavin saw Talianna lean forwards with concern. *She's going to think I'm being stupid. I shouldn't worry her.* A glance at Lord Corbel's unimpressed face wiped the momentary hesitation from his mind. He lowered his sword and stepped back a fraction, tempting Roderick to make a foolish move. Roderick took the bait, swinging forwards at Gavin's unprotected arm. Jumping backwards and stepping to the side, Gavin leveled his sword point at the back of his opponent's neck. "Yield."

"Don't let him beat you so easily!" Lord Corbel shouted, the words echoing across the arena. "Show him what you're made of!"

Gavin didn't think he was missing the anger that sped through Roderick's face as the other man turned to smash aside his blade. Just like that, the fight was joined again; backwards and forwards across the dusty sparring ring until Gavin's chest was heaving and his arms burning with exertion. He swung at Roderick's side, but his opponent managed to dodge aside at the last moment. Suddenly, his vision went white as something solid hit him across the shoulders. Crumpling into a heap on the ground, Gavin let go of his weapon as Roderick angled his sword at his throat.

"Yield!"

It took an agonizing long moment before Gavin found his voice again. When he could finally speak, it was as if through a mouthful of dust. "I yield." He blinked slowly as the pain shooting through his shoulders subsided. "You've been holding back."

Roderick offered him a hand up, the anger that had clouded his face replaced with cautious pride and respect. "So have you. You had me fairly, the first time." He flicked a gaze toward the grape arbor, where Lord Corbel's face had flushed with pride. "I'm sorry about him."

"I'm used to it." It was easier to say to Roderick than it had been to Talianna. "Some people only see my rank, not my title." He bent to pick up his practice sword. *And being used to it is my own lie.*

"I understand," Roderick said. He nodded toward the others. "Let's reassure your lady that you're all right."

The pain in Gavin's shoulder hadn't lessened by the time he stepped into the shade. Talianna had her hands on her hips, her beautiful face darkened with worry as Lord and Lady Corbel moved to congratulate their son. "Are you all right? Are you hurt?"

He shook his head, plucking at the ties on his jacket and shaking it free. "I'm all right, but I think—" Gritting his teeth against the pain, he dragged his shirt over his head. A damp patch slithered past his face, an unmistakable metallic tang warning him of what had occurred.

"Gavin—" Talianna's voice was hushed. "You're bleeding."

Something burned behind his right shoulder, and he caught a glimpse of fresh blood as he turned his head. One of the lash marks had split open. Before he could say anything, Talianna had pulled a handkerchief out and was pressing it into his skin. "Don't move," she murmured. "It's not that bad."

He looked up uncomfortably to realize that the others around the practice yard had gone quiet. In the shadow of the vines, Gavin could only imagine what they might—or might not—be able to see. He clutched his discarded shirt with both hands, the sudden warmth of shame sweeping over him.

"I—" Lady Corbel's voice had gone thin and shaky. "You mentioned there were injuries, but—"

"What happened?" Lord Corbel demanded, surprise overtaking the sneer in his voice. "What did he do to deserve this?"

Gavin's fists closed into tight knots around the fabric of his shirt. *Only slaves or criminals have scars like this. From now on, everyone will assume the worst.*

He was about to respond, and not politely, when Talianna stepped in front of him. Her spine was perfectly straight and her voice composed as she explained, "The bandits knew who they were looking for. Sir Gavin refused to turn me over, and they did this. They assumed he was dead, and if we hadn't come across a woodwife who helped us, he would have been." Her voice rang with authority as she added, “I owe my life to him.” The words settled like early frost over the practice arena as she turned to him. “Sir Knight, I’d appreciate it if you’d escort me back to my rooms.”

Weariness sank into his bones as he got up. “Yes, Milady.” He shook out the crumpled, bloodstained shirt and pulled it on over the open cut. It was better being in pain than being the object of everyone’s stares as he followed Talianna across the courtyard to the house. Behind him, he could hear Roderick’s and Lord Corbel’s voices, both intense with the heat of an argument. The defense heartened him, but nothing could quite undo the shame still burning his face and gnawing at his heart.

She’ll have to defend me like this as long as I’m guarding her. I love her, but I can’t expose her to that kind of contempt.

Not even the cold depths of her royal persona could temper the frustration churning through Talianna’s stomach. She threw the front door open and made for the stairs. Her skirts caught with each step until she grabbed them up out of the reach of her shoes. Gavin trailed her like a silent shadow up the stairs. He hadn’t spoken since she’d demanded to leave the practice courts, and it was a surprise when he finally said her name.

“Tali,” His hand landed on her elbow. “What’s the matter?”

She dropped her skirt and turned to face him, politeness vanishing in peculiar fury. “Him!” She began stomping up the last flight of steps toward her room. “Did you see the way he looked at you? *Talked* about you? Like you were only some foolish commoner!?”

"I noticed." An edge had crept through Gavin's voice, at odds with the stoic politeness he usually displayed around other nobles. "He doesn't seem to care much for me. At least your cousins don't seem to mind."

"Exactly! They don't care, because why would they? As a knight, you outrank them. You've seen battle and they haven't. But to my uncle—" Talianna's foot caught in her skirt, and she stumbled on one of the last steps.

As quick as thought, Gavin's hand was at her back, his other arm under her elbow to steady her. "To your uncle, I'm nothing more than a servant," he said quietly, as if he hadn't just saved her from falling. The arm around her shoulders tightened in a brief embrace before letting her go. "Don't worry about it. I'm not bothered."

They climbed the last few steps in silence. As they reached the door to her suite, the pressure against Talianna's heart built until something cracked inside. "Wait."

Gavin stopped behind her. "What is it?"

"Marguerite and Gabrielle will be inside. And I have something to say." She craned her neck to look down the hallway. For the moment, they were alone. "Gavin, I can't let this continue. What happened in the forest—it changed everything for me. I know we have to carry on acting like nothing ever happened, but I can't. I just can't."

For a moment, fierce hope flared in his eyes before disappearing under some invisible shroud. "Tali, don't," Gavin whispered. "We can't. Not here. Not around other nobles, not around anyone who won't understand." He looked at the floor, his hand tightening at his side and desperation pitching his voice. "Maybe not ever. I'm so far below you in rank; no one would accept it. And just now—that type of talk—you'd hear it for the rest of your life; people always whispering behind your back—"

"Our backs," she interrupted. "I meant what I said, in the woods. Father left the choice of my husband up to me, and while there were several good candidates, they all lacked one very important thing." She swallowed hard, remembering every ball, hunting party, and festival where the princess had blinded everyone to the girl yearning to be seen. "You looked past the princess and saw me. Just me. And you thought that girl was worth dying for." She caught her breath and pronounced, "I want to spend the rest of my life with you, and not just with you following one step behind me."

She hadn't realized she was crying until Gavin reached up to brush a tear from her cheek. "You really want this?"

She nodded. "It's the only thing I can choose for myself, and you're the only man worth choosing."

He took a deep breath, frustration and hope warring across his face. "Then," his voice came out hushed and helpless. "What would you have me do?"

"Ask." She smiled. "Just ask."

Gavin's eyes closed, brow creasing as some inner battle raged where she could neither see nor hear. Finally, his eyes opened to reveal green touched with gold as brilliant as the sunlight through forest leaves. He took a deep breath and said, "Tali, I've loved you for longer than I can remember. I know I'm below your birth, and you deserve someone who is more your equal. But there's no one else I can think of who I'd rather spend my life with." Her heart skipped a beat as he whispered, "Will you marry me?"

He'd kissed her in the forest, surrounded in a cascade of golden light. Now, in the darkness of the hallway and surrounded by the weight of duty, expectations, and contempt, she kissed him. Fabric rustled as he pulled her closer, the scars he'd earned saving her life pressing against her hands through the softness of his shirt. The warmth that normally guarded her back surrounded her as she whispered against his chest, "Of course, I will."

CHAPTER EIGHT

BETRAYAL

TALIANNA WROTE TO HER PARENTS the following day.

"I don't like it, Tali," Gavin warned. They were briefly alone in her sitting room as her maid Gabrielle ran an errand downstairs, and Talianna stood in the comforting circle of his arms. She rested her head against his shoulder with a frustrated sigh as he reminded her, "We still don't know who paid the bandits to kill you, and I'm afraid your letters to your father may not remain as private as any of us would like."

"They need to know, even if Mother doesn't understand." She pulled her face away from his shoulder to look up at him. "Father made things clear that he expected me to return from this summer with a choice in mind, so things could be announced after my birthday in the fall."

"So soon?" His arms tightened around her a fraction, the sheath of his wrist knife pressing against her shoulder blade with the reassurance that his strength could turn from comfort to protection in a heartbeat. "I thought—"

"Father's health isn't as good as he makes it appear," she confessed. "I think he's getting worried. He once told me that I'd have as long as I needed to make a decision, but lately he's been pressing me more and more each time the subject comes up. If I had to guess, I think he's nervous that he'll pass without my future being settled."

Gavin let her go, one hand going up to run through his blond hair in a helpless gesture. "I knew, but—"

"He hides it well," she said, stepping back from him as her maid entered the room with a tray of tea. "I understand it's a risk, but this type of information can't stay between us."

He nodded, a pained look crossing his face. "Send it, then."

Weeks passed. Gavin and Talianna did their best to behave as normally as possible, though Talianna soon suspected that her lady's maids had found out about their engagement. Although not of noble birth or court training, Marguerite and Gabrielle had caught on quickly to the duties of attending a princess—including noticing when their mistress needed privacy. The remainder of the family didn't seem to notice anything amiss between Talianna and Gavin, though Talianna assumed they were still too awkward with Gavin to notice anything else.

As the days slipped past, everyone fell into a peaceful routine. Still, between socializing with her aunt and younger cousins, Gavin's weapons practice with Roderick and Brendan, and the occasional horseback ride outside the castle walls, Talianna noted the passage of time with growing impatience.

"It's odd," she said one morning. Her maids perched on one of the settees in her sitting room and focused on needlework while she and Gavin read. "I sent that letter to Father quite a while ago, and I still haven't heard anything from him." She gave Gavin a significant look. "You know the one. I thought for sure he'd reply quickly, once he read it."

"That *is* odd." Gavin closed his book and frowned at the fireplace. "I also expected reinforcements from your personal guard to arrive, or at least a message that they were on their way."

The sudden silence in the room rang more fiercely in Talianna's ears than the noise of any crowded ballroom. She looked over at the older of the two conspicuously silent maids. "Marguerite, is something wrong?"

The woman didn't look up from her embroidery, giving an emphatic shake of her head. Gabrielle, the younger maid, set down her sewing and whispered something in her ear. With a frustrated look at her workfellow, Marguerite said quietly, "His Grace has been stopping your letters from leaving, Milady."

"What!"

The maids exchanged uncomfortable looks. "He gave us orders to give him any letters you sent," Marguerite said. "He told us it was for your protection."

Gavin groaned. "That *does* seem like something he'd do, and never mind telling us."

Talianna stood with a rush of skirts. "I think we need to talk to him." Lord Corbel's attitude toward Gavin had remained annoying as ever since the accident at sparring practice, and it didn't surprise her that he'd taken extra security measures without bothering to inform them. "Coming?"

Gavin picked up his sword from where it had leaned against his chair. "Coming."

Leaving her rooms, they passed the men-at-arms who stood on either side of the door and went down the stairs to Lord Corbel's study. Her uncle seemed taken aback when she explained her findings. "I'm sorry, my dear," he said, coming out from behind his desk to take Talianna's hand. She swallowed distaste at the feel of his clammy fingers as he said, "Given how perilous your situation was when you arrived, I thought it best that correspondence between the fife and the palace be temporarily halted until things settled. Though, here." Lord Corbel released her to rummage in an ornate box. He finally withdrew an envelope, sealed with the crimson and gold that marked her father's private correspondence. "This arrived just yesterday for you."

"And you didn't think to give it to me right then?" Talianna assumed the tone she typically used with minor courtiers—the tone that placed the title of 'Her Royal Highness' at the forefront of her voice. "Milord, regardless of your concerns, my correspondence with my father must take priority. There are urgent matters that need discussing, no matter the risks involved."

"Of course; I'm sorry for the oversight." Lord Corbel handed her the letter. "I'll ensure that there aren't any more occurrences like this. Unless you had anything else, Milady?"

"No, that was all," Talianna said. "I'm grateful we were able to clear up this misunderstanding." She glanced at Gavin, who'd taken up his usual spot behind her. "Gavin? Did you have anything you needed to bring up?"

"Actually, yes." He folded his arms. "I must also protest, Milord. I'm uncomfortable knowing that such an important aspect of Her Royal Highness's security was dealt with without being brought to my attention." One eyebrow raised, a challenge if she'd ever seen one. "Going forward, I'd appreciate any such measures being discussed with me *before* being implemented."

Lord Corbel gave an exasperated sigh. "Yes, yes, of course." He waved a dismissive hand in Gavin's direction as he ushered them out the door. "You have my word. Now please, I have to prepare for a meeting with my steward. If you'll excuse me?"

As the study door closed behind them, Talianna gave an annoyed huff. "Father would have never sent us here if he'd known how obnoxious my uncle was going to be." She shook her head. "He wasn't like this when I was a child, I promise you."

"I believe you. Your father isn't a fool." Gavin nodded at the letter in her hands. "I *am* grateful that he wrote, at least."

"Me, too." She frowned at the dimly lit hall. "It's too dark to read down here. Come on."

Gavin followed her up the stairs. The windows were large and graceful on the second level of the house, casting sunlight in regular rectangles on the carpeted corridor floor. Talianna broke the crimson seal and pulled several sheets of paper forth, eyes scanning each in turn. The sunbeams behind her edged her dark hair with light even as her face was thrown into shadow—a shadow that deepened the longer she read. When she looked up, her face had frozen into a formal, composed mask. "We might be too late."

Fear hammered at his heart. "What are you talking about?"

Talianna waved the papers. "M-my father. Before I left, I got fed up with his constant worrying over my marriage, and I told him he was free to make the decision for me if he thought he could choose better." She thrust the letter at him, her voice stretching dangerously close to a wail. "He always refused—he said he'd never take something from me that I deserved for myself. But now, he says that given how dangerous our journey was, he has no choice but to decide on my behalf. Look!"

Gavin stared, uncomprehending, at the words on the paper in his hand.

...harrowing journey leaves me no other option...confirm the line of succession before your return and lend stability to the realm...Roderick of Corbel, a man worthy of your time and attention.

It was instinct to reach out and pull Talianna close, holding her as tightly as he had the afternoon when they'd said goodbye as children. *We were so close to happiness.* He buried his face in the top of Talianna's head, the softness of her hair hearkening back to the moment when she'd hugged him in the forest. *At least, now, it doesn't hurt to hug her.*

At that, some part of his mind caught on the memory of new scars burning under bandages—and arrested his swirling thoughts. "Tali," he said carefully, "How did your father find out what our journey here was like?"

"I told him, remember?" she said, the thin disbelief in her voice layered under the kind of composure that said she was trying hard not to cry. "In the letter I wrote."

"The letter that was never sent." He released her to step back and look into her eyes. "It never made it to him; how did he know what happened?"

She shook her head. "It doesn't matter. He's made his choice; you saw the seal just like I did."

"I saw the seal," he answered as gently as he could. "Just—check again, please. Are you *absolutely certain* it was him who wrote this?"

He turned to look out the window as Talianna examined the letter once more. *I don't know which I hope for; to be right or to be wrong.*

A quick intake of breath sounded beside him. "This isn't Father's handwriting." Talianna looked up at him, her face painted with confusion. "I can't believe I didn't notice it before. Gavin, he *never* uses a scribe for personal letters. And—" She flipped between pages with a new urgency. "He always uses my nickname, no matter how serious the matter is. There's no mention of it here. I—" Her eyes darted at the stairs as a chambermaid walked past with a pitcher. "Something isn't right."

Gavin took her arm and drew her close enough to where no one could possibly overhear. "Someone else close to your father had to have sent this; someone who could get access to his seal. Someone who knew you were here but also knew what the journey was like."

"My uncle may have said something..."

"Perhaps, but if that were the case, why wouldn't your father have sent more men to guard you?" A warning hum had begun in the back of his head. "Your uncle may be stupid, but your father isn't. Tali, there's too much here that doesn't match."

A shadow passed over Talianna's face, as if a reflection of her royal persona had been cast over the woman inside. "You sent a letter of your own to the palace to request reinforcements, before my uncle arrived home and stopped our correspondence," she said, her voice low and filled with tension. "Who'd you address it to?"

"Lord Kelmar." Something grim yawned in the pit of Gavin's stomach, his muscles tightening as if to absorb an unexpected blow. "Something felt off about his story the night we left, but I trusted him enough to obey his orders." He caught his breath as another thought struck him. "The orders that were also sealed in your father's name. Lord Kelmar may have had access to your father's seal. And he's the only one, other than those here, who would have heard what happened in the forest."

A spark flashed through Talianna's eyes, and they narrowed. "The bandits had knowledge about the specifics of how we were traveling. You said they knew exactly who they were looking for."

He nodded helplessly. "There were only a few people who knew the circumstances of our departure, but Lord Kelmar knew the most. My only question is, how much of this does your uncle know? Is he conspiring with them?"

Talianna wrapped her arms around her torso. "I don't know! I would have said never, but with the way he's acted, I don't know any more." Her eyes locked onto Gavin's. "This was supposed to be a safe place."

"You're right." Certainty settled in his mind. "And if I have anything to say about it, it will be." He fished under his sleeve and drew his wrist knife, pressing the hilt into Talianna's hand. "Get to your room. Stay there."

Talianna nodded, icy strength filling her gaze. "Where are you going?"

"I'm going to find proof." He pointed to the end of the hall. "Go!"

She went, glancing back before vanishing around the corner. Gavin made for the other stairwell, moving as quietly as he could along the polished steps. "I hope Milord Earl actually *did* need to consult with his steward," he muttered, barely more than a whispered threat. "Otherwise, this conversation will be much more direct than anyone wants."

Luck favored him. Lord Corbel's study stood empty, the inkwell capped and pens set aside. With a rapid glance at the door, Gavin slipped behind the desk and began efficiently rummaging through stacks of documents. After long minutes, he found what he was looking for. In a box buried deep in one of the drawers, Gavin uncovered a document written in a familiar hand and sealed with a foreign signet. It was the work of a moment to read the contents of the entire missive, his heart thumping harder and harder with each passing word.

"Holy Lord of Light," he exclaimed under his breath, lowering the document with a pair of sentences burned into his mind.

With the princess well in our grasp, all that will remain is for an accident to befall the king. With His Majesty's failing health, no one will question his sudden death.

"It's worse than I thought," he gasped, stuffing the paper into his tunic. The sound of the drawer closing came mirrored, as the study door opened with such force that it rebounded against the wall. Two men-at-arms rushed in, weapons drawn and at Gavin's throat before he could free his own sword.

"Sir Gavin!" Lord Corbel's aristocratic voice was surprisingly strong as he strode into the room with another guardsman at his heels. "Why am I unsurprised to find you here, meddling in matters far above your station?"

Gavin's heart hammered in his chest. "Why?" he demanded, certain the paper tucked into his tunic was crackling loudly enough for everyone to hear. "How could you plot against them like this? They're your family!"

Lord Corbel shook his head condescendingly. "My brother-in-law has never appreciated true leadership. And with him out of the way, Talianna will need guidance. She may be my sister's daughter, but she's still a woman. She needs power surrounding her—men of true breeding and noble quality to guide her steps." The corner of his mouth twisted into a sneer. "It's something her father should've seen years ago."

"I don't care what power you think you deserve," Gavin snapped. "Plotting against His Majesty will always be treason. And Talianna doesn't need your help. She's brilliant without anyone at her side."

Lord Corbel smirked, the taunting in his voice coming straight from Gavin's nightmares. "That's exactly the type of thing a servant with everything to gain *would* say." He snapped his fingers at the guardsmen. "Get him out of here."

The men-at-arms lowered their swords only long enough to yank Gavin's arms behind him. He twisted and shoved as they dragged him out the door, shouting as loudly as he could before one of them slammed an elbow into the side of his head. Everything went dark.

CHAPTER NINE

ULTIMATUM

TALIANNA PACED HER BEDROOM, measuring the footsteps until she knew by heart exactly how many of her paces it took to cross in each direction. *Wait for me,* Gavin had said, but as the hours slipped past, dread began growing in the pit of her stomach.

Something is wrong. She bit the inside of her lip, worrying at the tangled knot of thoughts and emotion as if it were a logistics problem set by one of her tutors. *Lord Kelmar. The bandits. Father's letter. Uncle's strange behavior.* Eventually, her emotions settled, one unexpected thought rising to the surface of her mind as raised voices sounded in her sitting room.

Prepare for battle, Talianna.

She opened her bedroom door to find Gabrielle standing with her back to it, her hands outstretched and pleading. "I told you, Milord, Her Highness isn't well! She—"

"I'm here, Gabrielle," Talianna said, laying a gentle hand on the girl's shoulder. She locked eyes with her uncle, whose face was approaching the angry red ordinarily seen on midseason strawberries. "I'm feeling much better. It's all right; you can go."

Gabrielle gave her a stricken look before obeying, skirting the guardsmen and disappearing into the hall. Talianna took the moment of silence in the wake of the door closing to compose herself.

"I wasn't expecting to see you until later this evening, Uncle," she said as she stepped further into the room. "Is everything all right? Where's Gavin?"

Her uncle gave a short laugh. "Oh, him? He was found rummaging through my study."

Talianna's stomach clenched at the words, but she kept her face as smooth as possible. "That doesn't sound like him," she said. "It's possible there's been some kind of misunderstanding. Where is he now?"

"I've detained him. He won't be disturbing our conversation, if that's what you're concerned with." Lord Corbel nodded toward the paper she still clutched to her bodice. "I see you've read your father's letter."

Talianna glanced down. Her book still lay on the side table, the ribbon she'd used to mark her place a bright spot of color in a room devoid of sunlight. "I have," she answered cautiously. "I assume you received a similar one?"

"I did." Her uncle sat down without invitation, withdrawing a scroll case from his belt. "He included these." Papers crackled as he removed them from the case, their embossed edges curling across the table and hiding her book from view. "It's all arranged, and requires only your signature to complete."

Talianna tilted her head, a chill spreading through her at the sight of her father's official seal. *I need to play for time. Gavin wouldn't have been imprisoned unless he'd found something he wasn't meant to see.* "What exactly has been arranged? What is this?"

"A contract of betrothal to Roderick. Also, documents placing me in the position of advisor to your Majesty, once you take the throne."

Talianna paged through the documents, her concern deepening with each new revelation. *Betrothal contract, reorganization orders for my finances, the beginnings of a new household structure. If I go through with this, I'm reducing myself to a pawn in the hands of my advisors.* Deep inside, she had to offer grudging respect to whomever had devised the scheme. *This is much more sophisticated than merely attempting to stab me.* Finally, she looked up, simmering anger buried deep under ironclad composure. "I see here that you would also have control of my household once I am married."

"Acting in your best interest, of course." Lord Corbel crossed one knee over the other. "A queen will require a trusted advisor who can handle the daily affairs of her household. And who better than your own father-in-law?" He gently shifted the documents from her hands, pressing her fingers between his. "Tali, I know it can't have been easy, laboring under the weight of this choice for years. It's unfair to place the responsibility of the realm's future entirely on your shoulders. I'm only grateful that your father was finally able to lift the burden from you."

For a moment, he sounded like the affectionate uncle of her childhood. Tears unexpectedly welled from her eyes, and she bowed her head. *Rest and freedom, at last. An end to all the speculation. Someone else to share the load.*

It would be so easy, if only I wanted it like this. Talianna took a deep breath, the pressure of her uncle's pudgy hand against hers bringing to mind every stifling moment when she'd sacrificed the girl inside for the sake of the princess. Her hand curled into a fist as she pulled it free from his grasp.

"You have no understanding of what royal pressure feels like," she whispered. "And God help me, you never will." She raised her head, authority swelling in her voice. "My father gave me his word that my choice would remain my own. If this is truly his wish for me, then I need to consider carefully before I give any kind of meaningful answer. Even if I agreed to marry Roderick, there are certain things that will require alteration." She pinned her uncle with a clear-eyed stare. "As things stand, I'm unwilling to place so much responsibility in the hands of someone who's behaved so discourteously to me and demeaned those who I value most."

Her uncle's face flushed. "You mean Sir Gavin? Talianna, he's a *servant.*"

"He's not just a servant, Uncle," she said. "He's nobility, even if his bloodline isn't written in gold. He's earned the position he holds, and my father trusts him with my life." She nodded toward the door. "Thank you for delivering the documents. Please leave—*now*—so I can think this over."

She didn't think Lord Corbel was used to being ordered about in his own house. He strode to the door, hands clenched into fists. On the threshold, however, he turned to face her once more. "If what you said reflects your heart, then I'd caution you to think carefully of your next actions." He narrowed his eyes. "Remember, it is only you that is irreplaceable to the realm. Sir Gavin is of little consequence."

Talianna felt as if someone had poured a trickle of ice down her back. She shot to her feet, matching him stare for stare to cover her sudden fear. "Leave my rooms this instant," she hissed.

A triumphant light shone through the earl's eyes. "As you command, Milady." The door slammed behind him.

Talianna sank into her chair with shivers running up and down her limbs. The unexpected threat had completely disarmed her fearless persona, and her stomach clenched in knots at the realization of the powerful weapon she'd handed her uncle. "Oh, Gavin." She pressed a hand to her mouth. "What have I done?"

Blackness.

What in—Gavin's hands flew to his face. No blood or pain met his fingertips, and he breathed a relieved sigh. Blinking hard, he peered into the darkness until, finally, a sliver of light registered on his consciousness. He was lying on a chilly stone floor, the light a crack beneath the door of the room. Slowly getting to his knees, then his feet, he groped around until he was certain of his surroundings—a storeroom of some kind, most likely in the basement of House Corbel. The darkness was less disorienting with his eyes closed, so he shut them again and felt his way back to the door.

Sitting with his back against the wall, he pulled his knees up and wrapped his arms around them to conserve body heat. The movement made the paper in his tunic crinkle, and he pulled it free with a grim chuckle. The guardsmen had taken his sword and other weapons, but the hastily tucked paper had somehow escaped their notice. *They'll regret that, once their master finds out it's missing.*

He smoothed the paper across his leg before running his fingers down its surface until they reached the textured wax seal. *Lord Kelmar's handwriting; I'd recognize it anywhere. But a foreign seal—a Treluthian seal. And they're not only after Talianna, they're after the king as well. If His Majesty dies and Talianna takes the throne while in their control, we'll be at the mercy of our enemies.*

He sighed and let his head fall back against the wall, half-remembered visions of the border posting lurking past the edges of his mind. *His Majesty's staved off open war through diplomacy and subterfuge time and time again, but campaigns are never fought on just one battlefield. Us coming here was meant to avoid complications, but I didn't expect our enemies to be one step ahead of us.*

A thought occurred to him, so ironic despite his situation that he had to laugh. *This ploy of controlling Talianna instead of outright killing her really is their best one yet. I almost wonder if they're glad she survived the forest.*

The paper folded small enough to be tucked between his sock and his calf, in the spot where a boot knife ought to have rested. With the incriminating document hidden, he got to his feet and began pacing the small space. *Talianna can't agree to this. I don't think she will, anyway—even without knowing about the threat to her father, she's smart enough to recognize a terrible decision when she sees one. But more than that, we need to get word to the king—or warn him ourselves.*

Gavin halted his pacing, eyes now adjusted enough to the darkness to notice the shift in light at the bottom of the door as someone approached. The door opened in a squeal of ungreased hinges, admitting a blinding wave of light broken by the shape of a guardsman. Gavin flung himself toward the opening, smashing the man's head against the wall and bolting into the corridor beyond.

Torchlight pierced his vision, as blinding and disorienting as the darkness had been. Voices rang through the corridor, someone yelling, "Stop him!"

A hand caught at his shoulder, and he twisted wildly, his shirt-sleeve tearing. He punched the person holding him, and his fist ached as the blow connected. His assailant staggered backwards with a gasp, the sound familiar enough that he pulled his next punch long enough to recognize Talianna's cousin Roderick. "You!"

The hesitation was all it took. A spear haft thudded across the back of his head, and he staggered and fell. Voices swirled around him, mixing with the clank and rattling of metal on stone. He felt himself dragged, and something cold snapping closed on his wrist before the voices subsided. Eventually, the world tipped right side up once more. He was still in the storeroom—now illuminated by lantern light—with his right wrist manacled by a chain fixed into the wall. Roderick leaned against the opposite wall, his gaze equal parts concerned and wary as he said, "Welcome back. We need to talk."

Gavin's head spun as he dragged himself into a sitting position. "Why are you here, traitor?"

"The earl sent me." Roderick winced and put a hand to his collarbone where Gavin had punched him. "He wanted me to make sure you were well secured, and now, I think I understand why. At least you didn't break anything." He stopped and shook his head, voice growing exasperated. "Will you stop glaring at me? I promise, I'm not here to bother you."

"Really?" Gavin didn't bother hiding the sarcasm in his voice as he rubbed the back of his head. The dizziness was lessening, but a splitting headache had begun. "You did a really fine job of showing it."

Roderick held his hands up, his dark eyes flashing. "I'm not the one who attacked the first person through the door! And if I hadn't let them knock you out, they'd have kept hurting you." He looked away, his voice lowering in something that sounded like shame. "It's the earl's orders. He wants Talianna to sign over her freedom in exchange for your safety."

Pain welled in Gavin's heart. *I knew we'd been too obvious. How can I have been this stupid?* "I hope for her sake that she doesn't," he answered bitterly. "And you'd better be warned; it'll take a lot more than your father's bloodthirsty guardsmen to break me."

"I know." Roderick shifted his weight from side to side. "Look, I see how much you care about Talianna. It's obvious in how you've put yourself in danger to protect her." He raised an eyebrow. "That kind of disregard for your own safety goes beyond an oath of duty."

Gavin looked up in surprise. There was respect in the other man's eyes. "And?"

"My father's actions, whether successful or not, are going to ruin my life. If he succeeds, I end up a puppet king. If he fails, I'll suffer along with him for my part in his schemes." Roderick fixed his gaze on the floor. "I respect my cousin, and I do feel that she and I could make a good partnership, but I can see that I'm never going to win her heart."

Gavin forgot all about his headache. The chain around his wrist clanked as he got to his feet, using the wall for support before standing on his own. "Help us, then."

"How?" Roderick shook his head. "You don't know what I know. You don't know the—" His voice dropped, and he glanced at the door. "You don't know who he has behind him. Or what they'd do to my family if I did anything other than play along." He passed a hand over his face, desperation roughening his voice. "My mother, my brother—Holy Lord of Light, my *sisters*—they're trapped in this as certainly as I am."

"Trapped or not, we need to do something," Gavin argued. His stomach clenched at the panicked look on the other man's face, but he forced himself to keep his mind on the only thing that mattered. "Where is Talianna now?"

Roderick frowned. "Her rooms. She's not letting anyone in, and she threw my father out when he went to try and speak with her."

"That does sound like something she'd do." Gavin glanced at the door, uncertain if there was anyone outside who might overhear. "You know there's more to this conspiracy than just Talianna's future. Our entire country will crumble if your father and his allies get into power."

"You're right. That's why I'm here." Roderick sighed. "If it weren't for who he's working with, I'd have stayed out of this and done whatever I needed to in order to assure my mother and siblings' safety." His hand balled into a fist. "He's not really my father, anyway. Mother only married him after my and Brendan's *real* father got killed in a border skirmish with Treluthian outriders."

Gavin took a sharp breath and steadied himself against the wall, its bulk solid against his hand as visions of several years ago flashed through his mind in a blur of red. “Your father was there?”

“He was there. Mother knew marrying Lord Corbel would ensure our security, but I don’t think she ever expected he’d join forces with the men who were responsible for her first husband’s death.” Roderick’s face had been stony, as unmoving as Talianna’s face when she was at her most regal. Now, Gavin recognized the growing desperation in the other man’s eyes, and it brought to mind a piece of wisdom from his training master. *Never back an enemy into a corner with no way of escape,* the man had warned. *You never know what he might be willing to try.*

“If my stepfather’s masters take power, there’ll be violence. No matter what they think, they won’t find this country willing to fall into their power easily. My family’s story will be played out hundreds of times over.” Roderick lifted his head, light burning fiercely in his eyes. “Helping you is the only way I’ll have any hope of protecting my family *and* retaining my honor. I don’t know how we can stop them, but—” He took a single step toward Gavin and put out a hand. “Allies?”

Gavin eyed him for a long moment. Finally, the chain rattled as he extended his own hand. “All right.”

CHAPTER TEN

ALLIANCE

"I DON'T BELIEVE YOU," Talianna said flatly as she stared at Roderick across her sitting room. It'd been hours since she'd banished her uncle from her suite, and her tiny windows now opened only onto darkness. Her shoulders felt tight, and her head ached as if she'd been bearing the weight of her ceremonial coronet the whole day. *And in a sense, I have.*

Roderick crossed his arms defensively. He'd kept his distance since being shown in by the men-at-arms outside the door, barely stepping into the circle of light cast by the fire. "I've told you everything I can. I don't want my mother and sisters to suffer if Father finds out what I've done."

Some of Talianna's hostility drained away, replaced by exhaustion. "I can't fault that." She sank into a chair. The door to Gavin's room stood open beside the fireplace, his absence at her back sending a hollow, lost feeling through her chest. "How long have you known about the plot against my father?"

"Not until today. Father didn't see fit to mention it until after he'd arrested Sir Gavin." His voice dropped to an ashamed whisper, the echoes of a frightened child coming through it as he said, "He told me to go downstairs with the guards and hurt him enough to make you change your mind."

Talianna's head shot up. "And you *listened*?" She stormed across the room and yanked open the door. "Get out. I can't believe I thought for even a moment that you'd help me. You're as bad as he is!"

Something she couldn't name flashed through Roderick's dark eyes. "Talianna, stop." In one step, he was at the door, pushing her aside and closing it with such force that the frame rattled.

"Don't touch me!" she spat, drawing back a hand to slap him with all her strength. "Leave me alone!"

Roderick caught her wrist before the blow could land. "I *didn't hurt him*, Talianna. I swear." He released her and took a step away, holding open hands in front of him. "I did what I could to keep him safe."

Talianna drew instinctively back. Roderick was barely an inch or two taller than her, but in the darkness beyond the firelight, he seemed so much bigger. *I couldn't get past him even if I had a weapon.* "Then tell me the truth," her voice cracked. "Do *you* want this?"

"Do I—" Roderick's jaw dropped. "No!" He stepped farther away from the door, the firelight casting a glow over the side of his face. "I only want my family to be safe. I can't stand the way my father looks at my sisters—the girls *he* was responsible for bringing into the world." The glow spread over his face as he kept retreating. "He thinks they're nothing, the same as he thinks Sir Gavin is nothing. He can't be trusted with power, Talianna. And neither can the men he's working with."

Talianna took a deep breath. "Then who are they?" She pointed a warning finger at him. "You say you're on my side, so prove it. Who is directing your father in this lunacy?"

For a moment, she thought Roderick wasn't going to answer her. Then, he dug in his pocket and flipped a gold coin into the air. It flashed in the firelight, landing with a heavy thud on the rug. Even in the dim lighting, Talianna could make out the double-headed wolf of Treluthia.

"Them?" she whispered. "*That's* who's behind this?" She bent to pick up the coin. It felt every bit as heavy in her hand as it had sounded when falling to the floor.

"Father gave that to me when he explained the rest of his plan this afternoon." Roderick had stepped closer to the fire, its light edging his green tunic with gold. "Along with about ten others. He must think I'm as driven by greed as he is."

Talianna closed her hand on the foreign coin, its edges digging into her palm. Something dangerous had begun stirring in her chest at the sight of the crest, as determined as the light she'd seen in Gavin and Roderick's eyes each time they sparred. "He'll regret that decision soon," she vowed. The fire warmed her face as she crossed to stand in front of it, returning the coin to her cousin. "If we're going to warn my father, we need to move quickly. Can you get us horses and supplies?"

"Yes, easily. Especially with how much gold Father just tossed my direction. But my mother, my sisters." Roderick turned the coin over in his hand, a frown stamped on his face. "I can't leave them. You're going to have to escape on your own, and you know what happened the last time—"

Talianna took a deep breath, the popping of an ember falling on her ears like a whip crack. "I know. But last time, our enemies were ahead of us." She dared to smile at her cousin, the light playing across his form reminiscent of the sun shining through leaves. "This time, we'll be ahead of them."

Several days passed, as filled with tension as an archer's bowstring. For Talianna, the hours had become a deadly game of chess against her uncle, as she drew upon every ounce of diplomacy and strategy she possessed to avoid signing the documents that still lay upon her sitting room table. After the first day, she'd been confined to her room save for closely supervised walks in the grounds with Roderick.

"If I'm to spend the rest of my life with him by my side," she'd insisted. "I have to be given the opportunity to speak with him one on one. No matter what my father says, I *cannot* agree to marry someone I've had so little time with."

Her uncle had reluctantly agreed, and this afternoon saw her and Roderick walking between the grape arbors of House Corbel. The heat of summer lay heavy against Talianna's skin, and the scent of flowers and horses filled her senses as they passed the stables. "You *were* able to secure horses?" she murmured, quiet enough that the servants tending the gardens would be unlikely to hear.

"I did." Roderick stopped and directed her attention to one of the paddocks, where two horses—one bay, the other blue roan—were being exercised by a groom. "Those two, there."

Talianna nodded approvingly. "Thank you. I'm not the best judge, but I think they're beautiful."

She thought Roderick was about to say something else as they rounded the paddock, but his eyes flicked to something behind her, and his posture stiffened. Talianna turned with sudden fear clutching at her heart to see her uncle approaching them, flanked by two men-at-arms.

"Talianna," Roderick said from behind her, his voice low and urgent. "Do you trust me?"

Adrenaline shot through her veins, cold composure seizing her limbs. She lifted her chin. "I have to."

"Good." He stepped past her, posture and voice both shifting to something more confident as he addressed Lord Corbel. "Father, thank you for joining us."

"My pleasure. You did what we'd arranged?"

Talianna thought a shudder passed through Roderick's shoulders as he nodded. "I did. Perhaps you'd like to escort Her Highness?"

Sickening dread crept through Talianna's stomach as her uncle came to take her arm. "Of course. Milady, please join us." It wasn't phrased as a request.

"What's going on?" she asked as they entered one of the service corridors of the main house. "We'd barely started our walk, and—"

"Please, spare me," Lord Corbel said, releasing her arm as, ahead of them, Roderick struck flint to steel. Torchlight bloomed in the opening of a stairwell. "I'm a patient man, Talianna, but these delaying tactics are getting tiresome."

Talianna squinted in the dimness at the bottom of the stairs. The doors opening off the corridor looked like storerooms or wine cellars—*Or cells.* Her heart started pounding. *Gavin. He's here.* She turned to her uncle. "Why are we here?"

"I warned you that your servant meant nothing. So far, you seem determined not to listen." Her uncle rounded a corner into a passageway lined with storerooms. Two guards stood at the end of the corridor, Roderick already striding to join them.

Talianna stopped and pressed a hand to her mouth. One of the men-at-arms put a hand to her shoulder, urging her forward as her voice came out shrilly. "What did you do?"

"Only what I promised would happen if you continued to be stubborn. Open it," Lord Corbel ordered.

Roderick pulled a set of keys from his belt without meeting Talianna's furious gaze. The door squealed on ungreased hinges as he opened it. "Here."

Talianna wrenched her shoulder free and ran to the door. Her heart sank at the sight of Gavin, sprawled on the floor unconscious with his face bloodied. "Gavin!"

Roderick caught her with an arm around the ribcage as she pushed past him. "I'm sorry, Talianna."

"Let go of me! Let go!" she shrieked, all sense of princessly composure gone as she rounded on her uncle. "How could you do this!?"

"This doesn't have to happen, Talianna," Lord Corbel said from the corridor. "It can stop at any time." His expression hardened. "You can stop it at any time." He gave a curt nod to Roderick. "See if you can talk some reason into her, then take her back to her rooms. I'll be in my study."

As her uncle's footsteps retreated, Talianna managed to elbow Roderick in the side. "I trusted you," she hissed as he doubled over with a groan. "You beast!"

A familiar voice cut through her rage. "Tali, stop."

She looked up, wide-eyed. Gavin was sitting up, blood staining his sleeve as he wiped it away from an otherwise unmarked face.

He returned her shocked expression with a reassuring smile. "It's all right."

Talianna shoved Roderick away and fell on her knees next to Gavin. She wrapped her arms around him, fingers clutching his shirt in a fierce embrace. "You're all right?"

"I'm all right," he reassured her, his hands gently drawing her back before going to brush an errant curl from her forehead. "I'm not hurt, Tali. It was a trick."

"But the blood—"

"Not mine," Gavin said. He looked up at Roderick, still standing in the doorway. "I think it was a chicken."

"A duck," Roderick said. "And it was more difficult to get *that* than it was to get the horses."

The door screeched closed, leaving the three of them alone in the tiny room. "I'm sorry, Talianna," Roderick said as he came to kneel alongside her, eyes cautious as if he expected her to hit him again. "We needed something to happen that would result in you barring everyone from your rooms, and I couldn't risk your reaction being anything other than real."

Talianna sat back on her heels. "This was planned?" She shot Gavin a look that was meant to be fierce but dissolved into a smile. "You've been working together?"

"We came to an understanding." The chain trailing from his wrist clanked as he wrapped his hand around hers. "This part was Roderick's idea, though. We weren't sure how else to take your uncle's attention off you."

"I'm not sure how long it'll buy you," Roderick added. "Hopefully, enough for you both to get out of the fife without being pursued."

Urgency stirred, tempered by the reassuring warmth of Gavin at her side. "We're leaving soon, then?"

Both men nodded, but it was Gavin who answered. "Tonight."

The sun had long sunk below the horizon when Talianna slipped down the stairs behind Roderick. The brush of her cloak against the stairs, coupled with the feel of her boots against her feet, was so eerily reminiscent of the last time she'd fled under cover of darkness that she found her nerves coiling into tight knots as the sally port in the outside wall came into view. Gavin waited just beyond, holding the reins of the two horses she'd seen earlier that day. He met Roderick with a brief handclasp before catching her in a strong, one-armed hug and pressing a kiss into her temple. "No trouble getting out of the house?"

She shook her head and pulled her hood over the scarf she'd wrapped around her hair. "Not yet."

"You need to hurry," Roderick warned from the sally port. "The guards aren't the most attentive to this side of the house, but there's always the chance that one of them might decide to be thorough for once." He passed Talianna a satchel. "That's everything I was able to collect from Father's study. It should have the details a magistrate will need to bring him and his allies to justice. Just—" His features were dark in the shadows under the wall, but she could hear the uncertainty in his voice. "Remember my family when you decide my fate."

Regret stung Talianna's heart. Any magistrate would undoubtedly view Roderick's involvement with his father's plans as damning and treasonous—a fact he certainly knew as well as she did. "I'll try."

"Protocol may not allow her to speak on your behalf, but I can," Gavin said beside her. "You were handed the chance to take power for yourself and chose not to. That'll mean something in the right ears. I'll do whatever I can to keep you out of prison and away from the headsman."

"Thank you," Roderick said, taking a step backwards with a cautious glance at the top of the walls. "You'd better go. I'll stall my father as long as I can. You'll be all right traveling through the forest?"

Talianna accepted Gavin's boost into the saddle. "We'll be all right." She peered into the darkness, envisioning the green depths of the woods. "There are things in there that not even your father's masters could have predicted, and we didn't leave without allies."

They rode hard through the night and into the next day. Spurred on by the need to put distance between themselves and Fife Corbel, Gavin kept their pace as fast as he dared until the rolling plains melted into the fringe of the woods. Dismounting alongside a stream, he tipped his head back and looked up at the green canopy as the horses drank. Talianna slipped from her horse as well, coming over and leaning against him. Her shoulders hitched with sobs as she buried her face in his tunic front. "I don't want to be back here."

Gavin closed his arms around Talianna and held her tight, his own chest shuddering with suppressed tears. "I know," he whispered. "I know."

"I had to be so *royal* with Roderick," she said against his chest. "I had to be certain of everything, and there was no one to *see* me."

He drew back from their embrace and gently cupped the side of her face in his hand. "I see you, my sunlight. I always have. And we're going to be all right." He gave the treetops a glance. "Though, it would be extremely helpful if your hunch proves accurate."

Talianna nodded, drawing a deep breath as she stepped away from him. Gavin laid a cautious hand to his sword hilt as she walked between the trees in the little clearing, her fingertips trailing across the bark of each as she passed it. Finally, she gave him a sheepish smile, so far removed from her regal composure that he had to smile back. "I don't know what I'm supposed to do."

Gavin shrugged. "That woodwife said they liked you. And you *did* get their attention when I was in danger." He looked up at the canopy of leaves, intertwined branches blocking out the sky in a lacy labyrinth of foliage. The sounds of the forest filled his ears, thus far carrying no hint of danger. *I can't believe I'm suggesting she talk to the trees.* "Try," he finally said. "We never know what could happen."

"All right." Talianna crossed to the foot of an oak tree. With a deep breath, she splayed both hands across the craggy bark. The leaf-filtered sunlight seemed to hum, and Gavin could have sworn a tremor passed through the ground. For an instant, the brown and gold in her eyes became touched with green, the bizarre light fading like a forgotten dream almost as soon as Gavin noticed it.

"Anything?" he asked, half afraid of the answer.

Talianna frowned. "I think so." She raised a hand to her brow, voice going hushed. "I—I think they heard me. It was like hearing someone I'd known my entire life. Maybe Melina was right, after all."

Gavin nodded. "Old blood, hm? Perhaps the stories knew what they were talking about."

"Maybe. Though we should probably still travel quickly. We have a long way to go."

CHAPTER ELEVEN

NOBILITY

THE BLESSING OF THE TREES followed them through the forest for the next several days—revealing itself in leaves rustling counter to the breeze, a path unexpectedly smooth, and passage so swift that Gavin could hardly believe it to be true. Talianna alternated between cheerful and pensive, occasionally staring into the green depths with a look on her face that said she herself barely believed the favor that followed them. Sooner than either of them expected, they were nearing the edge of the forest. The canopy had thinned, and Gavin began to see the towers and crenelations of the palace in the distance as he and Talianna came over a rise, leading their horses behind them with slow steps.

"Home," Talianna said beside him.

He looked over to see a wistful smile crossing her face. "Didn't think you'd miss it as much as you have?"

She brushed a hand through the leaves of a weeping willow. "So much about me is different now. I hadn't expected it would still feel the same, but somehow, it's still home." The wistfulness faded from her face as she looked down the path, calculating intelligence taking its place as she asked, "Are you ready?"

Gavin nodded, turning to tighten the straps holding their bedrolls to his saddle. "We need to get inside and find Tristan.

I don't think it'll be safe to make any moves on Lord Kelmar until we've gathered reinforcements." He had to hide a wince as he faced forward once more, the scars across his back still tight and unaccustomed to the twisting movement. "I know I'm not supposed to admit to being afraid, but this number of unknown factors is frightening. We know their plan is for your father to suffer an accident, but we don't know when or where. And I'm not sure how to get close to your father to warn him without putting us both in danger."

Talianna's face pinched in a frown. "The servants' corridors, to start with. Though, now that I think about it—" She looked up at the sky, which was becoming more and more visible through the tops of the thinning trees. "What day is it?"

Gavin shook his head. "I have no idea." He counted back the days in his head from when they'd left Fife Corbel. "I think it's coming near the end of the month."

"You're sure?"

"As sure as I can be," he said. "We left at the beginning of summer, and it's getting close to Midsummer now..." A chill went up his spine at the thought. By the look on Talianna's face, she had come to the same conclusion. "If I were going to stage a fatal accident in order to create chaos in a kingdom—"

"They're going to make their move soon," Talianna finished for him. She eyed the distant palace with the same type of grim determination he usually associated with soldiers facing the enemy. "We may not have much time."

They skirted the edge of the woods until they reached the gate through which they'd departed so many weeks before. Once there, Talianna pulled her hood up to cover her face while Gavin talked in undertones with the guards. From the cadence of their conversation, and the body language that slowly shifted from suspicion to respect, she gathered that they recognized him—and that he'd managed to gain their trust.

Maybe it's for the best that others hear about the outside threats. Then, if we fail, maybe some will suspect that everything isn't as it should be. The thought of failure sent creeping fingers of dread up and down her spine, and she shivered despite the heat of the summer sun. *We're doing all we can, but what if it's still not enough? I've studied and prepared to the best of my ability, but I'm not ready to lead a country to war.*

She was shaken from her teeming thoughts by Gavin's return from his conversation with the gate guards. "Let's get out of sight."

He led her toward one of the stables, where they left the horses and their belongings in an empty stall. Talianna made sure to grab the satchel of documents that Roderick had given them before following Gavin into one of the service corridors that paralleled the main hallway of the palace. Servants scurried everywhere, most so intent on their work that they barely took a second look at either her or Gavin as he led the way toward the royal family's rooms.

Catching up with him at a corridor juncture, she whispered, "No one's recognized me."

He gave her a fleeting smile. "You're not supposed to be here, and you're wearing commoner's clothes. The servants are too busy, and the nobles won't see you at all."

Her hand went up to the scarf she'd hidden her hair in. Comparing herself to the servants bustling past, she estimated that she resembled a scullery maid or lower-class maidservant. "That's something my tutors never covered."

"It's easy to be invisible when all anyone sees is your job," Gavin said. Belatedly, she remembered all of her uncle's jabs as his voice hardened. "No one thinks a servant's life is worth much, anyway."

"I'm sorry."

"It's all right." He shook his head, but she caught the flash of a lie in his eyes as he turned away. "Let's get to your rooms. There's a good chance that some of the guard will still be posted there, and they can gather the others while we warn your father."

She nodded, resting a hand on the satchel at her side. The documents and foreign coins weren't heavy, but her shoulder still felt weighed down with the urgency of the situation. They hurried up the twisting stairs that led to her room, the lantern-lit stairwell echoing with their footsteps before Gavin pushed open the servants' entrance to the sitting room.

Immediately, his shoulders stiffened, and his hand went to his sword hilt. "Tali, run!"

She had barely enough time for a fleeting glance into the room before her vision caught a glimpse of armed men and the glitter of drawing steel. Then, instinct took over, and she sprinted, pell-mell, down the staircase and back into the labyrinth of servants' corridors.

Gavin wasn't sure who was more surprised; himself or the men-at-arms around Lord Kelmar. He took in the contents of the room—barred door, nondescript clothes, and more than one person with noble bearing—in the heartbeat before hands went to weapons and voices raised in surprise.

"Tali, run!" He kicked the door shut on the echoes of Talianna's footsteps, put his back to it, and drew his sword.

The door at the bottom of the stairwell burst open as Talianna stumbled into the servants' corridor on the second floor. She slammed it behind her and ran down the corridor, not slowing her steps until she'd turned two corners and gone down another flight of stairs. Once surrounded by the steam and clamor of kitchen, scullery, and laundry, she paused at a corner to compose herself. Her hand tightened around the strap of the satchel. *Gavin's bought me a few minutes, but it won't last. I need to get help.*

There's too many of them. Gavin gasped as one of the guardsmen's swords traced a stinging line along his arm. He stepped back as far as he could, his boot catching on the outflung arm of a downed man. Balance lost for a split second, he regained his footing only to find his grip on his sword hilt growing slippery as blood slid down his arm.

She still has all the proof her father will need, he reminded himself. *She just needs to make it to him.*

Gavin launched himself at the guards once more. This time, the exchange of attacks was shorter, ending with his back pressed against the door and nowhere else to retreat to. *That's all I can manage.* His sword slipped from his grasp and fell to the floor as the remaining guards leveled their weapons at him. *Sorry, Tali.*

"Hold!"

Lord Kelmar had rounded the table, his hand close to his own sword hilt with an amused look in his eyes. "You are *not* the man I expected to see here, Sir Gavin."

"I could say the same thing," Gavin answered, keeping his eyes on the man he'd once trusted with Talianna's life. "Though, I wouldn't put it past you to have commandeered the rooms of the woman you tried to murder." He laughed at the duke's raised eyebrow and the surprise on the faces of the few other courtiers in the room—men he barely recognized, who seemed rather perturbed by the turn of events. "Yes, we know about that." He clamped his hand against the wound in his forearm as the guardsmen who'd defeated him grabbed his shoulders. "We know all of it. No matter what, your plans won't succeed." *I hope.*

Lord Kelmar's eyes flicked to the dead and wounded guardsmen on the floor. "I underestimated you both. I won't do that again." He took a sudden menacing step toward Gavin. "Where's the princess now?"

Gavin shook his head. "I have no idea. Ideally, she's getting as far away from you as possible." He couldn't help the contempt that came through his words. "You swore just like I did to protect the royal family, *on your honor.*"

Lord Kelmar's laugh came out more like a snort. "Honor? I gave that up years ago. All that matters in this age is power, and there's no power greater than the one that sits on the throne." He drew himself up with a stern look at his allies—a general commanding his army. "Kennon, go secure His Majesty. If the princess shows up, do whatever you must to keep them apart." He leveled a stare colder than any of Talianna's royal looks at Gavin. "I'll be there after I deal with this...issue."

Sudden panic struck through Gavin's heart as the guards bound his wrists with what felt like knotted handkerchiefs. *I hope Talianna had enough time.*

"Find a bag to go over his head," Lord Kelmar ordered. "I don't want anyone recognizing him."

Even with the dire situation, Gavin couldn't deny a twitch of satisfaction as the men rushed to do their master's bidding. *At least one person doesn't assume all servants are invisible.* He gave the bonds around his wrists a cautious tug, wincing as the movement stung the cut running up his forearm. *I don't have much of a chance to escape from here. Out in the open, I might have more of an opportunity.*

"I'm surprised you survived the forest."

Gavin looked up in surprise as the duke spoke. Even with his suspicions, it was still shocking to hear the admission out loud. "You planned it?"

Lord Kelmar shook his head. "She was *supposed* to reach the fife unharmed; it wouldn't have been believable for her to mysteriously disappear in the woods. Some of my other compatriots took things into their own hands." Something like a thundercloud passed over the nobleman's face. "They've been dealt with." He crouched to pull Gavin's wrist knife from the body of a dead guardsman, examining the blade before tossing it across the room. "They didn't believe me when I told them it was a pointless endeavor anyway. I knew all along that you'd do whatever it took to ensure she survived the trip."

"I hold to my oaths," Gavin said from between clenched teeth. "Something you seem to have forgotten in your pursuit of power."

"Knights are all the same. Honor and duty, always." Lord Kelmar sighed as one of the guardsmen emerged from Talianna's bedchamber with a wide scarf. "It's a pity. I could've used a man like you." He gestured at the door with a curt order to the guards, "Get that over his eyes, and let's move."

Gavin closed his eyes as the blindfold went on, enveloping his head with soft blackness and distorting most sounds. The smell of lavender that normally clung to Talianna's clothes stirred his senses, and for a moment, he could picture her face silhouetted against the sunlit woods. He took a deep breath, the moment of peace broken as a firm hand wrapped around his bicep and shoved him forward.

Muffled sounds filtered through the blindfold as the guardsmen propelled him down the stairs and into what he guessed was the service corridor immediately below Talianna's rooms. While a few noises sounded like exclamations of dismay or consternation, he assumed that the presence of the duke—walking alongside the guards and their bound prisoner—was enough to deter most servants from voicing objection or confusion. *I can't believe I didn't see this in him before.*

After a few minutes of walking, a fresh breeze brushed across Gavin's skin. While he'd lost track of their direction, the warmth of sunlight on his clothes and the heady smell of flowers informed him that they'd made their way out of the palace and were somewhere on the grounds.

He dug in his heels unexpectedly, causing the guards to swear and one to lose his grip. The grasp on his upper arms renewed as Gavin demanded, "Where are you taking me?"

"To do what the bandits failed to do," Lord Kelmar's voice said coldly somewhere ahead of him. "I knew I should've gotten rid of you as soon as His Majesty began pressuring his daughter to marry. The two of you were becoming too close for my comfort."

"You don't know anything," Gavin spat. "All you care about is removing anyone who might stand in your way."

Brilliant sunlight streamed into his face as the blindfold fell away. As his vision cleared, he realized where he was. Rose beds surrounded a fountain and carefully trimmed grass, the hedges beyond rising high enough to seclude the garden from sight. Arched gateways guarded each cardinal point, their white-painted lattices overgrown with climbing roses in vibrant pinks, yellows, and reds. He caught his breath with a gasp as the memories swept in—laughter and play, his world crashing apart on the heels of a single embrace, and the vision of a small girl with the world on her shoulders.

It's the garden.

Too late, he realized that Lord Kelmar had said something else. Gavin's knees hit the ground, the sun warming the back of his neck as metal cleared a sheath with a ringing sound. *Sorry, Talianna. At least we had a little time.*

Before any blow could land, another sound broke the tension. An offset rhythm of clanging bells sounded from the palace, the clamor growing and inciting a surge of adrenaline within his veins.

The guardsmen both tensed. "What the—?"

Gavin doubled over as a boot slammed into his stomach and the duke's voice built to a scream. "What have you done?!"

He coughed, caught his breath, and—laughed. "You underestimated us again, *Sir.* You thought I was a threat, but you didn't stop to think what Talianna might be capable of." He locked eyes with his former commander, his fear swept away in the tide of bells and memories of children's laughter. "She's hidden behind her crown all these years, but you have *no idea* what kind of power you've been toying with. We didn't just know everything; we had proof, and you've given her time to get it into the hands of those you fear most. You're done for."

Lord Kelmar stepped back, fear mixing with growing anger in his face.

"Sir, you need to go!" one of the guardsmen urged.

"Not while he's still alive." A horrible sneer twisted Lord Kelmar's face, and his hand went to his own sword. The guardsmen's hands left Gavin's shoulders, and they took several steps away, fear almost palpable as their master advanced. "She may take the throne unhindered, but at least *you* won't be there to see it."

The ringing of the duke's sword being drawn echoed strangely through Gavin's mind, matched by dozens of others as a powerful voice resounded across the garden. "Stop!"

Lord Kelmar's head snapped around, and his eyes widened. In a heartbeat, he'd dropped his sword and was fleeing toward the opposite side of the garden, his men outpacing him as armed men poured through the archway that led to the palace.

Gavin blinked furiously; certain he was hallucinating as his second-in-command ran across the grass toward him with his sword drawn.

"Captain!" Tristan shouted. With a quick slash, the blood-soaked bindings holding Gavin's wrists fell away. Tristan pulled him to his feet, taking in his appearance with a whistle. "Holy Lord of Light, man. She said you needed us, but I didn't realize how badly."

"—she?" Gavin whirled in the direction of the gate just as a tall, trim figure in a plain grey dress and bodice stepped through the archway. "Tali!"

In an instant, he was ten again; and this time, the princess wasn't walking away from him. He was never sure afterwards which of them was running faster, closing the distance toward each other at a pace that made all the years seem to fall away. They met in a skidding rush, Gavin catching Talianna around the waist and spinning to dispel their momentum. The world swirled, then settled, as he and Talianna clung to each other in a desperate, relieved embrace.

When he could finally think again, he asked, "How'd you find us?"

"I realized the duke would've heard from my uncle. He would've known we meant more to each other than our stations dictated, and I thought he might try to kill you." Talianna nodded to the gate on the far side of the garden, this one made of wrought-iron and barring the way to the wilder portions of the grounds. "I thought I saw that gate, but from the other side—the forest side. The trees, they said—I *saw* you." Her arms tightened. "You were on your knees. I don't know how to explain it, but I knew you were in danger." Her breathing quickened, and she looked up in terror. "We were almost too late! He was going to kill you!"

"But he didn't," he reminded her. "You saved me." A laugh built in his chest, pouring out all the relief and hope that words couldn't express. "You've saved me twice now." He glanced at the side of the garden. Curses and shouts drifted through the air as the men of Talianna's personal guard bound and dragged Lord Kelmar and his men away. "It was close, too. I think I owe you a debt."

"No, that makes us even. Barely." She drew back from him and put her hands on her hips. "I don't care what protocol states, or what insanity you swore to. If I'm to be queen someday, that means I can release you. No more oaths."

Gavin pulled her back into his arms, the summer sun warm against his face as he kissed her deeply. "None," he whispered, running a finger down her tearstained face. "None, unless you count the ones we'll make to each other on our wedding day."

"Not that those are any better. Sickness, turmoil, poverty." Talianna gave a short laugh. "Maybe we should write our own."

He couldn't stop his smile. "I think you'll have enough trouble to contend with, once the court finds out that you've selected the younger son of a minor noble house as your intended."

She looked up at the castle with a set to her jaw—vibrant strength that had been locked behind the façade of royal perfection now released for the world to see. "Father will understand, and I don't care about the others. I know who I chose, and I chose the bravest, most stubborn, most sacrificial guardian the kingdom's ever known."

"Handsome, too," Gavin added with a laugh. He kept hold of her hand as they walked back through the rose garden, side by side.

"Handsome as well. And modest." The sunlight highlighted every speck of gold in Talianna's eyes as she stopped under the arch where, years ago, circumstances had torn them apart. She stood on her tiptoes to kiss him softly, the scent of roses and sunlight filling the air as she whispered, "I love you."

"I love you, too."

BEYOND

AS THE CHAOS ACROSS THE REALM SUBSIDED, the rumors spread. They spoke of foreign conspiracy, death and torment, a duke beheaded, and an earl's estate handed over to his stepson. By the day of the princess's wedding, a whisper had made its way through the countryside and into the surrounding lands: *cross the royal family, and you'd fail.*

Why?

The gossips were never specific. Some muttered darkly of sorcery, others of old blood. Others—those with clearer eyes and steadfast hearts—spoke of the unbreakable bond between the king, his daughter, and the guardian who'd given up his own safety to see theirs assured. Of such things were fairy stories made, yet hardly anyone knew how close to the truth the whispers *actually* trod.

The double doors swung open, allowing sunlight to stream into the hallway. Beyond the doors, the throne room was filled with people, their figures painted pink, green, blue and auburn in the puddles of light cast by the stained-glass windows.

Talianna took a deep breath, settling her shoulders as her attendants processed down the carpet toward the archbishop with baskets of rose petals. Her veil brushed against her cheek as she glanced over her shoulder. "Do I look all right?"

A forest green tunic came into her periphery as Gavin stepped up to stand beside her. He gave her a smile with a twist of mischief. "You look terrible. We'd better call this whole thing off and get married in the stables."

"You're the worst," she accused, not even trying to hide her smile. "Thank you."

A flurry of trumpets sounded a fanfare. At the steward's nod, she and Gavin stepped forward, walking into the throne room side by side. The sunlight kissed her face through the veil as they stopped before the archbishop, and the wedding ceremony began. As she and Gavin turned to face each other, the thought occurred to Talianna how unlike this day was to the night he'd sworn his oath of protection.

It was dark, that night, she thought as they clasped hands. *We didn't know how each other had changed over the years apart, or what would happen from that day onward. Yet, even then, we both knew it was a moment that would carry us through the rest of our lives.*

Gavin's fingers wrapped around hers. His voice didn't waver as he delivered his vows, a triumphant look in his eyes as the final words thundered through the hushed room. As the priest turned to Talianna, surety settled in her stomach.

Forever seen. Forever protected. Forever loved, now and always.

She released Gavin's hands to reach up and brush the veil back from her face. A flicker of uncertainty ran in whispers through the congregation—this wasn't the point in the traditional ceremony for such a thing to occur. *I don't want a single barrier between us. Never again.*

"I, Princess Talianna, pledge to take this man as my wedded husband, in accordance with the faith and in the sight of these witnesses. From this day onward, I promise to love, honor, and guard him through sickness, storm, and turmoil, for as long as we live." The sunlight warmed her face, gently washing away the fears of lonely years. Talianna took a deep breath and looked straight into the eyes of the man who'd seen past the crown to the princess.

"So do I swear."

FLIGHT OR FIGHT

Kaitlyn Carter Brown

When a prince falls from the skies and a princess flees her throne, they find their separate worlds aren't so different after all.

FLIGHT OR FIGHT

KAITLYN CARTER BROWN

CLOUDS PASSED IN A COLD RUSH OF VAPOR, blue sky distant above and the green ground approaching nearer and frantically nearer. Air ripped at his clothing, his hair, threatening to tear the circlet of gold from his princely brow—the same circlet his scheming brother ought to have stolen before pushing him over the edge of the sky palace's largest balcony.

Impact was imminent.

I won't die. I won't die. I'll...I can survive. Zarin clenched his smarting eyes shut. Unable to do more than fall, tumbling and hurling through the open air, he could only wait. Wait for the earth below to catch him.

The fall from the cloudlands might not end him, but the lands below might.

Saffron dashed through the thick underbrush, thankful for the leather boots that nearly drew up to her knees. Her cloak, woven with grass and moss and leaves, blended into the forest, but no amount of disguise could throw off her scent in the wolves' nostrils.

A long, mournful howl echoed through the forest, an announcement between the monsters that her trail had been located. In her mind, she could see them, hulking and huge, claws long and teeth sharp. The studded collars that encircled their necks bore a royal emblem, sent from the throne of Heimdym in search of her blood.

And so, she ran, fleeing those who sought her death.

Among other things. Heat flushed at her face. *My birthright is my own. It belongs to no one. Only myself.*

White light streaked across her vision, momentarily blinding her. Saffron skidded to a stop as the light fell from the sky, vanishing beneath the tree line. Her stomach dropped straight to her boots.

The cloud dwellers.

She'd heard many stories, mostly spun by the old women in the markets. A kingdom set among the clouds. Its people, summoners of lightning and mysteries. And sometimes, they flew down to walk upon the earth, among its trees and glades.

Although, that had looked like falling more than flying.

Little contact occurred between her kingdom and the one in the skies. Saffron adjusted her course, treading lightly toward the impact site.

Drawing a steadying breath, she pulled a slender arrow from her quiver and set it taut against her bowstring. If whatever she found proved a threat, they'd feel her arrow before they saw her golden braid laced with twigs and the green stripes of paint lining her cheeks.

Some princess you make. Saffron silenced the voice in her head. *Some princesses were meant to be forged into warriors. Even if the throne has been stolen from me, my crown given to another, and my flesh meant for the wolves, this kingdom is mine.*

A ragged cry echoed through the forest.

Saffron stiffened, her fingers tightening on the bow. Step by cautious step, she moved without sound, blending into the forest itself. The trees grew farther apart, allowing filtered sunlight to dance along the forest floor—and to highlight the vomit soaking into the earth. A young man bent forward on his knees, his stomach giving one last retch.

Lovely. Saffron stared.

Indeed, the stories were true. Cloud dwellers did possess exquisite silver hair, spun from starlight itself. Alabaster skin clothed long limbs and nimble feet made for walking upon the vapors of the skies themselves. He wore a loose, robe-like garment that wrapped about his body, girded with a gold sash, and left one sculpted shoulder bare.

Saffron might have called him beautiful, if the sight of the circlet upon his silver brow didn't leach the warmth from her body.

The young man coughed, wiping his mouth with the back of his hand, and then lifted his gaze. It seemed their astonishment was mutual. "Don't shoot! Please!" His voice rasped, probably raw from bile—and his fall from the skies.

Saffron's shoulders tensed. She took a step forward. "You're in my domain now, cloud boy, why shouldn't I let this arrow teach you a lesson?"

He opened his mouth to speak, but uttered no words. A dazed, confused look entered his eyes—the color of the skies themselves. He dropped his shoulders, visibly deflating, and hung his head in defeat.

He's not dangerous. Of that, Saffron was certain. Perhaps the stories were wrong. She let her arrow slack against her bowstring. "What is your purpose here, cloud dweller?"

The young man closed his eyes. "I'm not sure I have one."

The mournful refrain in his voice struck her heart. Not like lightning, but something like sympathy. Something that reminded her far too much of her sorry flight through the forest, running from the home where she was no longer welcome. Though she hadn't fallen from the skies, she had indeed fallen far.

The timbers of the forest rattled with the wolves' howls.

They're close. Saffron spun around, the tip of her arrow scanning the trees, seeking purchase. She watched for the glint of yellow eyes, her entire body on alert, waiting for the wolves that desired her flesh.

"W-what was that?"

Saffron spared the cloud boy a glance. His eyes were wide with terror, his skin turning even paler, if possible. "The pretender-prince of Heimdym sends his wolves to devour my flesh." Sarcasm lay heavy on her tongue. "We need to run, now." *We? Who is 'we'?*

The young man rose to his feet, his long limbs shaky. "The air—gravity—it works different here..."

"I'm not waiting for you." Saffron lowered her bow, glancing over her shoulder as she tore through the underbrush. "But a word of advice, the prince's wolves aren't picky eaters."

A groan escaped his lips as he jogged along behind her, making a great deal of noise. "I knew it! A prince will kill me!"

"Aren't you one?" *We're too loud. They'll find us.* Saffron ducked into a briar thicket, weaving among the thorny branches with an ease that would give the wolves pause.

The tromp of their footsteps soon became subdued by the gasps and cries as the young man's lack of agility and exposed skin proved too great a temptation for the thorns. "I, uh, I was one. I guess I could still be. Depends on how you look at it."

Emerging from the thicket, Saffron approached a stack of lichen-covered boulders. *Better than nothing.* Stealth wouldn't save them. "Got a name?"

"Zarin."

A few leaps and scrambles later, Saffron ascended the boulders, her eyes scanning the forest. "Well, Prince Zarin, can you fight?"

He huffed and panted, trying desperately to follow her up the rocks. He looked a sight, his robe stained with dirt and leaves and tiny rivers of blood running from the scratches along his arm. It seemed the rumors were true, and the cloud dwellers did bleed silver.

Caught between two boulders, he scrambled to gain footing. Panic skirted across his brow. "Um..."

Saffron knelt and extended a hand. *What am I doing?* Pathetic didn't even begin to describe him. This cloud prince wouldn't last an hour out here in the wilds, much less the treacherous cities of the Heimdyms. *It seems I was miserably misled about the cloud dwellers.*

Still, the light brightening his gaze as he seized her hand could've shamed all the stars in the heavens. Was that a smile upon his porcelain face? She could've laughed. He had no idea how much danger they were in.

"That's a no?" She grunted as she heaved him up. He didn't weigh much. *Perhaps that's the secret as to how they walk upon the clouds.*

Zarin didn't have the chance to respond. A monstrous wolf, roughly three times the size of a normal hound, burst through the trees. Mouth frothing, it snarled and prowled in a slow orbit about the rocks, its eyes burning like fire.

Saffron didn't hesitate, loosing an arrow. It pierced its hide but didn't slow the beast's pursuit. Bounding up the rocks as if they were pebbles, it growled and exposed the teeth that would soon have their flesh.

I didn't ask for this. Saffron drew her knife. Its edge was jagged, in need of care that she hadn't the ability to give. *I didn't want to lose my crown. I didn't want to fight for my life.*

But the usurper with his stolen crown had other ideas—and refused to suffer a rival princess.

"Get behind me." She took a deep breath. The wolf coiled, ready to pounce. One heartbeat. Two.

She didn't look to see if Zarin had obeyed. This may well be her last moments, her last moments as a runaway princess with a claim to a throne that would never be hers. She would die fighting out in the wilderness, far from the walls of her castle. No one would mourn, her life declared worthless by the one who had stolen her birthright. No one would remember. Even to this wolf, she was just another pursuit, another set of bones upon which to sharpen its teeth.

The wolf pounced, and the forest and its wilds faded away. Everything became obscured by glorious light. It filled the glade, spinning and spiraling in a kaleidoscope of shimmering gold.

Zarin stood before her, shaky and pale, his hand stretched out toward the wolf's maw. In his hand was a stone, flat and round and altogether too brilliant to gaze upon. It seemed made of glass, of fire, and turned Zarin's pale skin to molten gold. The silver blood upon his scratched arms shimmered white, and he and the stone were one—one blinding light akin to the glorious sun itself.

The wolf cowered and stumbled on the rocks. It backed away, its motions jerky and unstable. Once upon level ground, it clawed and scratched at its eyes, moaning and whimpering. Saffron blinked. Where the dilated pupils once had glimmered with hatred, now the wolf's eyes were pale and white.

Blinded.

Then it turned and floundered into the forest, bumping into trees and stumbling over the uneven terrain. Zarin lowered the stone, its glow fading. His chest heaved for air, and he wavered a bit before dropping to his knees.

"What...what was that?" Saffron looked at the stone in his hands. It had dulled and no longer possessed the power of the sun. Now, it gleamed like the purest pearl.

Zarin tucked the stone back into the folds of his clothing. As he braced himself against the rock, the corded muscles on his arms taut, Saffron's eyes widened. The scratches bleeding silver had closed, restoring his flawless, starlight skin. Where the light of the strange and wonderful stone had blinded the wolf, it had healed him.

"The reason I survived the fall from my world." He sighed. "And the reason why the prince will kill me."

It seems we've a rather large thing in common. Saffron sheathed her knife. "The prince from your world?"

Zarin nodded. "My brother. He did not wish to take the chance that I could be named heir in his stead, so he pushed me over the edge of the world and into yours." His hand went to his chest, where the stone rested. "That stone is the *mishelle*. It is held by the king, a mark of their heirship and their rule." He heaved a sigh that seemed too heavy for his frame. "My brother cannot ascend to the throne without it."

Sympathy, like the cool droplets of springtime, rained upon Saffron's soul. *Two worlds, above and below, same perils.* Perhaps they weren't as different as they seemed. "Will he come after you?"

"He'll come for the *mishelle*." His shoulders slumped. "Or to make certain of my demise. I'm not sure the stone will protect me from everything. I'll have to face him...eventually."

Eventually.

The word hung in the clean air of the wilds. Full of dread yes, but also anticipation.

Saffron glanced over her shoulder, into the forest. Somewhere, beyond the murk and the density, the trees and the rocks and the ravines, her kingdom lay waiting. It lay beneath the usurper prince's control, bound by his grasp.

Maybe running was not the answer. *Maybe I too will find my eventually.*

And that time, she wouldn't be caught off guard. She would stand and take back her throne.

Stepping forward, Saffron extended a hand. "You saved my life, Prince Zarin of the clouds. As a princess driven from her throne and fleeing a relentless pursuer, I do not think I ought to reject the kindness of a royal ally."

Zarin grasped her hand and stood, the tremors vanishing from his limbs. His eyebrows shot up his forehead, likely astonished that their paths, with all their similar complexities, had somehow converged. Then, he bowed at the waist. "Princess."

The sound of her title upon his lips birthed a warmth in her heart that she hadn't felt in a long time. The chill of her loneliness thawed at the edges.

"I...if I may?" Zarin blushed. Beneath his pale skin, it bloomed rather purple. "I think I'd like to help you in that endeavor."

Saffron permitted herself a smile. "Perhaps I can help you too. At the least, we might protect each other."

Hope kindled in Zarin's gaze.

For the first time in what seemed ages, Saffron laughed.

"A lost prince, a fleeing princess. I suppose this will be quite the adventure."

A MARRIAGE OF INCONVENIENCE: PART ONE

Robin Rakkeby

When Princess Myka begrudgingly agrees to a marriage of convenience to stave off planetary war, she expects to lose her old way of life and herself along with it. What she doesn't expect is Prince Laszlo's own proposition—a marriage of inconvenience, with tomfoolery in store for those who forced them into this situation.

A MARRIAGE OF INCONVENIENCE: PART ONE

ROBIN RAKKEBY

MYKA LOOKED LIKE A SLIGHTLY MORE ALIVE version of the taxidermied white-feathered huxxa that graced the palace's hunting display during Midwinter celebrations, though perhaps even that was too generous a comparison.

She shifted on her feet, rays of the evening sun shattering as they reflected off the yellow tourmalines stitched into the embroidered knotwork of her wedding dress. The skirt billowed around her hips, flowing into a puddle of honey-stained white at her feet. It might have been beautiful on another girl, or in another time but... *These blasted huxxa feathers.* The downy plumes tickled her skin as she ran her fingers across the trim. *Why is it tradition for a bride to wear them?* At least her dress fell on the subtle side of ostentatious.

The queen lifted a tiara of feathers that radiated upwards like beams of light on a cloudy day. "Ready for the finishing touch?"

Myka directed a sour look at the monstrosity but held her tongue, ducking her head so her mother could affix it to her auburn hair.

"You look beautiful."

She rolled her eyes. "Yes, I'm sure all the birds would find me ravishing. If only I weren't marrying a human."

"Myka," her mother chided softly, taking her hands in her own. "I know this isn't the duty you expected to fall upon your shoulders, but I'm proud of you. And I know your father is too."

"I don't want you to be proud of me." The words came out before Myka could stop them. She was a princess; she knew her place. It did nothing to make stepping into it any easier. "I don't want to go," Myka whispered.

"I know." The queen pulled Myka into a delicate hug. "I know. But you must."

The golden hue of light drained away as Myka followed her mother into the shadowed hallway. When was the next time she would see the sun? Feel the kiss of its morning rays on her skin? Witness its evening light bathe the city in a honeyed gold, or its midday fury flood the air with waves of heat? When would she be able to tinker in her workshop? Would Isyjin royalty allow her to bring her tools? To build anything with her hands?

Her mother halted abruptly and Myka barely stopped herself from running into her. Wedding music swelled from behind the carved wooden doors of the ballroom. An attendant bowed to the queen, to Myka, and then—with a finality that sent a shiver down her spine—pushed open the doors that lead to her fate.

Myka kissed him—she remembered that much. It was hard to forget the horror of hundreds of eyes watching, waiting for the kiss that would seal the treaty and usher in the glory days of a warm, bright tomorrow. No, whatever warmth that kiss was supposed to invoke was more akin to the heat of the failed compressor that had blown a hole in her pod racer and sent it to the junkyard. A thermal catastrophe.

There was a feast. And dancing, if her aching feet were any indicator. But trying to block out memories of her fate did little good when it—her husband—was sat across from her, his dark brown eyes locked onto her blue ones in a silent battle of wills.

Laszlo did have nice eyes, at least. And he looked nice too. Not *nice* nice, though he wasn't lacking in that department. No, what caught her attention during this staring contest was the kindness that softened his features *just so* and tilted his lips into an expression too inviting for its own good.

It only soured her mood further.

"Remind me again why we're staring?" His deep voice drifted across the silence between them.

"It's supposed to intimidate you off the bed."

"Right. And we're allowed to blink during this contest?"

"No." Her eyes twitched. "Yes." She scratched her arm. "Why aren't you moving?"

Much to her dismay, Laszlo settled further into the pillows and tilted his head at her. "I'm trying to figure you out," he admitted. "And the floor has a draft."

"What have you surmised?"

Laszlo twisted his wedding band around his finger. By the nervous expression that peeked through his collected calm, the repetitive motion was doing the opposite of helping him think. His hands fell back into his lap, any hint of nerves falling away with the gesture. "That you don't want to be in this situation," he finally said.

"A master of deductive reasoning." She rewarded him with a slow clap. "At least I haven't married an idiot."

"Which is incidentally convenient, as I don't want to be in this situation either."

Her hands stuck together. "Then why did we do this?"

Though her question settled into a heavy silence between them, panic bubbled up within her. When all else was stripped away, this marriage wasn't simply a joining of two Hemis—it was a joining of two people. That was the crux of what terrified her—how sharing her life with another might change her, how Laszlo might change her. As the youngest in the royal family, she never had the pressure to marry, and with the freedom of choice, she chose to pursue mechanics. In a hemisphere with a sleepless sun giving rise to unlimited energy and her natural penchant to tinker, innovation was inevitable. It also supported her mildly secret guilty pleasure—pod racing.

Now, she would be trapped in a sunless hemisphere sealed by an unbreakable, unwanted marriage. If Laszlo didn't want to accept her as his wife, the royal family would never accept her as herself. She already knew losing herself was a possibility. Now, for the stability of the treaty, it was an inevitability.

"I don't know about you." Laszlo's steady yet reassuring voice drifted through her haze of panic. "But planetary warfare doesn't sound pleasant." He leaned forward, catching her gaze. "I'd like to propose an accord."

Myka's spiraling thoughts screeched to a halt. He did want this? Or didn't he? "I'm listening," she managed to say.

"You didn't envision this future for yourself. I didn't envision this future for myself. But we can't do anything about it lest we condemn the planet to burn," he began. "I'm not sure how this arrangement was proposed to you, but in Isyjin law it's called a 'marriage of convenience'."

"In Pykos it's called an arranged marriage, but close enough."

Laszlo nodded thoughtfully. "They arranged this into something to convenience themselves and our hemispheres. I don't want to risk the safety of our people with foolishness, but that doesn't mean we can't, ah, work together to inconvenience those who forced us into this?"

"So you're proposing..." Hope fluttered in her chest. Skepticism reached out to squish it, but the delightfully mischievous look that graced Laszlo's features forced her to pause.

"A marriage of inconvenience," he said.

Myka stared at the man before her. The endlessly confusing yet strangely endearing man. Who was also her husband. Who had also just proposed...

An un-princesslike snort escaped her as his words settled into her mind. "Are you a child?" she laughed.

"No, but I'm responsibly petty." An easy smile spread across his lips, one that made her want to return the gesture. One that gave her the feeling that, perhaps, life with this man wouldn't be so bad after all.

"What kind of inconveniences?"

"Minor ones. Nothing harmful." He shrugged. "My parents as 'mother and father' are lovely. My parents as 'king and queen' are stifling. I think breaking the mold would do all of us some good."

"Inconveniences like...?" She looked out her window, watching as the evening sun coated the city in liquid gold and trying to gather ideas. "Inventing our own language so no one can understand us?"

"That sounds like a lot of effort, but yes." He nodded thoughtfully. "I do like that idea. Disappearing on unimportant days to explore is another one."

"Have you been pod racing?" she asked, hope stretching its wings further.

"No, but I think you'll find skjza racing to be an enjoyable alternative."

Myka leaned against the bedpost, a sense of peace washing over her as his proposal settled comfortably in her mind. "Deal, but I'm still not sleeping next to you. And I'm not sleeping on the floor either."

"I have an idea." Stray pillows fell to the floor as he extricated himself from the copious pile of cushions.

Her brow wrinkled in thought. If she timed this right, she could burrow herself deep enough under the blankets to claim her territory. As soon as Laszlo stood, Myka made to jump, but a hand on her shoulder grounded her mid-flight. "I'm not being chivalrous."

She craned her neck to look up at him. The filtered light of the evening sun softened Lazlo's sharp cheekbones and cast shadows over his brow where dark locks of hair fell over his eyes. It took everything within her to not reach up and brush them back into place. "Then what are you doing?" Myka whispered.

"Proposing a compromise." He gave her shoulder a squeeze and let his arm fall to his side. "Step back please."

Myka complied, trying to ignore the heat rising on her cheeks as she did so. A task that became immeasurably easier as she tried to figure out what in the seven suns he was doing.

Laszlo knocked the remaining pillows onto the rug before turning his attention to the crisply tucked in blankets. He tugged the corners free, and, with great finesse considering the size of the bed, pulled them off in one fell swoop and deposited them onto the ever-growing pile.

"What are you—?"

"Trust the process," he interrupted without looking up as he set to untangling the blankets. Two found a home on one side of the bed, one on the other. He frowned, shook his head, and moved the lone blanket to join the other two. Then, he started piling the pillows right down the middle.

"You're making a fort," Myka observed, a strange combination of excitement and endearment filling her heart.

He nodded to the side with blankets. "You can have the left."

"I thought you said you weren't being chivalrous."

"I'm not; your sun is blisteringly hot. My act of chivalry is not sleeping naked."

If Myka thought her face had gone hot before, it was absolutely burning now. She opened her mouth. Closed it. Opened it again. Nope, her brain circuitry was fried and all coherent thought gone with it.

Laszlo seemed to have the same conundrum as he slowly turned toward her with a sheepish expression that contradicted his flippant boldness. "Sorry. Um. Isyji is cold. A hundred and fifty degrees colder than Pykos on our warm days. We have internal heating, but with your sun, I feel like I'm melting out of my skin."

"No, yeah," she squeaked. "Of course. Yes, well, I prefer blankets. And clothes. Clothes are great."

"Good."

"Grand." Myka picked at a loose thread on her shirt. The cool, thin silk of her well-loved pajama set felt like nothing more than a whisper against her skin. Never before had she felt so betrayed by fabric. Was it too late to put on something *less* intimate?

"I can get the curtains," Laszlo offered.

"Okay." *Definitely too late.* Myka gave him a wide berth as she walked around the bed and clambered under the blankets. It would be a miracle if she fell asleep, but tomorrow held a long day of travel to Isyji and she would take all the rest she could get. Even if it meant sharing a bed with—

"Are you comfortable?"

—a man she had no idea what to do with. She sighed internally. "Yes." *No. Yes, in a very no sort of way.*

Darkness engulfed the room as the curtain fell over the window. Maybe if she closed her eyes...Myka snuggled deeper under the covers. The soft rustle of fabric hitting the floor sounded in the room, and she cracked an eye open even though it was too dark to see. "What are you doing?"

"Letting my eyes acclimate. I don't want to stub my toe."

She cleared her throat. "What was that sound?"

"My shirt." He paused, seeming to consider his next words. "I, uh, sweat through the fabric. I promise I'm not indecent."

"Because sleeping half-clothed with your wife is sure to cause a scandal," she deadpanned.

Laszlo huffed a laugh in response. It was another minute before he padded across the room. The bed dipped and shifted as he got comfortable, then all was quiet until—

"Good night, wife," Laszlo whispered.

A small smile grew on Myka's lips. "Good night, husband."

The engine of the Isyjin RoyalClass Dryfter hummed in the walls as they flew. The design looked similar to the dryfter they took from Pykos Proper to the hemispheric arc separating Pykos from Isyji, but somehow that made the differences stand out more. The frequency of the engine wasn't quite right. The composite material of the aircraft body shimmered unnaturally in the low light of the cabin. Logic demanded that Isyjin technology utilize different engineering techniques to account for the drastically different atmospheres that defined the two hemispheres. But Myka hadn't considered how that, of all things, would be what broke her. Her face stayed glued to the window as they flew over her home, Hemi, but now that they traversed Isyjin airspace, she couldn't even bring herself to raise the window shield.

A small downy huxxa feather clung to her trousers, and she choked down a strained laugh. Of course that would be the one thing to follow her from home. Taking it between her fingers she twirled it slowly, watching as fine threads of gold shimmered amongst the white plumes under the artificial lights.

"What kind of animal is that from?"

She glanced across the aisle to see Laszlo watching her with an unreadable expression. "A white-feathered huxxa. Do you not have them?"

"No. Our side of the planet has birds, but it's too cold for huxxa. Its feathers are beautiful though. I've never seen anything like it."

Myka gave the feather a sad smile before tucking it safely into her pocket.

Laszlo glanced out his window. "You should take a peek. We're far enough into Isyji to see the Kuzjarani formations."

Dread settled in her stomach. "I'd rather not."

"It'll help you take your mind off things." He patted the seat next to him. When she didn't move, he added, "I wouldn't be saying this if I thought it would hurt you."

Myka tentatively unbuckled her seatbelt and slid across the aisle into the seat next to him, her back ramrod straight as she stared a hole into the headrest of the seat in front of her.

"Hey." The soft timbre of his voice caressed her ear.

Turning her head, she met his gaze and froze. His irises were pools of liquid amber with constellations of sunkissed honey swirling in their depths. They were beautiful, alluring, and not the color they had been on their wedding night.

"What happened to your eyes?" If this was his plan all along, he'd certainly succeeded in taking her mind off the distance that grew between her and Pykos by the second.

"Oh." He sat back. "It was a protective coating. Your sun's heat *might* sear my skin, but even its filtered light will permanently blind me."

Right. Pykos Hemi held the everlasting sun. Isyji Hemi stared into the lightless void of space. It would make sense, then, that Isyjins had adapted to frigid temperatures and infinite darkness.

"Why should I look outside if I won't be able to see anything?"

"Trust the process," he reminded her.

Myka sucked in a breath, released it slowly, and peered around Laszlo before she lost her nerve. The sight that confronted her would have taken her breath away if she hadn't just exhaled. Towers of jagged crystal deposits pierced the land, shifting from an electric green to milky blue to blush rose as they reflected the dancing colors of the aurora zephyralis. Snow-covered gorges scarred the landscape surrounding them, while veins of ice emitted a soft bioluminescent glow from the depths of the planet.

"It's beautiful," Myka breathed. Glancing up, she caught the tail end of Laszlo's tender expression as he directed his attention from her to the window. It did nothing to hide the smile in his voice.

"I'm glad you like it."

As soon as the aircraft landed, time seemed to accelerate. Myka was launched into meeting after meeting, introduced to so many people she barely remembered her own name, finally had a proper conversation with the king and queen who were just as stuffy as Laszlo warned, and given an extensive tour of the palace, which was unsurprisingly made of ice. She wanted to pay attention, truly, but when hallways mazed together and the fifteenth room started looking too much like the third, her mind unhelpfully locked onto a singular question and the rest of the tour was lost—how many people had licked the walls?

Her body was frozen from the cold while her mind felt full of buzzing sandflies by the time Saran? Jaran? deposited her in front of the singular set of doors she actually did remember—Laszlo's chambers. Mumbling a 'thank you,' Myka stumbled through the doors, vaguely registered crossing the sitting area, and flopped face first onto the fluffy but deceptively-not-warm bed. A grumble of indignation rumbled in her chest as she tried to burrow herself against the blankets without spending the energy to crawl under them.

"That bad, huh?" Laszlo spoke from the sitting area across the room.

Myka grunted, then mumbled into the blankets, "The seamstress turned me into a living pincushion."

"Did she now?" He laughed. The soft snap of a hardbound book closing punctuated the melodic sound. "Do you know when your new clothes will be ready?"

"End of week."

"Good, you'll need them."

Myka snorted and turned her head to face him, the sight of Laszlo completely engulfed by a massive fur blanket chasing some of her fatigue-fuelled frustration away. "You think?" she retorted. "I've never been so cold in my life."

"Sorry, here." He rose from the sofa with surprising grace and brought the blanket with him, arranging it over her as he sat on the edge of the bed. Its preheated warmth flooded her weary bones and she relaxed deeper into the mattress.

"Thank you," Myka said, eyes drifting closed. "Aren't you cold now?"

"No, not too cold." There was a tenderness to his voice that warmed her further. "I am glad you went to see the seamstress though. You'll be needing your thermosuit sooner rather than later."

That piqued her interest. "For our first round of inconveniences?" she asked, looking up at him. "What did you have in mind?"

"Guess." Laszlo nudged her playfully. "We already talked about it."

"I'm too tired to guess."

He beamed at her. "Skjza racing."

Myka blinked, her brain attempting and failing to process what he said. There was no way, *no way* he'd actually chosen the Isyjin version of pod racing as their first inconvenience. With the way her heart pounded against her chest as if trying to go racing that instant, he couldn't have suggested anything else.

"Are you serious?"

"Yes?" He laughed. "I thought you'd like to start with that one."

Maybe she would never be able to race a pod again, but this might fill that void. She could learn to adapt to frozen mechanics too. Maybe, just maybe, she didn't have to lose herself in her new life. Myka closed her eyes and snuggled further under the blanket, a warmth filling her that had little to do with the furs draped across her back. "I think I love you."

"We are married," Laszlo teased, though the featherlight touch that brushed a strand of hair off her face sent her heart fluttering in her chest and coated the words that followed in a vulnerable truth. "I'm relieved to know the feeling is mutual."

The week blurred together into a whirlwind of events, made manageable by the promise of skjza racing. Though now that the day had arrived, her excitement to race and the feeling of existential dread at spending two days on the open tundra of Isyji threatened to overwhelm her.

Unfortunately, there was little she could do about the existential dread—they were already deep in the heart of Isyjin wilderness. Fortunately, she was too mesmerized by the world around her to notice. Prior to sneaking out of the relative warmth of the palace, Laszlo had given her an eyedrop solution for people with degraded darksight. *It's made for the elderly*—that clarification had earned him a thwack—*and honored guests of Isyji.*

Much to Laszlo's credit, the drops did help. Though they were in the hemisphere of eternal darkness, it was bright. Not as the day was bright, but bright like night, as nonsensical as that sounded. The darkness held a richness in its color she never noticed before. And the light? It looked to be infused with life itself. The bioluminescent glow of the ice transformed into its own galaxy of frozen constellations, while the snow dusting the landscape shimmered as if made from the stars.

Laszlo nudged her shoulder and nodded toward the pass between two mountains. "We'll get through, then we'll camp for the night and carry on to the finish line tomorrow," he shouted over the wind rushing around them. "Once we're in, we can't stop."

"How long is the pass?"

"Three hours, give or take."

Myka nodded. It was a long time to be exposed in hostile terrain, but she trusted Laszlo's piloting skills. She trusted her mechanics skills too. A week wasn't enough to learn all the ins and outs of a skjza, but the Isyjin engineer she'd wrangled into giving her a crash course was more thorough than even she would have normally requested.

Spires of rock and snow laden trees clawed their way out of the once barren tundra as they approached the mountain pass. Flurries swirled down like unburning embers, carrying with them an ominous softness that sent a chill creeping through her veins. Flexing her fingers in her gloves to rid herself of the sensation, she glanced at Laszlo. A frown marred his features as he looked rapidly from his armband to the mountains ahead.

"What's wrong?"

"I'm not sure, I..." He trailed off, hands dancing across the controls. "I need you to monitor the electromagnetic coupling readings." Laszlo nodded to a display on the skjza. "Tell me when it passes the threshold and—"

The world flickered and plunged into blinding darkness as a moaning whistle wrenched itself from the bowels of the mountain pass. Myka's blood curdled in her veins. Laszlo muttered a prayer only the stars could comprehend. But time? Time held its breath, awaiting the inevitable. It arrived in the form of a wind raging from behind, barreling over them as it siphoned into the mountain pass with an echoing shriek. The skjza lurched and twisted as the force of the wind sucked them along with it. Laszlo pulled back on the throttle, trying to gain control of the skjza.

They only accelerated faster.

Myka watched in horror as they raced toward the maw of the mountain. She didn't register Laszlo's brief 'I'm sorry' until strong arms wrapped around her waist.

And then she was floating. Falling. Air left her lungs as snow sprayed around them in a powdered explosion, every bone in her body aching as they tumbled across the frozen ground in a tangle of limbs. And then they stopped. Laszlo lay next to her, unmoving, his arm draped across her waist.

"Laszlo?" Her voice came as a croaked whisper.

"'m fine." She felt, rather than heard his answer.

Myka moved to sit up, but Laszlo's grip tightened. "Stay down." His voice intertwined with the roar of the wind.

"We need to find shelter! We'll get buried."

"No! That was a coronal mass ejection." He shifted next to her, curling around her as a protective barrier. "You need to stay down."

Before she could say anything more, the mountain pass they'd almost entered, had almost been sucked into, imploded. Ice and rock folded in on itself, shaking the ground as sheets of snow carried by the wind whipped around them.

Laszlo spoke again before it had a chance to settle. "Now we find shelter."

"Now?!" Myka tried to look around, but any semblance of visibility she'd once had was gone.

"I didn't know if it would implode or explode." Laszlo pressed himself up and hauled Myka to her feet, his arm looping through her own as he pulled her into the unknown.

ALL IN JEST

Annee Clark

Sparks fly and anything can happen when the enchanting court jester catches the eye of a princess destined for an arranged marriage with the steely prince of a neighboring kingdom.

ALL IN JEST

ANNEE CLARK

THE PRINCESS WATCHED HER JESTER the way one might watch the stars in the night sky. His eyes twinkled with mischief above the two white diamonds painted on his cheeks, as, completing a cartwheel, he straightened just before her seat at the head of the table. She sucked in a soft breath, forgotten silverware clattering against her plate. He struck her with the same wonder as the smear of a bleeding sunset, or the crest of a wave.

The jester's gaze, intent and roguish upon her own, seemed to narrow the world into just the two of them. With a twist of his hand, he snapped and revealed a white rose, missing from the table's centerpiece. The dinner guests murmured their awe as the jester deftly held the flower out to the princess, balancing its stem on the tip of one finger. "Your Highness."

The princess swallowed. Accepting the rose, she hoped there was no tell-tale flush to her cheeks. When her fingers closed around it, the previously white petals bloomed into a blood red. She barely heard the delighted gasps of the crowd as she studied the flower, turning it over in her hands before looking at the jester again.

He tossed her a wink, so brief and so intimately for her that she could have convinced herself she'd imagined it. He spun away with unmatched fluidity and ease, even while feigning clumsiness here and there to coax laughs from his willing audience. The princess's eyes never left him for a moment, tracking his every twirl and flip, his every jest and trick. He was silver-tongued and graceful, drawing her eye with all the spectacle of a natural phenomenon.

The prince at her side rested a hand over hers, startling her attention away from the jester with a stony expression. "I grow bored of these antics, my dear. Might we spend a quiet moment alone before retiring for the night?"

The princess's excitement wilted, stealing a last glance at her jester. Was it her mind playing tricks, or was he watching her even now, tracking her through the edge of his gaze, even as his performance carried on?

"Certainly," she answered at last.

Her betrothed rose from his seat, offering her a hand. The princess's fingers closed around his palm as she stood, clasping her rose in her other hand.

He led her away from the tumbling laughs and cheers of the dining hall and down the corridor. Her heart ached to return to that dining table, to watch her jester dance and quip and tease. Instead, the quiet swept the night bare like a creeping tide. So much of her future was decided for her—even now, the evening did not belong to her.

The two royals stepped out onto the balcony, cool air brushing their skin in a velvet caress. The princess had always liked the cold more than most; it narrowed her senses into something familiar. The night smelled sharp with the promise of snow. It stole her attention away from the worries churning her mind until the future king spoke again.

"I know that you are not satisfied with our arrangement." His voice was different now than it had been while in view of their subjects. It leveled into something a little less diplomatic, less cushion to the blunt teeth of him. "My father and I have been more than gracious to offer you my hand. For your own kingdom's sake, you would be wise to drag your head down from the clouds and back to the earth where it is"—he paused after letting the uncharitable words fall—"best suited. Under my direction, by my side. You understand, don't you, dearest?"

The princess surveyed the unfamiliar kingdom. Its rolling hills and valleys twinkled with the village lights beneath a sleeping sky.

"I understand."

"Good. I trust that with time, you will grow to be content here with me." His voice sounded like the color grey, steely and dull.

"I hope for the same," the princess said in answer—mechanically, politely—always the amiable princess first, and never just a girl.

The prince nodded in her periphery, his fingers slipping from hers. "Then I bid you goodnight, my dear." His words shifted to something almost concerned—though for her or for his future plans, she couldn't decide. "Don't stay out too long. You'll catch a chill."

Though his footsteps faded away behind her, she waited until the encroaching silence enveloped her whole, only then certain that she had been left alone.

The princess stayed on the balcony until the air numbed her face and fingertips. Overhead, the clouds parted, the moonlight slashing silver over the world below. Beneath its glow, she examined her white-turned-red rose once more. That same excitement and wonder that had stirred beneath her skin then bubbled up anew, coaxing her again to hope for even a sliver of agency in her own fate.

"Aren't you cold, princess?"

The princess paused, lifting her head. The familiar voice, warm and lilting, seemed to fill the very cracks of her.

"I like the cold," she answered, turning to face the speaker.

The jester shifted with leisurely movements to lean against the rail beside her. Something sparked in the pit of her belly, to have him so close. If anyone saw, their mere proximity would cause a scandal. Still, she turned to the railing once more, facing the same direction as her jester. "How did you turn my rose red?" she asked, glancing at him.

The light of the moon highlighted the white diamonds painted over his cheeks as his mouth lifted into a smirk. "You know what they say about magicians and their secrets."

"You are a court jester," she reminded him, "not a magician. Though your tricks are...impressive."

"I impress you, princess?" His smile widened, sly and teasing.

Heat flooded her cheeks and she turned her head to hide the sudden flush. "I believe that is what I said, yes."

"You didn't see the end of my performance."

Her gaze flicked back to him, eagerness betraying her. His eyes glittered beneath the dance of moonbeams, knowing and patient as he awaited her reply. The princess's mouth felt slightly dry. "All right, then. You may...repeat the end of your performance for me."

He clasped his hands in front of him, attention still affixed to her. The amusement was clear on his face. "I may? Do you command it?"

The princess's cheeks burned further. "I only mean—if you should like to. I would...I wouldn't deny you."

The jester took a single step closer, and the princess felt as if all the air had vanished from her lungs. "Would you like to see how it ends?" he pressed gently.

She swallowed. "I... Yes. Please."

"I could do more than that." He spoke softly. "I could get you out of here—for a little while, or for good."

The princess turned away, forcing down the longing jolt in her chest. "Don't be foolish."

He reached out, brazen and delicate all at once, to catch her wrist, spinning her back around. His other hand raised to just barely brush a finger down the line of her jaw.

The world around them flickered in a kaleidoscope of color, then vanished all at once. The princess blinked and they were in her own kingdom's village, her castle towering within sight.

The princess spluttered, trembling, and looked at the jester, her jester. Her fingers were gripping his. "What—?"

He grinned, something else—magic—sparking behind his eyes. "I'm afraid being the fool is precisely my job, princess. Now. Your Highness. Anywhere you'd like to go?"

The princess stepped close, looking up at the court jester. A million thoughts wanted to flee the confines of her mouth. She looked around at her kingdom, her home.

Everywhere, her heart whispered. Then, for the first time, she spoke the word aloud.

A MARRIAGE OF INCONVENIENCE: PART TWO

Robin Rakkeby

Myka and Lazlo's hijinks have stranded them in a frozen wasteland, but a chance encounter uncovers an even bigger threat than anything wielded by the Isyji hemisphere.

A MARRIAGE OF INCONVENIENCE: PART TWO

ROBIN RAKKEBY

THEY COULD HAVE WALKED FOR DAYS, for all Myka knew. The windstorm left her completely blind. Disorientated. Frozen. The sudden lack of sensation when they stumbled through a portal of salvation—the opening of a cave—was the sweetest pain she had ever felt.

Laszlo dragged her away from the entrance before letting go of her arm and slumping to the ground, Myka following suit.

"What," she breathed, "was that?"

"Coronal mass ejection." Laszlo hunched further into himself. "They mildly affect our weather patterns, unless there's a big one like that."

"Then they have a big effect?" She leaned her head against the icy wall of the cave.

"Yeah. Yeah, you could say that."

A hysteric laugh bubbled out of Myka's throat before she could stop it. "In Pykos, CMEs trigger volcanic eruptions. In Isyji, they cause mountains to fold in on themselves?! You know these events can be predicted, right?"

"I know." He ran a hand over his face. "I've been monitoring it. There was nothing. Nothing to indicate an event like this. I like racing. I also like staying alive." Laszlo met Myka's gaze with wide eyes. "I swear to you I wouldn't have brought you out here if I knew this would happen."

Her fear-fueled frustration ebbed at the panic in his voice. He'd gotten them out safely and calmly when she would have led them to their death. She needed to be that rock for him now. Myka shifted closer to him and rested her head on his shoulder, a smile growing on her lips when Laszlo wrapped his arm around her waist and settled his head atop her own.

"What do we do now?" Myka asked softly.

"Wait it out," he said with a resigned sigh. "Re-evaluate when we can."

And if the entrance gets buried? She wanted to ask but held her tongue. With the way Laszlo had his head tilted toward the entrance of the cave, he was thinking the same thing. If they went back into the storm now, they would die. At least here, their probability of survival was higher. As for how much higher, that was one calculation she wasn't going to make.

Myka pushed herself up with a groan, the bioluminescent glow of ice illuminating the cave. At some point during the storm they had fallen asleep, though now Laszlo was nowhere to be seen. He couldn't have gone far; the cave entrance was completely covered by a layer of thick ice over packed snow. There was no way they were getting out the way they came in. She sucked in a deep breath, releasing it slowly in an unsuccessful attempt to quell her rising panic.

At the sound of footsteps crunching through snow, Myka turned to see Laszlo emerge from the shadows covering the back of the cave. "I thought this was the cave I'd been to before, but I must have gotten mixed up in the storm. There's nothing. No exit."

Myka felt herself deflate, vaguely registering Laszlo's movements as he plunked onto the ground next to her. This was it. This was how she died. In a foreign place. A frozen place. Never to feel the sun against her skin or sand between her toes. The embrace of her mother and idle chatter with family during breakfast lost to time. She'd never even see another stupid huxxa again.

She pulled the feather out of a zippered pocket on her thermosuit and rotated it between her fingers. She'd thought herself a fool when she tucked it there before leaving the palace. Now she was grateful for the reminder of home. The white plumes took on a muted blue tint from the glow of the ice surrounding them. Draping her hands over her knees, she resigned herself to staring off into space with her fingers grasped around the tiny scrap of sunshine.

"Myka?" Laszlo's voice cut through the silence. "Are you moving the feather?"

"No."

"Do huxxa feathers naturally move on their own?"

She frowned, squinting at the feather as he leaned closer. Sure enough, the feather's downy edges were stirring. "...No?"

"I don't think we're trapped," he breathed. "Airflow. There's airflow somewhere in here."

Laszlo stood, patting the walls and kicking the snowy junction between the ground and the ice as he made his way around the perimeter of the cave. Myka tucked the feather into her pocket and copied his movements, following the contour of the opposite side of the cave. She felt like a fool, but a hope-filled fool was better than a dead one. She was about to ask him if he'd found anything when her boot plummeted through the ground and she fell against the wall, her shout echoing in the enclosed space.

"Myka!" Laszlo's shout echoed back. Moments later he came skidding to a halt next to her, steady hands settling on her waist as she balanced on one foot. "Are you okay?"

"Yeah." She relaxed into his embrace and looked up at him with a cheeky grin. "Found something."

He gently tucked a wayward strand of hair behind her ear. "You're impossible," he chided affectionately. "Come on, let's get you out of the wall."

Laszlo helped Myka extricate her foot from the snow and they knelt, digging the frozen ground away with renewed fervor. Shards of ice and clumps of snow piled behind them as they cleared a path to reveal a tunnel just large enough for the two of them to crawl side by side.

"This *was* the right cave." He sat back on his heels and laughed, then looked at her with a smile so bright it could rival the suns. "I didn't kill us!"

Myka tried to return the gesture, but the gaping maw of the much too small tunnel demanded far too much attention. It was reassuring that Laszlo wasn't alarmed, because there was no way she would consider climbing into that unknown void otherwise.

"What is it?" she asked.

"An ancient system made by ice eels."

She tilted her head at the tunnel and let out a soft 'huh.' Somehow that fact made the abyss seem less intimidating.

Laszlo smiled and brushed a flake of snow off her cheek, the warmth of his touch taking its place. "Come on."

Crawling on hands and knees, Myka followed Laszlo into the winding system of tunnels. The melted and refrozen ice made it difficult to gain traction. Eventually she devised a wiggle-scoot system that worked, made slightly more awkward when she had to slither on her belly through some of the smaller tunnels. Sliding out of one such tunnel, Myka bumped into Laszlo as he looked around the new tunnel system they found themselves in. Though 'tunnel' was too unimposing of a word—it was *massive.* Myka stood, brushing flakes of ice off her thermosuit as Laszlo found his feet next to her.

"What is it?" she asked when his frown deepened.

"This tunnel wasn't here last time. This is freshly carved. I—" A look of horror flashed across Laszlo's face, and he froze.

Myka felt, rather than heard, the low groan of the ice surrounding her, as if it was trying to resist bowing to the will of another but was powerless to stop it. The sound built in intensity, crescendoing until the ice hummed with the need for release. Beneath her thermosuit, the prickle of charged air licked at her skin.

And then her world exploded with light.

Myka fell against a solid mass that wrapped itself around her as she stumbled forward, the contact sending lightning through her veins. She couldn't breathe. Couldn't think. Couldn't see.

"Don't move."

She vaguely registered the sensation of something shifting. A haze of iridescent lilac veiled her vision. Disappeared. And then she felt...nothing. Or, at least the absence of pain, which was as good as nothing. Myka blinked, her jumbled thoughts coalescing until she registered Laszlo's presence against her. "We need to stop meeting like this," she mumbled, though his sturdy presence felt like a haven after near-death-by-underground-lightning. "What did you do?"

"Shield. Ice eel," he bit out, drawing her closer still.

She nodded and squeezed her eyes shut, relaxing into his embrace as the adrenaline began to wear away. Only then did she realize she wasn't nearly as shaken as she thought she had been. No, it was Laszlo. *He* was shaking.

"They carve through the ice by emitting an electric field over their scales. It prevents them from freezing and—" His hand briefly left her back as he made what Myka assumed was a vague gesture. "Tunnels."

"Are they dangerous?" she asked into his chest.

"The eels? They're gentle giants. Their electricity—" He cut himself off with a shuddered breath.

Myka waited for him to finish his thought, but when he tucked his face against the folds of her hood, she didn't have the heart to prod. Instead, she held him in silence. Ice eels were a new, albeit, unpleasant experience for her, but she suspected this went much deeper than a quick shock for him. Myka tilted her head up to look over Laszlo's shoulder. Muted electric blue lightning strobed through the ice, highlighting the slowly undulating form of a shadowed behemoth as it moved as if drifting through water. The flashes of light faded as the eel disappeared into the distance, becoming fainter and fainter until—

"It's gone," she whispered.

"I know. Just. Give me a minute." Myka rested her head back against his chest, breathing deeply so he could breathe with her.

Listening as his heart slowed from an erratic pounding to a steady, reassuring beat. Laszlo finally sucked in a breath and released it slowly. "Thank you," he whispered, sliding his arms up her back and fiddling with the armband of his thermosuit.

The shield reappeared, shimmering lilac in the air around them before disappearing once and for all. Laszlo stepped back, tilting his head up and turning in a circle. "They shouldn't be within ten klicks of Isyji Proper."

"Everything is ice; don't they go wherever they want?" Myka absentmindedly rubbed her arm, watching as he tried to pull himself together.

"Yes and no." He faced her again, his panic smoothed into something more akin to concern. "The ice isn't stopping them, but we have magnetic fields around the city to deter them from burrowing under and weakening the infrastructure. If their electric field hits a concentrated mineral deposit in the ice...the explosion is something better observed at a distance."

She grimaced. "So, what does this mean?"

"I'm not sure yet, but it's not good." Laszlo held out his hand. "Side quest to our mayhem mission?"

She intertwined her fingers with his. "You sure?" she asked. He nodded resolutely. "Then lead the way."

Myka had no idea how Laszlo knew where he was going. Maybe he didn't, and they were merely going on a wild huxxa chase. But every fifteen minutes or so he would pause, check the electromagnetic readings on his armband, and carry on with the confidence of a man who took strolls down eel-made ice tunnels on the regular. Though with the way his eyes darted around looking for danger she doubted he was truly as confident as he pretended to be.

Laszlo flinched as the familiar prelude of ice eel-induced lightning rumbled through the tunnel, but he maintained his stride as he wrapped his arm around her shoulder and activated the shield. "I think we're getting close, if the increase in eel activity is any indication."

"You said they shouldn't be able to bypass the magnetic fields?" Myka asked. "It's not something they could have adapted to over time?"

"No, there are fail safes for that exact reason. There haven't been any breaches since they were redesigned after the explosion fifty years ago."

"How easy are they to disable?"

Laszlo raised his brow at her. "Nearly impossible."

"Check." She tilted her head toward his armband.

"It's not magic. You can't just *will* it to read something it's not entirely attuned to."

"Fine," she huffed. "Then I'll check."

Laszlo shot her a bemused glare as she stopped walking, but stood patiently while he watched her fiddle with the settings on her armband before powering it off. Myka took a small screwdriver out of a pocket on her thermosuit and removed the face of the armband to expose the wiring below. She pulled wire cutters and a portable soldering iron from another pocket, a smirk tugging at the corner of her mouth as Laszlo's jaw dropped.

"Trust the process," she said as her smirk changed to a genuine smile.

He shook his head. "I can't decide if I want to kiss you or feed you to the ice eels."

"Neither is preferable." She squinted at the wires before choosing which ones to snip. "That would be distracting, and I only have one"—she cut through three of them—"chance to get this right."

Myka twisted two of the wires together before soldering the third to another part of the processor. Screwing the face back on, she powered up the armband and tapped on the screen, navigating to the menu where the newly wired magnetic datafield was held.

"Does this look normal for general Isyji Hemi magnetic readings?" She held her wrist out for Laszlo to see.

"Yeah."

"And for Isyji Proper?" She switched the settings again, and the field around the city pulsed like a faint heartbeat.

"Absolutely not." His brow furrowed as he leaned closer to glare at the data. "Those readings are barely high enough to be considered anything other than noise."

Before she could talk herself out of it, she pressed a featherlight kiss against his cheek, smiling as his frown disappeared, replaced by a look of peaceful delight.

He turned to face her. "What was that for?"

"You've been frowning too much."

Laszlo grinned and tucked her closer against his side, pressing a kiss against her temple before guiding them further into the maze of tunnels.

"What was that for?" she asked.

"I wanted to." His arm brushed against hers as he shrugged. "And my wife is a genius. I'm not an idiot, mind you. But I think you might have uncovered something very, very interesting." He scratched his head. "And concerning."

"All right, out with it." She poked Laszlo's side. "Isyji's problems are my problems too, and we're on this side quest together."

"That's the thing, for as long as I can remember there were problems. Massive ones. Black markets, civil violence, mysterious disappearances—whether they were murders, kidnappings, or something else entirely we're still not sure. Rumour said it was all organized by a crime syndicate—the Kuzik Tïj—but any leads our spies followed only produced a trail of corpses and more questions than answers. It was terrifying, especially for those living in the outskirts of Isyji Proper. We started negotiations with your parents last year because of how dangerous it was becoming, and it was spreading toward Pykos. If these issues became a planetary threat?"

Myka shuddered at the thought. She knew how dire the situation was, but hadn't paused to reflect on the consequences of what was happening in Isyji, or what could happen should those consequences reach Pykos.

"Violence at the border from frightened Isyjins was already causing enough trouble and was well on its way to inciting a war with Pykos if it wasn't stopped," Laszlo continued. "We would be decimated if there was a war on two fronts. We needed peace with your Hemi, help from your Hemi."

"And so we were wed."

He gave her shoulder an affectionate squeeze. "And so we were."

Myka smiled at the warmth that trailed through her. "What happened, though?"

"Six months ago, everything stopped. The black markets, the violence, the disappearances. People were skeptical. How could they not be? But they trusted that we took care of the problem. The thing is, we didn't do anything, and the harder we looked, the less we found. We moved forward with the treaty since it would benefit both hemispheres and, well, we didn't quite trust the silence. As it turns out, you, my wife, found a way to make the silence speak."

Myka shrugged. "I believe we have my huxxa feather to thank for that. We would still be stuck in a cave without it."

"Thank the stars you're a sentimentalist, then."

The sound of grinding metal on ice echoed down the tunnel, halting them in their tracks.

"Time to see what silence has to say," Myka said. "Let's go."

"Stay close, I don't want to remove the shield and I'm not sure what we'll find. Today is for recon. Later, we'll cause whatever's down there a massive inconvenience."

Frozen ground dug into Myka's knees as she and Laszlo crouched behind an ice formation, but she didn't dare shift. Not that the movement would have mattered; the cavern they found themselves in bustled with activity, suffocating the air with frenzied anticipation. Shouted commands echoed off the walls, melding with the crack of chisels biting ice and the occasional roar of a blowtorch. Ice eels rested in docking bays, as workers attended to metallic sheaths fitted over several eels' bodies. Others pushed pods filled with firearms and unlabeled sacks and tarp-covered lumps. But it was the cargo held in the crates in the far corner that caught her eye, froze her lungs, and stilled her heart. Not even her nightmares could hope to replicate such a sight.

It was spreading toward Pykos, Laszlo had said.

No. It had arrived. It had stolen. It had consumed.

Even at this distance she knew how the curvature of the small device would feel tucked against the palm of her hand. Knew the crystalline matrix of fused Pykänosti Desert sand would warm her skin with the controlled kiss of lightning as it hummed with a frequency engineered to precision. Knew that its chemistry was beautifully stable under the conditions for which it was designed to be used. She squinted at the energy cores she'd designed. The ones meant to regulate the temperature of the homes of her people, and act as a conduit for desert storms to prevent cities from annihilation. The ones that, even under the bioluminescent constellations emitted from the ice surrounding them, should not have been emanating a deadly, oil-slicked hue.

The mixing of Hemis created an inconvenience at best, and devastation at worst.

"We need to leave. Now." Laszlo tugged on her arm, but she couldn't move. "Myka, love." She tore her eyes away from her creation and met his panicked gaze. "We need to go."

Myka resisted the horrible urge to laugh. Where could they go? The Kuzik Tij was going to implode the city. With *her* device.

"I figured out how they've disabled the magnetic field." Laszlo's throat bobbed as he swallowed. "And they're mining ijnakt."

Of course they were mining the one substance impossible to find in Pykos. The one substance that would destabilize her design.

"Exit?" she croaked out.

He nodded toward a small tunnel tucked behind another outcropping of ice formations. Before he could move, she grabbed his wrist.

"Myka, we need to go," Laszlo hissed, using her grip to guide her toward the exit.

"I know," she conceded. But he had to know too. "They're going to bury the city. We're going to die."

Myka stood in a daze before the Isyjin king, queen, and counsel. Shouts danced around her—something about 'acting recklessly.' 'Disappearing for a week.' Had it really taken so long?

Laszlo's voice danced back. Sharp and angry and—his fingers intertwined with her own—protective? She'd told him of her discovery. Of the purpose of the device she designed, the failsafe she'd implemented that could never be overridden in Pykos, the way the addition of ijnakt and bitter cold would destabilize the energy core and turn it into a ticking time bomb. One that, if placed in the meticulously carved tunnels under the city, would sink it as if it never existed.

Myka had expected retribution. To be left alone in the vast Isyjin tundra to die as Laszlo carried on to the palace. She had inadvertently doomed his home. His people. Instead, he had gathered her into his arms and kissed her. *Your design saved your people from extinction*, Laszlo had said. *It has done nothing to harm my own. And if it does, that blame falls entirely on the heads of the Kuzik Tij. Not you. Never you.*

A door slammed, bringing Myka back to the present as the last council member exited the room. Silence rained like a sandstorm against flesh. Someone shifted beside her. Laszlo. He stepped into her field of view. Slowly, gently, his arms wrapped around her, tucking her against him as if her body were a puzzle piece that fit with his alone.

"What did? What...what decision?" Numb fear twisted Myka's words.

"They're going to change the magnetic field so the syndicate's inverse field no longer interferes with ours." Laszlo's quiet voice wove through the haze. "Spies are investigating the tunnels as we speak. We will bring them down, once and for all."

Myka nodded, the softness of his shirt caressing her cheek and his arms around her waist the only things keeping her from succumbing to panic. He tilted her chin up, and as she met his honey-colored gaze, the trepidation within her stilled—as if holding its breath. Waiting. Then, in the brush of his thumb against her jaw, it melted away with a sigh as he shouldered her burdens with him.

"You and I, my beautiful," Laszlo kissed her forehead, "clever," the tip of her nose, "wife," his lips brushed against her own and her eyes fluttered shut. "Shall cause such an inconvenience that has never before, nor will ever be seen again."

Myka tilted her head and sealed his promise with a kiss. Her partner in mayhem, her partner in life. Come sun or storm, she was his strength and he, her shelter. Laszlo rested his forehead against her own as they broke apart, and in the space between breaths, Myka whispered her own promise, "To inconveniences, and those who cause them."

GREEN GLOVES

Katie Fitzgerald

One green gardening glove is the only memento Princess Kendra has from the week she spent with Felix, the landscaper who stole her heart during Easter break at the royal villa. Now she's back for the summer, wandering the gardens and wondering if Felix will ever return...

GREEN GLOVES

KATIE FITZGERALD

ON WEDNESDAY MORNING of the first week of university summer break, Princess Kendra Fairfax de la Paz wandered her mother's flower gardens behind the royal villa. Up and down the gravel pathways she inspected the queen's rhododendrons and delphiniums, snapping photos on her phone of roses and peonies. It would be easy for any outsider to believe she was a devoted horticulturist, given how much time she spent among these blooms.

The pocket of her jacket held the real reason for the visit: a thick, two-toned gardening glove, grey on the palm and green everywhere else. It was all she had of someone special she very much wanted to see again, if only she knew where to find him.

Three months prior, it had been Kendra's Easter break. Queen Amelia had just left for Venice, and in her absence, landscapers were to lay mulch and prepare the flowerbeds for the spring season. The princess had been instructed to make the occasional appearance on the veranda, to show that a royal eye was watching.

Kendra had been recovering from a particularly tough term filled with political science courses where no amount of effort had seemed enough to satisfy the expectations her parents or her professors had for the future queen. They were especially disappointed that Lady Famke van der Meer was now first in the class, with Kendra trailing a quarter of a point behind. The idea of manual labor in the fresh air appealed to her immensely. By the second day, she was tired of observing. She went down to the garden, picked up a rake and fell into step beside one of the workers. He was about her age, tall and muscular, with genial brown eyes. If he was surprised to see a princess stick her hands in the dirt or break a sweat, he didn't show it. He had simply grinned and demonstrated how she could effectively spread mulch over the empty beds of soil.

"It must be so refreshing to work outdoors every day." Kendra raked as she spoke, keeping pace with the crew. "I spend so much time in ballrooms and lecture halls."

"Well, sometimes I think the occasional ballroom wouldn't be so terrible. Especially during a snowstorm when I'm out shoveling. Did you know eyebrows can freeze?" He raised and lowered his brows several times in rapid succession, and she laughed out loud.

The daylight hours flew by as they worked side by side, sharing pleasant conversation. Kendra learned that his name was Felix, and he was a part-time student taking plant science classes. He had dozens of lines of Robert Frost poetry memorized to suit the tasks his work required, and he quoted them freely. He had an older sister who was newly married, a dog named Flora, and his favorite foods were burritos and oatmeal cookies.

Despite being a committed night owl, Kendra rose with the sun every morning that week to meet the landscaping truck when it arrived. She spent the days with Felix, neatening gravel and trading jokes, clearing dead brush and quoting comedy films. On Friday, they raked leaves away from the gazebo while singing pop hits loudly and off-key. When her palm blistered, Felix removed one of his own gloves and passed it over to her. He was slow to pull away, his hand warm as it brushed against hers. “You should take a break,” Felix said gently. “That blister looks nasty.”

“But what would you do without me?” Kendra bumped her shoulder against his.

There was a pang near her heart when he said softly, “Honestly, at this point, I don’t know.”

Kendra’s heart pounded harder as she turned to face this thoughtful man whose company she so deeply enjoyed. Looking up into his eyes, she said, “Felix, I think—”

“Kendra!” The queen’s anger was unmistakable not just in her voice, but also in the flash of her eyes and the purposeful click of her heels on the gravel path. “What are you doing out here? You know tourists are lurking this time of year.” She gave Felix a disapproving glance, then continued to scold. “Get inside before someone takes a photo of you looking like that.”

Kendra looked down at her mud-smudged jeans and dirt-caked sneakers. Her tee shirt, too, was a mess, and she knew her ponytail had come loose. “Honestly, look at your hair,” the queen went on. “Get cleaned up at once.”

Forced to relinquish her rake, and too embarrassed to even glance at Felix, she took off running into the house and didn’t stop until she reached her private bathroom. It was only then that she realized she had accidentally stolen Felix’s glove. By the time she had scrubbed away all the dirt and put on a fresh dress, he and the rest of the landscapers were gone.

The truck returned several times during the second week of Easter break. Kendra never caught a glimpse of Felix, though she ran outside with the glove each time the green-painted truck pulled up. When asked, the queen insisted she had only requested that the gardeners stay away from her daughter, but Kendra had her doubts.

Walking past the gazebo now, Kendra rubbed her thumb over the rough surface of the glove in her pocket. After a whole term away at university, she had given up hope of seeing Felix again. Most of the gardening work was done, other than lawn maintenance, and only a small team handled that. Her time in the garden was really just a chance to relive her memories, and bask in the feelings they gave her.

Unfortunately, it seemed like today's nostalgic walk was about to end. Gloria, the queen's chief of staff, was jogging down the garden path calling Kendra's name. Gloria slowed as she reached the gazebo, and, catching her breath, she gave a small bow of her head before speaking.

"Your Royal Highness, there's a call from the gatehouse. A young man from the landscaping crew says he left something here. He asked for you by name, so I wanted to check with you, but of course I can send him away."

"No!" Kendra's forceful objection caused Gloria to jump, and the princess inhaled slowly to steady herself. "Sorry, but I have what he's looking for. I'd like to take it to him myself."

"Are you sure that's—?"

"Quite sure!" Kendra called over her shoulder as she took off running toward the gate leading to the villa's entrance.

As the gatehouse came into view, she saw him. He had the right build, yes, and that was his hair, definitely, and there was the smile. Kendra felt her heart grow warmer at the sight of it.

Felix raised one hand to wave as she approached. The hand wore a green glove. Then, laughing, he raised his other hand, which was bare.

"I was starting to think I'd imagined you!" Kendra slid to a stop in front of him, breathless, ignoring the puzzled look of the gatehouse security guard. Fumbling in her pocket, she produced the glove and held it out to Felix. "I didn't mean to steal this, I promise."

He chuckled. "I considered it a loan, don't worry."

Ignoring the stares of the bewildered gatehouse staff, Kendra began to talk with Felix as though no time had passed since their last meeting. Felix truly had not been back to the royal villa since the day her mother had interrupted them. "It was in my contract," he explained, "not to fraternize with the royal family. I didn't want to cause any trouble."

"We were raking," Kendra said, taking a step closer to Felix and smiling up at him. "My mother overreacted. That's not really fraternizing."

"No," Felix said, and he leaned in so close that his features blurred. "But this probably is." Before Kendra could speak, his lips claimed hers. The guard gasped but held his tongue. Kendra stepped in even closer, wrapping her arms around Felix's torso. This reunion was everything she had pictured in her daydreams, but better because this time it was real.

After the kiss, Kendra said, “Did I get you fired?”

Felix shook his head. “I quit. That day, with the glove. I couldn’t be here and not see you. It would have been torture. Then I had to find another job; I’m pretty sure it’s poor form to ask a princess on a date when you’re unemployed.”

Kendra looked into his face, studying the long nose and warm gaze, the freshly kissed lips and slight stubble. She giggled nervously. “Is that why you’re here?”

Felix nodded. “That, and I need my gloves to do my job.”

Kendra smacked him playfully. “Does your contract at the new job say anything about me?”

“Nope.” Felix shook his head and pointed down the road. “Now I’m not allowed to fraternize with Lady Famke van der Meer.”

“You’d better believe you’re not,” said Kendra. Pleased that both she and the green glove had found their matches, she emphasized the point with another kiss.

THE COTTAGE COURT CHARLATAN

Hannah Carter

A tiny kingdom ruled by mushroom fairies is rocked by confusion when a well-dressed frog interrupts the princess's birthday celebration.

THE COTTAGE COURT CHARLATAN

HANNAH CARTER

DANGER HAD COME to the Cottage Court.

This was something unusual, for King Helianthus and Queen Zinnia protected their people with unrivaled love and care. In fact, life in the Cottage Court was so safe that more adventurous fairies might call it mundane. So long as one stayed away from the giants, the Bubbling Bogs, the dreaded witch frogs, and the Sinking Swamps, one could almost guarantee that no harm would befall them.

So how, in the middle of Princess Amaryllis' twenty-first birthday ball, could a frog appear?

The dapper amphibian in the blue suit hopped onto the cobblestone-and-grass ballroom floor. The sparkling magic that illuminated the world glinted off the copper buttons on his white vest, and a scarlet cravat completed his ensemble. But no amount of genteel dressing could conceal his true nature: his true, slimy, green, froggy nature.

"Ladies and gentlemen of the Cottage Court, I have come to address the royal family." The frog's suave baritone voice might have convinced some to listen to him, had he not finished with a large croak that echoed throughout the open country air.

A few of the fairies gasped; one yellow chanterelle mushroom fairy fainted in the corner. A black trumpet fairy guard unsheathed his rapier and leveled it at the intruder. "How dare you approach the court?" He was long and thin, with a mixture of black and white skin like the mushroom he resembled.

The frog's wet feet slapped on the cobblestones as he approached the throne. Above, fireflies flashed in a hectic dance while the king, queen, and princess sat regally upon their mushroom cap thrones: none more beautiful than the princess herself, the only Amanita fairy in the land. Poets regarded her as the most beautiful creature in the Cottage Court, from her red-and-white toadstool top down to her matching pointed shoes.

"I have come," the frog said, punctuated by another ribbit, "because the princess has bewitched me."

Amaryllis remained stoic, her mouth pursed in a plump little line. Luscious brown locks framed a pale face, while permanent pink blush colored her cheeks. Her black eyes and crimson wings sparkled in the evening glow. "I have no business with—nor romantic interest in—a frog." She turned to the guards, more black trumpet fairies. "Guards, escort this emerald interloper out."

"By the laws of the fairies," the frog interrupted, a glint in his beady eyes, "the royal family is required to see all visitors who come to them with an appeal. Therefore, I appeal to the generous King Helianthus and the glorious Queen Zinnia to hear my plea."

King Helianthus stroked his yellow-and-brown streaked beard. He was a plantpot dapperling fairy, whose golden head resembled a turban. His long Rubakha and loose pants shared the same coloring, while umber threads wove intricate, flower-shaped designs across his clothes. "I admit it is quite unusual to allow a frog at court, but it *is* in our law that no creature, should they come with an appeal, be turned away."

Amaryllis let out an annoyed puff of air. "But he is a *frog*. Surely we don't have to hear the pleas of a slimy creature."

The queen rested a hand on her husband's shoulder—the blue on her arms resembled gloves, which stretched from fingertip to elbow. "As rulers of the Cottage Court, we try and be fair to all, no matter how ugly or...slimy they might be." One hand smoothed down her dress, a strapless ball gown that ended with a wide flare. It perfectly matched her large mushroom cap, for, as an indigo milk cap fairy, the top of her head resembled a wide-brimmed hat.

The frog adjusted his cravat. "As I said, the princess has bewitched me. From the moment we met, I have not been able to think of anything else except to find her." He croaked, and Amaryllis shuddered. "I request but one thing: allow me a dance with the princess."

More guards moved to defend their princess, so beloved by all. They raised their sticks with tiny thorns attached to the ends, their makeshift spears.

"Never!" one of the more eager black trumpet fairies bellowed. He even jabbed at the frog and almost cut through the fine silk of the guest's suit. The frog slid sideways to avoid the blow and pushed the spear away.

"What a presumptuous plea," a female plums-and-custard fairy said with a sniff. "Especially with so many men vying for Princess Amaryllis' attention on her birthday."

"Ah, but if the princess will not dance with me, then she would be denying an innocent guest their plea." The frog bowed low and tilted his face to gaze upon the object of his desire. “And no fairy of the Cottage Court would dare deny such an insignificant request.”

Princess Amaryllis met his gaze. Though her face betrayed no emotion, there lurked a fire in her eyes that met the frog’s in a challenge. This would be no dance—this would be a duel. A duel of wits and wishes.

She walked down the dais to meet the frog as the crowd gasped and whispered. Though smaller in stature than her opponent, the princess’ spirit could devour him whole. “Shall we dance?” She raised one hand to his shoulder and refused to flinch as his viscid hand slid around her petite waist.

“Raise a waltz to my daughter on her birthday,” King Helianthus commanded. At his words, the short and stout porcini mushroom fairies in the band began an elegant tune, slow and alluring.

The frog took the lead, though his webbed feet stepped on Amaryllis’ at every turn.

“My apologies,” he said. “You see, I am not quite used to dancing with these feet.”

“Perhaps that is why frogs should not dance,” Amaryllis said icily, “so that they do not embarrass themselves in front of the whole court.”

The frog chuckled. “Ah, is that why you detest frogs so?”

“I have many reasons to detest frogs.” Amaryllis’ eyes flashed. “You should go back to the swamp.”

“It is awfully lonely there,” he said, a thoughtful tone to his voice. “Especially when you are ostracized for being a frog—hideous and hated. As I have learned, it is rather hard to be green.”

"Do you want my sympathy?" Amaryllis snapped. "Have you come to woo me with a tale of woe?"

"I think not." His voice dropped as he leaned in, his mouth right by her ear. "Shall we cease this charade? I came to offer you a choice. You may tell the Cottage Court of your deceit, or I will. But you cannot continue this ruse forever."

Amaryllis met his gaze. "You think that they would believe you—a frog—over their princess?"

"We shall see." The music reached a crescendo as the frog pulled Amaryllis closer in a twirl. She shuddered as her toadstool cap brushed against the slimy underbelly of his chin. "But I wished to give you the chance to repent of your ways and become an honest woman. You have until the end of the dance to decide."

One-two-three. One-two-three. One-two-three. The waltz continued, every step as crucial as a move in chess. The princess and the frog, two opponents caught in a battle. They swept across the ballroom while magic whirled around them.

"I am not without sympathy, you know." His webbed feet slapped across the floor. "I know why you did what you did. I can help you if you just trust me. Tell the truth, Amaryllis. The end has almost come."

Her hand tightened on his shoulder. "I shall not."

He ribbited. "I will still give you every chance to change your mind. We do not have to be enemies here at the Cottage Court."

As the music died, even some of the more heartless mushroom fairies clapped, as if the duo had ensorcelled the crowd, too. And the frog and princess stared at each other, hands still in position.

"Shall you or I speak the truth?" the frog croaked good-naturedly.

Amaryllis' eye twitched. "Guards!" She dropped the frog's hand and stepped back. "This frog is not a simple frog—he's a witch frog! Escort him back to the Sinking Swamps immediately!"

The black trumpet fairies must have been waiting for such an order. They rushed the frog, who merely turned his attention to the king and queen.

"I wonder," the frog began, "how the princess knows that I came from the Sinking Swamp, unless she had been there before?"

Amaryllis clenched her fists. "Don't be ridiculous."

The guards twisted the frog's arms behind him and forced the emerald interloper to his knees. One soldier stripped the frog of his cravat, while another ripped the jacket from his body—as if a frog did not even deserve dignity.

"One final plea?" The frog lifted his head, spearing the royal family with his gaze.

Amaryllis lifted her chin. "You wasted your plea on a dance."

"Only because I wished to be generous," he said. "But now I only ask for a kiss from the princess."

Several onlookers burst into laughter. King Helianthus stood as if their guest had insulted his daughter's honor. Queen Zinnia, too, shook her head. "You could never demand such a thing from the princess—"

"Amaryllis is not the princess of Cottage Court," the frog announced. He let out two ribbits. "I am its rightful prince."

The guards wrenched the frog to the ground and dragged him away. But before they could reach the edge of the Cottage Court, the frog called, "It's all true! I am Prince Coriander. Amaryllis is a witch frog who approached me as I patrolled the Sinking Swamps yesterday, in order to keep witch frogs like her away from our humble court. She spied me and forced a kiss upon me, which made us switch places." A few croaks interrupted his impassioned speech. "She has enchanted all of you with her magic to believe that she is the princess, when she is the true frog."

"Silence!" Amaryllis trembled with rage, her jaw clenched, her face as scarlet as her mushroom cap head. "These are lies!"

"If they are lies, then you will have no trouble kissing a frog, just once, before you never see him again." The frog kicked his legs and wrenched in an effort to twist away from his guards, but he only managed to slow their progress. He flinched as they punctured his skin with their spears, and blood bubbled out of the wounds.

"I will not." Amaryllis pivoted, only to face her father, who stared at her with a curious expression.

The onlookers slowly began to whisper amongst themselves. Some cast shifty glances between the princess and the frog, and a few of the less ardent guards dropped their hold on the miscreant.

"If you speak the truth, then clear your name and kiss the frog." King Helianthus' forehead furrowed, and he tightened his grip on the arm of his throne. "No daughter of mine would balk at the idea of clearing her name and quelling the gossipers."

Amaryllis tilted her chin. "I should not need to. I am your daughter, and I have always been your daughter—"

"Then kiss the frog, love." Queen Zinnia waved her daughter on. The gesture might have seemed dismissive to some, but a challenging fire brewed in her eyes. "For, if true, his accusations are monumental. It would be best to get this matter over with before you one day ascend to the throne."

Amaryllis stared at both her parents. Her fists unclenched; her shoulders drooped a bit. Betrayal and despair flickered through her heart before resolution firmed her spirit. She turned around, shook her hair over her shoulder, and marched toward the frog like a soldier marching into battle.

Her opponent, already battered and bloody, stared up at her. "I am sorry," the frog croaked again.

He raised his head; and Amaryllis closed her eyes, sighed—and bolted away, her dainty little shoes tapping against the ballroom floor.

"Guards! My daughter!" King Helianthus cried. They needed no more prompting than that to chase after her, and the black trumpets seized her before she could disappear into the sunflowers and daylilies in the garden.

"No! No!" Amaryllis screeched. She kicked as the guards hoisted her in mid-air. "Please—" They deposited her in front of the frog and held her in place, while another black trumpet fairy placed his hand on the back of her head. "Please, no," she whispered. Desperate, sad eyes met the frog's. "I used up all my magic for this." Her bottom lip trembled, and tears trickled down her pretty face.

"A life built on lies can never be happy," the frog said. "But the truth will set you free. It will set both of us free."

Her beautiful cap drooped. With the guards still holding onto her arms, she glanced up at the frog through dark lashes. "I suppose we'll have to see."

Her lips met the frog's mouth in a kiss.

Sparks erupted from between them, and the courtiers all covered their eyes. And when they opened them again, they still saw a frog and the royal child—

Though the positions were now reversed.

Where the frog once knelt, now Prince Coriander stood. Tall and gangly, with mottled white-and-plum skin as befitting a violet webcap mushroom fairy. Under his rather plain lavender mushroom cap, black hair with purple streaks fell to his shoulders.

Amaryllis, defeated, slumped to her knees and bowed her froggy head. No hair adorned her emerald skull; no clothes protected her from the elements. And the crowd blinked as if a fog had dissipated in their minds.

"I remember now! We—we never had a princess! We had Prince Coriander all along!"

"She's the witch frog!"

"She cursed our prince!"

"Throw her back in the swamp!"

"Kill her!"

"Guards!" King Helianthus bellowed. He rose from his throne, face glowing a radiant golden that it only carried in his most irate moods. "Remove the charlatan—the witch—!"

The guards wrenched Amaryllis away from the crown prince, and—

"Wait." Coriander held up a hand. The flurry of motion around them stopped. He reached down and swiped away a tear from her cheek. "Amaryllis."

She covered her face with a webbed hand as if to protect herself from his eyes. "Don't look at me."

He shooed the guards away from her, and though a few protested, he silenced them all with a princely stare. "Why not?"

"Because I'm hideous!" She curled more inward like she could somehow convince her large body to disappear. But she could not, especially when Coriander reached for her again.

He placed his hand between her eyes. "Ladies and gentlemen of the Cottage Court—Mother—Father—I come to you with a new plea. Not as an intruder, but as your prince."

Queen Zinnia paused in the middle of her attempt to leave the dais.

"Perhaps you should know what it is like to be a frog, as I have. Then you would feel the loneliness, the yearning. Life in the Sinking Swamp is miserable. There are no flowers, there are no dances, no luxuries. It is only brown, dead, hollow. I did not even come across another frog while I was trapped there." Coriander patted Amaryllis' head once more as she sniffled. "And I admit, we at the Cottage Court have not been fair with our neighbors. We treat them as exiles, banished from the light. Amaryllis was wrong to bewitch me and take my place, but she fought to remain in the light and love she had found."

"She lied!" Queen Zinnia swept toward the two, her regal chin raised. "She made me forget my own son." She cupped Coriander's chin and gazed at him lovingly. "How can I ever forgive her?"

"In the same way I can, Mother." He smiled softly as he extricated himself from her embrace. "After all, was the offense not mine to forgive?" Coriander turned to Amaryllis. "Though I offered you a choice before and you rejected me, I extend the hand of mercy one more time."

Amaryllis wiped at her tears. "I...only wanted..." She croaked. "I was so lonely. So ugly. I thought—I thought if I was beautiful..." She uttered a series of croaks and ribbits. "I'm so sorry."

"There. You see?" Coriander leaned down and took her webbed hand in his. "Mercy is mine to give, and I freely give it." To the whole Cottage Court, he announced, "I decree that Amaryllis is now forever welcome at the Cottage Court as a beloved friend, the past forgiven with grace." He helped her to stand and dusted her off. "Now…shall we dance?"

CALLISTO FALLS

C. Ash

It's Prince Luke's birthday, but instead of celebrating with his people, he's a prisoner of war in a foreign kingdom. Illustration included also by C. Ash.

CALLISTO FALLS

C. ASH

"YOU LOOK REMARKABLY CHIPPER for someone whose execution is tomorrow night."

Prince Luke crossed his arms, trying to ignore the cold, metal cuff on his right wrist. A single blue light flashed steadily from a panel in the metal, indicating that he was exactly where his captors expected him to be. He hated that light.

He scraped together a response after a beat. "Well, it would have been sooner, but they didn't want me to miss my birthday."

His eyes flicked upwards to the security cameras stationed at the ceiling, then back to the tablet on the table. The simulated voice issuing from the screen sounded robotic, but there was most likely a human behind the words. Another official, perhaps, or an analyst on one of the starships in low orbit.

"I didn't know I was being sent tutors anymore," he told the tablet. The blank screen reflected back silver walls and silence. When Luke had first arrived at the capital, instead of being locked away in solitude, he was sent to expert after expert who taught him the propaganda of their kingdom. He was told that Calisto was a beautiful empire of progress, and that his kingdom was evil. The reality he'd seen with his own eyes began to blur after months of their version of history. Kadim wasn't perfect, but his people were like family, tight-knit and loving—and many of them were now scattered because of the war.

"We will discuss Kadim's two kings," the tablet's voice stated.

Luke rubbed his eyes with his thumbs. *Not this again.* "It's not like that. Our God is our King. My father's simply an ambassador."

"Can any kingdom manage with two kings?"

"Thus, the hierarchy." He didn't want to explain, not to a robotic voice who wouldn't understand. Behind his exhausted words, his mind stayed busy, incessantly repeating a familiar line about ever-present help in times of trouble.

"And this king is everywhere?"

Luke hesitated at the phrasing of the question. How would this voice know what he'd been thinking? "Yes, everywhere," he murmured, staring at the blank screen.

The voice floating through space somewhere must not have been terribly bored, because after a few more questions and vague comments about his kingdom it announced, "Now, you can stay here with your invisible king until you are summoned."

The harsh overhead lights clicked off. After sitting in the darkness for a minute, Luke relocated to the floor to lie down. It all felt like carbon steel anyway. He closed his eyes as the thrum of a waterfall spilled from an archway to channel through the palace. Behind closed eyelids, he tried to picture his fiancé aboard the flagship of their fleet. She'd be suspended in space even now, fighting against the darkness that threatened their people. Her grey eyes would be squinting in concentration out the windows of the ship's bridge, her uniform the cold blue of Rigel.

Between the two of them, Lyra had always been the large-scale strategist, while he'd gravitated more toward tactics. "Don't worry,

Princey," she'd remind him every time they were in a difficult situation. "Help is ever-present."

"That's because you know how good your backup is," he'd respond, complimenting her admirals.

Now, Luke hoped she was leagues away, nowhere near Calisto's capital. He remembered the chaos on the bridge of his ship when he'd surrendered. Past the sprawling windows into the stars, his smaller craft was being annihilated in bursts of white. The admiral had singled Luke out from the rest of his crew, snapping, "This one we need. I know a troublesome general who might want him back. She won't be able to resist a rescue." He'd grinned eagerly at Luke. "How would you like to end a war, young prince?"

Stay away, Lyra. Stay safe.

A flood of light assaulted his eyes as his sleep bled into dreams. He sat up slowly, blinking away blindness as sunlight spilled in the open door. How long had it been?

A guard in a silver uniform stood in the entrance, waiting for Luke to emerge from the dark room. As he crossed the threshold, the doors hissed shut behind him. Once outside, he squinted at the waterfalls, his eyes gradually adjusting to the white glint reflecting off the water.

The outer courtyard was a spectacle of grand stone clouded by mist, a hubbub of voices filling the halls as the silent guard led him toward the inner world of the palace. The guard didn't stop Luke as he approached a wide balcony to look over the flurry of activity. People scattered around like ants with bolts of silver cloth, hovering carts of dishes, and vivid bouquets of flowers.

"Do you like it? It's all for you." An elegant voice from behind him caused Luke to spin, startled. The queen stood near his balcony, arm resting against a pillar. Selene's dress was glimmering silver, morphing to a fiery orange gradient. Jewels glinted from her earrings and armbands. He even caught a few diamonds flashing in her hair, hard and flashing above the eyes that never stopped scanning for weaknesses, like a virus searching for weaknesses in code. She was sophistication personified, yet she'd personally killed his officers on the bridge of his ship when he'd been captured. With the horrific images never far from his mind, he couldn't help but see her as most other things in this palace: a beautiful mask concealing something monstrous.

Luke focused on the decorations below the balcony to avoid her gaze. "Silver's not really my color."

Luke had already been briefed on the festivities for the night. His birthday celebration would be a Calistan showcase—their silver and vivid orange national colors covering the palace, their breads and sausages and gelatins spread across the tables—with his lone figure standing out as a spot of blue in a sea of silver. They wanted to make him feel alone. But he didn't. He was never alone.

The queen laughed lightly behind him. "Well, I'm sure you can appreciate it for one more night." Her voice lowered as she spoke to the guard, "Make sure he's ready at nineteen hundred hours."

Luke only turned around as she walked away, her orange dress trailing across the marble floors. The queen had much to prepare for, between this party and her attempt to force a battle between Calisto and Kadim in Calisto's own airspace. Nerves churned in Luke's stomach at the thought, and he prayed his people wouldn't take the bait. Allowing Calisto to execute him would make his forces appear weak, but a rescue attempt could lead to devastating loss.

A few short hours later, the party began in earnest. Music and laughter from a sea of orange nobles echoed across the ballroom. Robotic trays hummed as they sped across the room, filled to the brim with meats, fruits, and cakes of all sizes. Also in prominent evidence—Calisto's weird, orange gelatin with cucumbers floating inside. Luke had never tried it, but it looked disgusting. If that gelatin was offered to him as a last meal—and tomorrow might indeed be his last meal—he might turn it down.

Part of the 'charm' of his birthday celebration was his position in the room, bookended by guards at the end of a long, food-filled table—yet with every dish carefully positioned out of his reach. It was maddening, and after a day of this, he was beginning to get dizzy. At least tonight, his incessantly glowing blue cuff had been exchanged for the towering gentlemen keeping an eye on him.

Queen Selene rose from her chair and led the guests in a series of toasts commemorating Calisto's victories in battle that year, honoring her generals. The honored officials sat at their own tables, dressed in military uniform with sleek, silver helmets. Since Luke couldn't see their faces, he didn't recognize any of them but the commander of the low-orbit fleet. The man was a beast of a strategist and had given Luke and Lyra more than a little trouble over the past year.

After the feast was served and nearly everyone had eaten their fill, the military leaders and nobility met at the ballroom floor and began dancing. Calistan dances were far more formal and systematic than Luke was used to. The counterclockwise motion paused only as a pair at one of the four corners of the room executed a stiff turn before settling back into the flow.

After the first dance, a captain approached him and held out a hand. She wore a space combat medal, which meant she'd possibly fought his own fleet at some point. Killed his comrades. He studied her featureless silver visor for all of three seconds, but she remained silent. He begrudgingly accepted the gloved hand and followed her to the dance floor. *What would the Calistan have said if I'd rejected the offer,* he wondered.

They slipped into the fringes of the circle, and the captain began easing into the steps of the waltz, simple but quick. She spun on the toe of one boot as they turned, gracefully back into place. Luke half-heartedly tried to keep up, feet a half-beat behind the tempo of the music and mind lagging even further. The thought of learning his enemies' dances? Absurd. All the colors and sounds of Calisto only made him miss his country, his planet. *Lyra*.

He made his first true mistake near the center of the room. The music swelled, and he lowered his arm instinctively in a waist slide move that reminded him of home. As he dropped his arm, the captain matched his footwork, swinging effortlessly in a way that tugged his arm just as he'd have expected. He paused, head spinning.

"Sorry Princey," came the apologetic voice, muffled behind the helmet but as piercingly familiar as his own heartbeat. "I've been in space too long. I'm forgetting how to dance."

His hand tightened over hers. He didn't dare say her name out loud. It was as infamous as his in this city. He worried he might be hallucinating, but he felt her grip. Knew in his heart. Lyra was *here*.

She pulled his arm, bringing him once more into the pattern of the dance. Silver and orange figures spun around the edges of his vision, all a blur. How was this possible? He swallowed, throat dry. "You came all the way from space just to dance with me, is that it?"

"You can think that," she said teasingly.

"In the middle of a war? Sounds like you live dangerously." He tried desperately to say anything that she could safely respond to. All he wanted was to pull her close and never let her go.

"Well, you count the cost. Plan ahead. Leave a capable crew in orbit. Anyone would do it."

"Not anyone."

"Well, some of us can't miss a royal birthday party." Before he could say anything else, she spun to the outside of the circle, silver helmet glinting under the lights. "Come. I want to see the famous waterfalls."

As she led him to the arched balconies at the back of the ballroom, he resisted the urge to glance behind him for his assigned watchdogs, certain that at any moment he'd feel a firm hand on his shoulder and a stern voice commanding his compliance. The roar of water grew closer as the music faded to the background. The palace courtyard stretched beyond the walls, and beneath the moonlit stone terrace, the largest waterfall in Calisto snaked into the night. Mist hung thick in the air.

When he looked back at Lyra, she was unzipping the tactical pockets of her uniform. "Here, take this."

A tightly packed jumble of straps and rope appeared, spilling over her hands as she thrust the climbing harness and anchor set urgently at him. They geared up in seconds before Lyra reached behind an innocent-looking balustrade. She unhooked a metal clip, handing him a line that disappeared past the balcony into the mist.

He stepped up to the marble rail. "You're about to tell me we have to jump, aren't you?" Applause erupted from the crowd behind them, the waltz ending. He craned his head anxiously toward the ballroom. Someone would follow them at any moment.

Lyra handed him a pair of gloves. "We're jumping," she confirmed, a note of apology in her voice.

He'd never rappelled down a waterfall before, but he pulled the gloves on wordlessly and threw a leg over the railing. Lyra gripped the length of rope near her waist and nodded her silver helmet at him. Luke swallowed hard against the panic roiling in his stomach. He hadn't set up this equipment, couldn't see past the spray of water that trailed into black, wasn't even certain there was anything safe to land upon.

Lyra released the balcony and let herself fall back. Luke watched her right arm as she let the line slide, then tightened it several meters down. He waited to pinpoint the spot where she disappeared, then fixed his eyes ahead at the archway. All he could hear was the roar of the water behind him. *Lord help us*, he thought, heart pounding.

Then he let go, falling into the mist. The first moment was pure adrenaline. Stomach dropping. Weightlessness. Then, he swung toward the waterfall. He closed his eyes and ducked as he crashed through the icy curtain of water. Shocking cold. Then the invisible line above him began to pull back the other direction. He saw points of light on the dark stone behind the waterfall. He looked down, keeping a death grip between his gloved fingers, swinging more gently now that he was underneath the place where the rope was hooked to the ceiling.

He caught his balance on a slick platform and turned a circle to take in his surroundings. The air was cold and humid. A tunnel of black, wet stone led underneath the palace, likely connecting back to the rivers in the courtyards. The capital was a maze of waterways, their labyrinthian depths the weakness Lyra's crew had exploited to get into the heart of the city. Three helmeted figures waited inside the tunnel, holding narrow beams of light.

Lyra pulled her helmet loose with one hand, releasing a cascade of brown waves. She jumped over a narrow channel of water to the raised platform he'd landed on. He hadn't seen her face in what felt like forever. Even now, he only caught the shape of her smile, her sharp grey eyes reflecting the edge of a light beam. The rappel line still bisected his vision, but Lyra ran up and pulled it away from his face so she could kiss him properly. He'd missed her so fiercely that it still felt like a dream—except that he was soaked and shivering from the waterfall. She fit her head against his shoulder, and he wrapped his arms around her back.

She let out a relieved breath. "Thanks for waiting so long. We ran into some traffic over the ocean."

That meant they'd battled part of the eastern fleet to get there. She sounded somewhere between laughing and crying, and he was so overwhelmed he felt the same. "Well, I know how good my backup is," he finally managed to reply.

Lyra lifted her head, smiling reassuringly and gripping his arms. "We know how good *our* backup is," she said, and Luke thought of the screen blaring lies and the near-invisible line that he'd trusted as he took the plunge.

She was right. An ever-present help in times of trouble. He held Lyra close, drinking in the moment of peace before they'd have to fight their way home. Above them, the waterfall drowned out the music of Calisto as it plunged noisily into the night.

THE QUEENS UNDER GLASS

Danielle Robertson

When The Gardener comes to town toting a greenhouse full of beautiful flowers, The Queen of Hearts is enamored. Her sister, The Queen of Diamonds, is not as trusting.

THE QUEENS UNDER GLASS

DANIELLE ROBERTSON

THE QUEEN OF DIAMONDS WAS SEVENTEEN, and she felt her life stretching before her like a hall of mirrors. There were a million fractured possibilities, but all of them ended up the same way: her, alone, staring into her own eyes.

The Queen of Hearts had fallen in love with a suitor who possessed bad luck in spades. How could The Queen of Diamonds let herself love after she watched her sister lose the thing for which she was named?

Because of this, she vowed only to ever love diamonds.

That summer, a scented breeze had fluttered in through the windows of The House of Cards. It ruffled the tapestries and sent the lady's maids into a tizzy, grasping for linens as they swooped across the courtyard.

Someone new had trotted into town, lugging a greenhouse of wonders behind him. The glass glint of it shone in the sun. Inside, the heat felt like a sugared rose petal softening on the tongue—the delicious graze of teeth against its melting sweetness.

And within that heat, nourished by sunbeams captured in the panes: a village of flowers, bright and mysterious, turning toward the viewer like shy dancers. Such flowers couldn't possibly exist outside of a dream—could they?—and they captured everyone's attention.

Nobles excused themselves from lunches and bridge games to peer into the greenhouse. Workers stole moments away from factory lines and shop counters to breathe in the intoxicating perfume. Everyone sighed over the soft flashes of purples, pinks, and magentas; the coquettish flirt of yellow, white, blue, and orange. The colors promised heat, and light, and love.

The Queen of Hearts fancied herself a Queen of Flowers, of sorts, because what better way to a person's heart than a bright bouquet? Despite her soft-spoken nature, she imperiously demanded to be shown the greenhouse wares that afternoon. She paraded through the gleaming glass walls with her entourage. She swept through the rows of plants, silk skirts brushing through the soil on the floor. She pointed out the flowers she wanted for The House's gardens, her fingers trailing against their soft petals and gem-green leaves. Her servants dutifully lugged pots as young attendants stood by, loading wares into carts. Her heart-shaped face, tilted up to the sun, gleamed like a flower itself. Her fair hair caught the gold of the sunrays, warm and bright. She was a wonder, in that greenhouse: a flower who had taken twenty years to bloom, and now stood resplendent.

And at the end of the greenhouse's many rows, like a proud minotaur in the center of his labyrinth: The Gardener, wiping the fine peat moss of his orchids off his callused hands. Dark-haired and tall, his eyes gleamed as each new customer stumbled in amongst his flowers. He had a smile that flowered like night-blooming jasmine, offering the sharp, fleeting promise of possibility.

It was that smile that captured The Queen of Hearts' attention—and her oft-famed heart.

The summer was all revelry, a carnival without end. The Queen of Diamonds heard her sister's laughter more in those months than any other. People traveled from all over to see the colorful parade in the gardens of The House of Cards. The Queen of Hearts had purchased nearly all of The Gardener's greenhouse stock, and now the flowers marched in proud rows in her gardens, brandishing gleaming stems. Their petals were the blood-red splendor of the sisters' army uniforms.

The Queen of Hearts' silvered laughter rang out in the early morning, through the bright afternoon, and into the star-speckled evening. And underneath the sound, like a drumbeat keeping time: the deep, honeysuckle laugh of The Gardener.

"What a spectacle," The Queen of Diamonds told her sister. They watched from the windows of their library as the townsfolk oohed and aahed over the vivid displays. The Gardener showered the flowers with sprays of water, the droplets glittering prisms in the hot summer sun.

"Father talked to us about Dynasty," The Queen of Hearts said. "Bloodline, the line of succession. I look out this window and everything feels possible."

The Queen of Diamonds tapped on the windowpane. "Flowers aren't children." She wanted to feel joy for her sister. She wanted to give in and wrap herself up in the heady kaleidoscope of colors in the gardens below, just like the townsfolk had. But she couldn't stop thinking of the gleam in The Gardener's eyes, that first morning in the greenhouse.

"These flowers are miracles," The Queen of Hearts said. "And they're all my own."

One morning, the sisters met for breakfast in the garden. The summer was drawing to a close, and the sisters were wrapped in furs to keep out the early morning chill. Before they sat, The Queen of Diamonds leaned in to kiss her sister—and caught the scent of woodsmoke and peat in her blonde curls. This, combined with the impish glint in her sister's eye, gave her the distinct impression that this was not The Queen of Hearts' first rendezvous of the day.

The trees of the surrounding forest turned orange and gold in time-lapse as the sisters sipped their coffee. Various servants scurried about, pouring more coffee, and offering trays of biscuits and dried fruit. A jar of honey from a neighboring kingdom caught the pink of the sunrise in its amber. The glow, like stained glass, cast itself on the queens' faces. Seeing her sister's face framed in such a light, The Queen of Diamonds was reminded of a time when the sisters were very young and shaking with fever, twin shades haunting the halls of The House. How they had both claimed to see things—people, fairies, creatures—crossing the halls and courtyards. Their mother had called it "flights of fancy," but The Queen of Diamonds had only felt terror.

The Gardener wheeled his cart back and forth over the cobblestones, hauling pruning shears and soil through the rows of flowers. Each pass of his cart was more deliberate than the last. The Queen of Diamonds took a moment to study this person who had captured her unshakeable sister's attention: his angular jaw, his storyteller eyes. She decided to put them all out of their misery.

"Dear Heart." She touched her sister's wrist, felt the pulse jump underneath her fingers. "Why don't you invite him over for a cup of coffee?"

There was a terrible rush of clattering cups and silverware, and a big show surrounding the pulling up of a chair. But when The Gardener settled down with many thanks, his hands dwarfing the dainty china cup he held, The Queen of Diamonds witnessed a settling in her sister. The Queen of Hearts pressed her palm to her chest, as if to calm herself. And when she looked into The Gardener's eyes, her sweet smile rivaled the honeyed brightness of the sunrise. This gave The Queen of Diamonds hope.

Until she felt something soft brush against her foot. It was a petal, brittle and dry, curled up like a sleeping child as it drifted to the flagstones. She crushed it to dust underneath her slipper.

The miracle, it turned out, wouldn't last the fall.

The sisters now looked out onto a courtyard of brown. The once-tidy rows of flowers were trampled and defeated without the summer sun to strengthen them. The townsfolk no longer came to cheer, to wander the gardens and admire the spectacle. There were whispers at the gate of waste and wanton excess. A family gone to ruin, gamblers dealt a bad hand.

The Queen of Hearts had a fever that leaked from her eyes; her face shone with it. Earlier that morning, The Queen of Diamonds had heard her sister arguing with The Gardener, begging him to fix the mess. Surely something as simple—as commonplace—as the changing season wouldn't be enough to kill off his miraculous blooms. His response had been low, the rumble of a thunderstorm far away. Too low to hear through the bedroom walls and the sweep of tapestries.

The House of Cards had been carefully constructed by the sisters' ancestors—a feat of clean lines and perilous, balanced design. The Queen of Diamonds often wandered the halls in the evenings, brushing her fingers against the cool marble and brocade fabrics of the home's interior. Reliable, solid. When so much felt ready to careen to the ground outside, the rooms stood strong. The tall spires of shelves in the library were the backbone of the home, and upon those shelves were the answers—the queen hoped—to all their questions.

When The Gardener's attempts to revive the gardens proved unfruitful, the sisters called in experts, people who might be able to assist with the failing ranks of flowers outside. The courtyard no longer held a military parade of blooms, prideful and brash, but rows and rows of wounded soldiers—sickly, despondent—who may never see home again.

Dynasty.

The memory of the word clacked in The Queen of Hearts' mouth, all teeth.

This was her dynasty now: broken stems, curled leaves. A carpet of petals crunching underfoot.

Each expert called in, ushered from some tropical climate or stuffy university, was a stab to The Gardener's heart. And The Queen of Hearts knew all about that: it was the best place to strike. Her eyes had hardened to gemstones, shining and cool. She had taken a page from her dear sister's book, it seemed. The lovers no longer simpered across the breakfast table, or brushed fingertips over passed coffee cups.

Every meeting the sisters took, however, may as well have been with a snake oil salesman. These men looked down on the sister queens, telling them tales of miracle potions, new kinds of soil, or shamans who could bless the land and make it fertile again. One decreed that the sisters were being punished for the indiscretions of their great-great-grandmother, a notorious flirt who handed out precious family heirlooms to her paramours.

"What was so different?" The Queen of Diamonds wondered aloud. She could scarcely look out the window for thoughts of the dying flowers. The smell of it punched at her gut, sickly, like rotting fruit.

"They never looked more beautiful," The Queen of Hearts whispered. She pulled her shawl tight around her shoulders, like she couldn't shake a chill. Like winter was even closer than they realized. "They never looked more beautiful than that first day. How gorgeous, to see them all sun-dappled. To walk through the rows in the greenhouse and feel so transported."

And both sisters, startled by the realization, nodded.

"The greenhouse."

So by the light of a candle, The Queen of Hearts and The Queen of Diamonds crouched over a book on the floor of their library. For a moment, they were children again, huddled around fairytales, with the candlelight providing a dreamy quality to the act. Only now, instead of fairytales, the sisters dreamed of buildings. Of a structure, like their House of Cards, that would stand strong and protect their dynasty.

"We'll build a greenhouse," The Queen of Diamonds said. "It'll look beautiful in the courtyard. Like a dazzling jewel in a crown."

Her sister looked out the window, toward the small hut where The Gardener slept more often these days. "It's not enough," she said. "It's not enough to cover the courtyard. They're laughing at us—laughing at me—beyond the gates. I can't even keep my garden safe! How am I supposed to be trusted to guard a whole kingdom? We can't box ourselves in, all alone."

In a fit of inspiration, or desperation, or both, The Queen of Hearts hired the most capable architects in the realm to construct a greenhouse that would not only cover the courtyard, and not only cover The House of Cards; it would, in fact, cover the entirety of her kingdom.

"Think of it," The Queen of Hearts addressed the curious crowds. "To have warmth and beauty, always at our beck and call." And nary a townsperson missed the meaningful look she shared with The Gardener, who stood slightly to the side of the crowd. The fever had come back to color The Queen of Hearts' face. The Gardener's smile had come back to color his. And to her sister's right, The Queen of Diamonds looked on, and once again hoped.

If she shut her eyes, The Queen of Diamonds could imagine what only existed now as pen and ink drawings: clear panes and lofted ceilings of shimmering glass. Fractals playing out across courtyards, squares, thatched roofs, fountains. The sheen of glass in rolling green fields, and the animals corralled by it, never needing to find shelter elsewhere. Because why would they need to stray when the sun would warm them, and the grasses and plants would grow so beautifully for them to eat?

And the flowers! If she shut her eyes, the colors of them burst behind her eyelids like fireworks. A carnival without end. Surely the parade would march again.

The Queens surveyed the progress from the library window as the first panes of the greenhouse were erected around The House of Cards' courtyard. The walls and the supporting beams. The panes of the roof, sliding carefully into place. The greenhouse stood tall and gleaming in the autumn sunlight, casting the sisters' home in orange and gold.

The Gardener and his assistants set to work, watering the listless flowers. Again, the sprays of water shone on the leaves, like stars plucked from the sky. The Queens stood in the center of it all, inhaling wet earth and dreams.

On that first day, the pen and ink plans came to life, dancing across the courtyard in graceful lines.

On that first day, the tired flowers stood a little taller. The Gardener stood taller. The Queen of Hearts stood taller, too.

On that first day, The Queen of Diamonds felt beads of sweat begin to roll down the back of her neck as the sunlight beat down. But she brushed them away and kept dreaming. To see her sister smile was the only cool breeze she required.

But as the weeks passed and the greenhouse grew—the glass walls stretched from the courtyard and down the hedge-lined paths, toward the gates to town—The Queen of Hearts found her smile shrinking, and The Queen of Diamonds couldn't tolerate the heat. The sisters may as well have been butterflies frozen in the paperweight in their father's old study: pretty things, trapped under glass.

The sun shone down beautifully at first. To step into the warmth of the morning on what outside of the walls might be a blustery day was a treat. But even clear walls and subtle warmth can stifle. Beneath their new roof, the petals of the flowers stayed brown, their scent cloying. Something refusing to die, or something already dead.

The Queen of Diamonds looked on from the shadows as her sister sank to her knees in the garden, her skirts fanning about her, and dug her fingers into the earth. The Queen of Hearts pulled up flowers by their roots and cried.

Seeking relief from the heat and the emotion building in her chest, The Queen of Diamonds wandered the halls of The House of Cards. And down a corridor, curled against the cool marble of a column, she found The Gardener. With rumpled clothing and fingernails caked in dirt, he stood out against the clean lines of the hallway.

She sat down next to the man who had paraded into town and captured her sister's heart. His beard was greying now, a shocking sight in someone so young. Like his flowers, he was fading.

"I never intended to stay so long," The Gardener said. His voice was full of gravel, not as soft as it had been in the spring and summer months.

"You never intended to stay with my sister."

The silence stretched between them. Then, The Gardener spoke, "Your sister has a smile that needs to be cultivated, and I'm not—" His voice, once so strong, cracked. "I'm not so sure I can usher it through the changing seasons."

The Queen of Diamonds felt tears burn behind her eyes, but she blinked them away. "She deserves someone sure."

He shrugged. "I can't even keep the flowers alive."

"And now we're all trapped under glass," The Queen of Diamonds said.

"Trapped." The Gardener considered her, the walls, his wasting hands. "Maybe."

The Gardener was gone by daybreak.

The Queen of Hearts' anger simmered, streaking her skin scarlet.

"And he left me with what?" she asked her sister. "A garden of dead flowers?" She kicked at the corpse of a rosebush, then swiped at her brow. "And why is it so bloody hot?"

The sisters looked up at the greenhouse ceiling above their heads, like the fine point of a diamond.

The Queen of Hearts clutched a shovel in her shaking hands.

With croquet mallets, with garden spades, with teaspoons from their coffee cups: they shattered the glass that stifled them.

The shine of it, the delicious shimmer. A treasure trove of diamonds, falling to the earth. The glass crunched underneath their heeled shoes. It was an embarrassment of riches.

The servants stood by, slack-jawed, as the two sisters wrecked months of work in mere moments. And suddenly: the sounds of life surged forward. The bird song, the buzzing of insects. The tinkling of windchimes in the breeze.

The glass looked like sugar in the dark earth. Enough for a tea party for the whole kingdom. Who wouldn't want to attend?

The Queen of Diamonds stooped down, touching the glittering soil with her finger. Was it possible the ground was holding the heat, captured by the sun? Could anything grow there? Could anything thrive, picking its way through crystals of glass to reach the sunlight?

The sisters would learn. They would consult the dusty tomes in the library. They would curl up with whole stacks, if need be, and devour them like their fairytales. They would send for the best consultants and search far and wide for answers. For themselves. They would learn what their kingdom could grow.

The Queens stood strong, clutching each other, as the House of Cards seemed to sway, sway, sway in the breeze behind them. Then it righted itself, and stood strong.

THE DISHEVELED KING

Anne J. Hill

The Disheveled King is a dark poem about a king who chose to save himself over his kingdom, and the consequences of this choice.

THE DISHEVELED KING

ANNE J. HILL

He sits on his throne
His scepter rests in his palm
His crown weighs down on his skull
Gold embroiders his armrests and
a silver crow sits perched overhead
its wings spread wide with
an unheard croaking

The king's eyes are heavy with
the sights before him
His heart is cold and lifeless
A thousand bricks press his chest
The echoes permeate his ears
His sword lies limply at his side
dust gathering on the hilt

His head is nestled against
the side of his throne
His only support to stay upright
His limbs are stiff from the hours of endless battle years ago
Blood still on his fingertips

The lifeless crow sneers down
at the disheveled king

Spider webs weave the scepter to the bird's wing
He hasn't bothered to swat them away
The act would cost too much
Red is splattered like paint across his body
The blood of his enemies forever staining
His mistakes lingering for eternity

He should have done something
To save them all
But he
Didn't

Memories—
The screams. The cries. The blood. The innocence lost.
—Forever floating through the halls of the battered castle

He rewatches the horrors daily
Chained to this disheveled throne:

The Queen spread out on the floor
His daughter screamed out his name
and begged him to save them

But he is frozen, forced to just
sit there, reliving the fatal scene of

his enemies tearing his world apart
Helpless

He chose not to help then
And now, there is no one
Alive to help
Just a king and his throne

Peasants outside pounded on the castle walls
begging for their savior as one by one
they all succumbed to his enemies
But the king's armies were too small
and his strength had grown weak

He locked himself in his throne room
Safety for himself as his kingdom fell
the crow silently laughing in his ear

Chains bind his wrists and ankles to the throne
that once had been a symbol of hope

Forever alone
This is his Hell
This is his fate
The disheveled king
And his throne of hate

LESSONS OF KINGSHIP

Amber Kirkpatrick

As a young boy aids a dying soldier, he reflects on his father's words about what makes a good king.

LESSONS OF KINGSHIP

AMBER KIRKPATRICK

THE AIR HUNG HEAVY with the stench of blood.

Sniffing and gagging, young Emery looked across the field where the dead and dying lay. Flies were already thick, and it grieved the boy to see carrion birds circling above. There was never enough time to remove the dead before the birds would be upon them.

But when the birds went after the soldiers who still lived, it was far worse.

This had been the bloodiest battle he had ever witnessed. A hole gnawed at his insides and a rank fear tugged at his heart. It wouldn't be many more years before he would be expected to join the soldiers, and he wasn't sure he would have the courage—or the stomach—to do so.

The murmur of voices caught his attention, and he pulled his gaze away from the circling birds to a cluster of men nearby. The king stood among them, speaking in a hushed voice. Despite obvious wounds of his own, he limped among the fallen men, bending down now and then with his head bowed. Emery knew the king prayed over them. He could read the man's deep distress in his posture.

What did it mean to be a king? So great a burden. Emery could only imagine what weighed down that man's mind. He was a good king, too. Never seeking war for the sake of greed.

Many nights Emery had spent at his father's knee, hearing stories of past wars and battles, of heroism and grand feats. But his favorites were the lessons of kingship. His father would sit with a smile, expounding all his own ideas of what made a good king.

The man who knelt and prayed over the body of a dead soldier was a good king.

A cry of "water" broke the boy from his reverie. He slumped to ease the yoke off his shoulders and withdrew a wooden cup from one of the two buckets he carried. He offered it to a fallen soldier, who drank greedily.

His father's voice rang in his memory. *A king is first and foremost a servant to the people.*

"Any news?" the soldier rasped.

"I believe the day is ours," whispered Emery.

"Not for most of these poor devils." The man nodded to the dead who surrounded them.

Emery glanced over the man, assessing his injuries with an eye far too experienced for his ten years of living. That leg would have to come off.

The boy flinched as the soldier's gaze met his, pain-filled eyes full of awareness. With a groan, the man clunked the cup into the water bucket and eased back to the blood-soaked earth. Emery made a move to lift the heavy yoke again, but the soldier grasped his hand.

"Do ye see the king?"

"Aye."

"He's a good man. He led us well."

A good king is the first to lead in battle, and the last to retreat.

Emery did not answer, arrested by the glassy look in the soldier's eyes. He knew that look—the man did not have much longer. He glanced about, wondering what he should do.

"Hot," muttered the man. "The sun beats down."

A king always remembers his soldiers give their lives for the kingdom and crown.

Emery tugged off his neck scarf and dipped it into the water. He wiped at the soldier's fevered brow.

"Thank ye, lad. You're very kind. I'm sure there are others who need ye."

"I can stay a bit."

"It won't be long..." The soldier groaned even as he spoke, his one good leg kicking at the ground helplessly as his grip grew weaker. Emery strengthened his own grasp.

"Lad, I cannot see ye."

"I'm here."

"The king...he is safe?"

"He is well."

"And we won the day?"

"Aye, because of courage like yours."

The soldier blinked slowly, a tear trickling down his grimy cheek. "My wife...we weren't married long. Sweet lass."

"I'm sure she is very proud."

"She was that, when I set off. But now...my Gwyndolyn..."

The soldier shuddered once more, his body hitching in pain. His last breath eased out in one long sigh. Tears stung the boy's eyes. He started to wipe them away, ashamed.

A good king is unafraid to weep, or show his grieving heart.

His grief welled up, and the hot tears fell faster. He wished he was back home, in the arms of his mother. She was a bright counterbalance to the harsh world he had been born into.

A warm hand pressed against his shoulder, and the groan of the man who knelt beside him tugged at his heart. Arms encircled him, and the boy sobbed. At last the grief eased, and Emery pulled away.

A greater consternation took hold of him when he saw who had held him as he wept. It was the king. "I'm sorry, sir," he whispered. "I shouldn't have—"

"Say nothing more."

A long silence followed, and the boy stared down at his hands. Blood stained them both.

"I saw what you did for this man," came the rich, deep voice, beloved by so many people. Most especially the boy. "You have done well, son."

Emery shook his head. "I just gave him water."

"You gave him much more than that. He did not die alone, and you gave him peace in his last, most difficult hour. You're a better king than myself, already."

"Thank you, Father."

The young prince stood. Without another word, he bent to lift the yoke onto his thin shoulders and went on with his duties, ministering to the men who served his king.

THERE WAS A KING

Amelia E. Clawford

A free verse poem, *There Was a King* tells the story of a kingdom in need of a new king.

THERE WAS A KING

AMELIA E. CLAWFORD

There was a king.

He wore a crown of glass and gold, and sat upon a throne of the same.

There was a king.

He led a nation most prosperous, its cities laden with trade.

There was a king.

He cloaked himself in royal purple, and led his troops to battle with a shining banner and a glimmering sword.

There was a king.

There *was* a king.

But he is gone now; he was lost, long ago.

He left no queen, nor an heir.

And now, every day, in the city square, the town crier cries out:

"Who will pick up the fallen crown?

Who will ascend the crumbled throne?

Who will lead the drowning nation?

Who will feed the starving cities?

Who will don the faded purple, and raise the threadbare banner, and shine the rusted sword, and shout the forgotten anthem, and lead the tired soldiers to victory?"

And every day, the answer remains the same: silence, only silence.

Until

One day

A young man strides to the front of the milling crowds, and answers:

"I will not wear the king's crown,

I will not sit upon his throne,

I will not don the purple robe, nor wield the king's sword.

"But I will lead the drowning nation.

I will feed the starving cities. I will sing the anthem and raise the banner and lead the soldiers—perhaps to victory, perhaps to defeat, but I will lead them all the same."

"Then," says the town crier, "you will be our king!"

"No," answers the young man, "I will be your servant."

The young man keeps his word. But though he does not wear the crown, and though he does not sit upon the throne, and though he does not don the royal robe nor wield the royal sword, the people know.

They know he is their king.

RUNAWAY PRINCESS

Marie Lynch

This photo was taken to represent a princess who ran away from where she was meant to be because she felt unqualified and unworthy. But, the crown remains where she left it, which shows how God doesn't abandon us if we run, that we can come back, and that things aren't as hopeless as they may seem.

OASIS

Kristen Bazen

Between the sandstone ridges and endless dunes of the Southern Desert, a wayward princess tries to outrun the choices she's made.

OASIS

KRISTEN BAZEN

BLOWING SAND STUNG NADIRA'S EYES, and she pulled her ripped shawl tighter across the bridge of her nose, fighting for a clean breath. There wasn't much left of the blue fabric. Pausing at the summit of a sandstone ridge, she glanced over her shoulder, chest heaving.

A burly merchant in camel-colored robes approached the base of the ridge, a shamshir sheathed at his side. Between two hazy rock formations in the middle distance, an archer jogged through the sand, a crossbow slung across his back. Farther yet, a prince rode a desert-bred stallion, its coat gleaming metallic gold.

Nadira's three pursuers were catching up. Whirling, she gathered her tattered skirts and ran down the slope, sliding through sand, stumbling over rocks. Dried blood glued her sleeves to the cuts on her forearms, pulling painfully with each movement.

I can take care of myself just fine, Baba. I don't want your so-called protection. I don't want you.

Her barbed words, spoken to her father ten months ago, came back to taunt her. Baba's face had crumpled like a palace built of sand, and he had let go of her hand. She had stalked away, and later under a canopy of stars, left her family in exchange for the sweet whispers of Prince Hakeem of the Eastern Desert.

The prince her father had warned her about. The prince who was now chasing her.

Some distance ahead, the Red Canyons loomed with welcoming shadows. The twisting fortress would be too narrow for the prince's golden stallion, and the shade would offer relief from the scorching sun. On the far side of the Canyons lay an oasis, where she could at last refill her waterskin.

Nadira tried to moisten her cracked lips with her tongue, but it felt thick and dry. When had she tilted that last swallow of water into her mouth? Yesterday? Two days ago?

An arrow hissed behind her, falling at her heels. The archer had gained the ridgeline. She was almost within range of his crossbow, and there was nowhere to hide—not until she reached the Canyons.

Nadira struggled into a sprint, wincing as her oozing blisters rubbed raw against her leather sandal straps. If only Baba were here. With his Gift, he could—

No. Baba would never speak to her again after the way she had shamed him. After she had stolen from his royal treasury. After she had thrown to the dog's mouth her duties as princess of Sahraa'u, the southern desert kingdom. She had made her choices, and now she must harvest the consequences. All that remained to be seen was which avenger would reach her first. And she deserved whatever violence they intended to inflict.

Five more paces. Nadira fought the loose sand that seemed determined to hinder her momentum. An iron crossbow bolt tore across her shoulder, and she slammed against the red sandstone of the Canyons with an agonized cry.

If she could, she would take her family back. All of them. Even her perfect older sister Meriem, who never disobeyed Baba and Mami, who always did what was expected of her, who conducted herself with propriety and wisdom and grace. But Nadira had hamstrung all the camels in her caravan.

Why can't you be more like Meriem? Mami's words, spoken in exasperation on multiple occasions, still stung.

A sob pressed against Nadira's tightly closed lips, and she lurched into the narrow entrance to the Red Canyons, clutching her arm. Fierce pain bloomed from her shoulder, rivaling the pain in her heart.

Dusky red shadows enveloped her as she pushed herself farther into the slot canyon before the archer could reload his crossbow. The sudden relief from afternoon sun and stinging sand cleared her mind enough to form a plan. She knew the canyons of the Southern Desert as well as she knew the colorful rooms and corridors of Qalat—the palace fortress she had once called home.

Fingers trembling, Nadira twisted a gold ring from her right hand. Briefly, her thumb moved over the exquisite ruby that marked her a daughter of King Shafiq, Lord of the Southern Desert and Exalted Steward of the Gift. When the canyon divided in two, she tossed the jeweled ring into the sand of the wider path.

The restrained sob escaped in a strangled gasp, and Nadira pressed a fist against her mouth, sagging against the curved layers of red sandstone. The weight of her choices was too much to bear. It had seemed so right in the moment to give in to the desires of her heart. To believe Prince Hakeem's starry promises and rose-colored plans.

For the first two months, life with Hakeem had been intoxicating freedom and wild adventure as they roamed the Eastern Desert and the palace of his elderly, lenient father. No more scolding from her parents for leaving Qalat after sunset, no more running from her ever-present guards. She thought all her dreams had solidified into reality.

Until Hakeem met a beautiful nomad on their adventures and discarded Nadira like old scorpion skin.

Prince Hakeem is a spoiled, arrogant child, her father had warned. Normally, Baba's voice brimmed with an undercurrent of mirth, but that day, it had been as solemn as his vows spoken on Coronation Day, when he received the Gift. *He enjoys the chase, nothing more, and will use you for a while until he tires of his new plaything.*

You don't know Hakeem like I know him! Nadira had spat. *You never consider my happiness—only your own!*

Suddenly hungry for air, she pulled the blue shawl from the lower half of her face, let the tail float free from where the rest wrapped around the crown of her head, and continued running. Strands of dark hair stuck to her sweaty brow and neck.

The passage narrowed and tightened until she was forced to turn her body sideways to fit through the canyon. Twice, she bumped her injured shoulder, hissing as fresh agony radiated through her body. Blood trickled down her arm and shoulder blade, seeping into the embroidered blue and green dress Hakeem had given her—or what was left of it. Once silky and pristine, the fabric was now soiled and threadbare. She had worn it every day for the past eight months, since Hakeem hadn't spent a dinar on her after meeting the sultry-eyed nomad.

By the time she reached the place where natural handholds and steps knobbed the sandstone wall, Nadira swayed with dizziness. Her cracked lips had split, and the metallic taste of blood filled her mouth.

Twenty feet upward, and she would be safe.

"I know you're in here." Hakeem's voice snaked toward her from the way she'd come, echoing through the Canyons.

Oh no. Nadira anchored a sandal on a rock ledge, wrapped shaking fingers around a misshapen sandstone bulge, and pushed herself off the sand. *No, no.* The prince was too close. Had he not fallen for her ring trick?

"No one gets away from me that easily."

Nadira was Hakeem's lover, prisoner, and prey, in that order. Soon to be prisoner once more if she couldn't reach the plateau in time. She hadn't thought the prince would chase her himself, and for the first few days after climbing down the wobbly trellis of roses outside her upper-level window, he hadn't. Apparently her other two avengers hadn't caught up fast enough. Or maybe he didn't want her to die; he wanted her as a living trophy.

He enjoys the chase, nothing more.

Gritting her teeth against the fire in her shoulder, she heaved herself, upward, upward, desperately hoping that the blood seeping from the arrow's gouge wouldn't color the sand, marking her trail in red. She could not, would not, be Hakeem's plaything ever again. She refused to be a captive in his palace, forced to watch from afar as he whispered endearments to his beautiful nomad. Too late, Nadira had discovered the prince kept all the women he had wooed, so that when he tired of one, he could move to the other.

I desire far better for you, my rosebud. Baba had been right all along, and now it was too late, too late.

Nadira gained the rim of the Red Canyons and rolled onto the flat sandstone, safe. But it was a tainted victory. The realization settled into the pit of her stomach and flipped. She would never have the strength to climb down and continue to the oasis for the water she so desperately needed.

And there was so much blood. It soaked her sleeve and trickled down her back and chest in small, steady streams as she crawled farther from the rim. Her shoulder spasmed, and she collapsed to her stomach. She should untwist the blue scarf from her hair and make a bandage, but all she wanted to do was close her eyes.

"You can't hide forever, Nadira."

The prince's voice floated up from directly below her, and she went rigid, hardly daring to breathe. "You belong to me."

Not anymore. She belonged to Sahraa'u, the Southern Desert, and its howling night winds, endless dunes, and twisting canyons. The hidden springs she had refreshed herself in and the towering date palms she had danced under. Once, the desert had been her friend, but now it would claim her life. A fitting end.

Maybe her pursuers would have offered a more merciful death. The archer with his wicked crossbow, a brother or cousin of the guard to whom she had given a cup of poisoned wine so the palace gate would be unguarded. Or the merchant with his curved blade, whose entire collection of woven shawls and robes she had torched, creating a flaming distraction in order to escape Hakeem's city.

Shame burned into tears that pricked Nadira's eyelids at the memory of the guard writhing in pain under the arched gate, bloody foam on his blue lips. Of the horror in the merchant's eyes as a year's stock of wares morphed from artistry to ash.

She had fallen so low from her family's legacy. Her father had received the Healing Gift at his coronation. At a touch from his hand, tendons mended, bleeding staunched, pain eased, and broken bones became whole. And many years before, her grandfather had received the Light Gift when he became king. Whatever object he blew upon would glow with an inner light that penetrated all shadows and gloom. And her? She lacerated with words and snuffed out the light in her father's eyes with her actions.

Lifting her head, Nadira scanned the horizon through hazy vision. No movement except a camel caravan far to the north, so her three avengers were somewhere in the Canyons. Her ring must have fooled the other two, for she heard no soft swish of sand under boots, only...only the gurgling grunt of a camel.

Nadira tilted her head. That wasn't right. The merchant and archer were on foot, and the prince must have left his stallion near the canyon divide. Maybe thirst had made her delirious. The caravan couldn't possibly be heard from that distance.

The setting sun painted the Red Canyons in shades of scarlet and dusty gold in one last show of brilliance. Long shadows made wavy ripples across the sand. Nadira lay flat on the sandstone plateau, chest rising and falling in shallow breaths. Nearby, a jackal howled.

Another grunt—a human one, this time—prodded Nadira's consciousness. The gentle scuff of leather boots on stone. Her eyes snapped open. So, Prince Hakeem had found her at last.

With the dregs of her strength, she pushed herself into a sitting position and drew a dagger from the bright green sash around her waist. She wouldn't win, she knew, but she wouldn't make it easy for him to reclaim her. Taking a shuddering, parched breath, she waited, resolving to bravely accept her fate.

Wavy black hair streaked with silver crested the lip of the canyon. A brown face weathered by desert wind but creased with kindness. King Shafiq, Lord of the Southern Desert, wearing plain brown robes instead of his embroidered finery.

"Baba," Nadira gasped. Tears flooded her eyes and she dropped her dagger, burying her face against her knees in shame. How had he found her?

"Nadira, my daughter."

At those tender words, sobs shook her shoulders, spiraling fresh pain through her body. Her throat tightened, and she curled into a ball, unable to face her father.

Linen rustled as he knelt beside her. A hand touched her arm, and she flinched, pressing her face harder against her knees. She had done too much, spoken such cruel words, perhaps killed a man—

"Do not hide your wounds from me, rosebud." King Shafiq's voice was low, urgent. "Where are you bleeding?"

Nadira tried to form words and only managed a whimper. He still wanted to heal her? After she had cut his heart with her tongue?

"Nadira." His hand rested on her hair, dark and wavy like his. "I cannot heal your wounds unless you let me touch them."

She lifted her face smeared with sweat, tears, and crusted sand. *I'm sorry, Baba.* Her swollen tongue refused to obey.

One look, and King Shafiq instantly unslung the waterskin from across his shoulder. Pulling out the stopper, he offered it to her, and Nadira pressed the opening to her lips, gulping greedily. Sweet, blessed water. She couldn't get enough. She would drink it dry, and maybe at the oasis, drink five more skins.

"Slowly, slowly." Gently, King Shafiq pulled away the waterskin. "You will be sick if you drink too much at once."

"I'm sorry, Baba." Her tongue could at last form the words, and now they surged forward like a flash flood through the Red Canyons. "I should have listened to you. You were right about him—"

"Shhh." King Shafiq touched a finger to her lips and Nadira held still as dried blood dissolved and flaking cracks reformed into smooth pink skin.

New tears stung Nadira's eyes. How often she had come to her father as a child and never once doubted his willingness to heal? As she had grown into a young woman, she had come less often with her hurts because they were usually a direct result of disobedience. "My right shoulder..."

Still kneeling in front of her, King Shafiq deftly peeled away the torn, crimson-stained fabric, exposing the jagged gouge still leaking blood. "What happened?" he asked quietly, a subtle distraction before pressing his calloused hand over the raw wound.

Nadira cried out. Pain swelled and stole the breath from her lungs, but King Shafiq didn't let go. Steadily, tendons and muscle and blood vessels stitched back together, a strange, unsettling feeling. Skin pulled tight, and the pain receded, allowing her lungs to expand again.

When King Shafiq lifted his hand, Nadira reached up to touch the smooth olive skin in wonder and stark relief. "An archer's crossbow bolt," she said, her voice unsteady. "I...I poisoned his comrade trying to escape from...the prince." She didn't meet his eyes.

King Shafiq only nodded and lifted her dirty, blistered feet. "And here? Running for too long?" He removed her sandals and wrapped his hands around her oozing sores.

Nadira took a sharp breath, but as before, the pain vanished after its brief reappearance. Her normal calluses reformed, and even the ache of running from the Eastern Desert became a distant memory. "Yes, Exalted One."

"That's 'Baba' to you, daughter," King Shafiq chided. He pressed his thumb into a tender spot on her cheek. Probably a bruise. The long scratches on her arms peeked through rips in her sleeves, and he healed those too. "Where else does it hurt, rosebud?"

Just my heart, Baba. Nadira picked at a loose thread on her sleeve. "Prince Hakeem is also here in the Red Canyons, hunting me."

"And?" King Shafiq lifted his chin, brown eyes flashing. "The Southern Desert belongs to me, Nadira. He has no jurisdiction here. My guards are waiting nearby with the camels—they spotted you crossing into Sahraa'u and sent me word." He pulled her into the shelter of his arms like a little child, though she was as tall as him now. "Stay close to me, and nothing can hurt you."

How she wanted to, and yet she hesitated. Coming back to Qalat meant admitting to her entire family she had been wrong. The shame would hound her for years.

"Your mami and Meriem cried for a week after you left, you know."

Nadira's heart stilled. "Meriem?" Perfect, rule-following Meriem? She rubbed her bare forefinger. "I threw away my ruby ring," she said, looking down at her hands. Why was she still making excuses?

"My goldsmith can make another, if you wish it." King Shafiq opened his satchel and offered her a handful of dates. "When did you last eat, rosebud?"

Nadira's mouth watered, and she abandoned the weak protests crowding her mind and leaned into the comforting strength of Baba's shoulders, plucking the dates from his hand. The thick, chewy sweetness drew out a contented sigh.

Yes, she would go home to Qalat. To Mami and her sisters and the cousins who enjoyed pestering her. To duties she didn't always enjoy and rules she didn't always understand—though a few she had more recently come to appreciate. But there would be safety and protection. Love she didn't have to earn. Rest for both her heart and body.

Knowing Baba, he would probably have a clean shawl and an embroidered dress waiting for her in his camel's saddlebags—maybe even her gold circlet. She could wash at the oasis and ride through the arched gate of Qalat with all the honor due a princess, undeserved though it be.

But for now, her oasis was right here, sitting atop the Red Canyons in plain brown robes, offering her another handful of dates.

THIRST

Brittany Eden

A flash fiction in verse exploring an unquenchable thirst in the desert and a search for the true King.

THIRST

BRITTANY EDEN

Was that the moon still ever shining
Above this wretched wasteland hoping
Thus far regret, no rain descend
No drops or hint of any end

My heart—it broke by arrow, bow
The sky a blue-toned jewel aglow
And beating like a drum, dreams
Awakened day, soon future seems

Pattering songs since eternity
Sapphire downpours infinity
To thwart the drought I raised my hand
I prayed amid the sun-scorched sand

The light betrayed our greater need
For flooding streams, for heavenly seed
Is it my heart or the expanse
Horizon stretched by loss—a dance

Is there an enemy, or just inside

A desert with nowhere to hide
The rays of light, the kiss of night
Both dawn and sunset feel too bright

If I could gaze beyond and see
A storm cloud destiny, a sea
A healing rain, a history
Sundrop soon sweet victory

Jewels soared behind my shut eyes
Dream ended with a heaving sigh
The skies will bleed a river free
A holy shower for you and me

I felt alone, lost trail a mess
Yet forward pressed, through wilderness
Diamond starlit fire by night
Hasty dayclouds 'ere in sight

A call was heard above the dunes
A ringing more than ancient runes
Shrill lonely horn and fractured lie
Sojourning souls not left to die

Followed a sound, a seed like hope
One dared to do much more than cope
The fiery heat, the narrow road
The bearing of a heavy load

The journey on this sparkling sand
Called love or life—I raised my hand
Again, because I saw a form
A figure, healer, through the storm

On long-awaited clouds he'd come
To wet and wash the feet of some
Who chose to cross far desert road
How tortuously was there a load

But then the man who sailed the storm
From where the scent of rain was torn
And future hoping less a dare
My dreary desert seemed more fair

That I would leave it some way soon
So soft the hurt of waning moon
Unless the rain-King reached it first
This soul to drink and forget thirst

The parched heart heat, a dusty swirl
A new world would at last unfurl
These souls beneath a raging sea
No longer 'fraid or far, in He.

THE LIGHT WE NEED

Liz Koetsier

Layla, the last royal heir of a country separated by mists and deception, must choose to take up the crown and bring light and truth to her people.

THE LIGHT WE NEED

LIZ KOETSIER

THE TAXI COACH THAT WAITED for us beneath the white, all-seeing moon was plain, unassuming. Matthias entered first. When I paused at the step, Zech bent and held out his hand to me, inviting. Pleading. It was as if he was sorry for having nearly dragged me from the tavern without a minute to think. When I accepted, he whisked me up as quickly as a hawk, and the door slammed behind me.

Once settled across from the boys, Matthias bumped his rifle butt against the roof of the coach, and it lurched forward.

The knock had come a half hour after I had blown out the candle, when the faint aroma of waxen smoke still lingered in the small, musty hotel room. Thin, white curtains had lifted with the breeze and blue-white beams of moonlight poured like translucent milk across the room. I laid awake, heart-tired but eyes wide open. It wasn't the lumpy mattress or poor, scratchy sheets that kept me from falling asleep. I was used to these things in Foxfield.

Whenever I blinked, I could see *him* behind my eyelids. His sallow unshaven face, sad eyes, arms no more than bones. To have met one's father for the first time, and in the next breath to learn that he was dying chilled the body in a way the mists never could.

I'd tossed and turned. *So many unanswered questions, and so little time to answer them.*

Then, the decisive *knock knock knock*. "Layla of Foxfield, are you there?" The voice had been low and urgent.

Jerked from memory by the motion of the carriage, I flipped my braid forward and began to finger-comb my hair to perfection, partly out of necessity, and partly because it calmed my rising anxiety. It felt like tiny fluttering mist dragons dancing in my stomach as I gazed across at the same soldiers that had escorted me from Foxfield, across the Mists, and into Owlslight—Matthias, with his straw-colored curls, always fidgeting, and Zech, with his serious and unwavering gaze. I found myself staring at Zech, the dancing mist dragons taking flight again. He caught my gaze, and I looked away, embarrassed.

Both had been out of breath by the time they'd come upstairs at the inn to get me. Zech leaning into the door frame and rasping into the shadows, saying I must come immediately. The king was asking for me, and he did not have much longer to live.

"How is he?" I asked across the carriage as we rattled away from the inn.

Zech shook his head. "Failing quickly. He didn't think you would come. I suggested we use a taxi coach rather than a royal one. Less conspicuous from the crowds, less threatening for you." He bent his head at an angle that hid his eyes from me and looked out of the coach window, as if searching for something—or *someone*. Threats, maybe? It wouldn't be unusual to hear of some radical patriot shooting down a coach suspected of carrying royals, or royal goods. No one trusted the king anymore.

Everyone wanted him dead. Well, they were getting their wish, because he nearly was.

I shivered at these same thoughts that had sought to drown me earlier tonight, when I'd wriggled deeper into the hotel mattress and pulled the sheets up to my chin. By the time I had begun contemplating whether it was worth waiting for impossible dreams to whisk me into blissful unawareness, I had heard heavy boots clodding up the hotel stairs. There'd been no use in ignoring the men sent to take me back to Foxfield.

With a lengthy sigh, I'd pushed away the thin sheets and padded barefoot across the creaking wooden floorboards. Before I opened the door, I hastily pulled on my threadbare robe in a chilly swoosh. Like wings, opened, then closed.

A wave of grief and confusion churned inside me. A part of me wanted to cry, a part of me couldn't. I'd never known the man until days ago, and only minutes after meeting him he'd asked me to make a life-changing decision.

He'd said I had weeks to decide. Now, it seemed, that timetable had been moved up.

"Who else knows about me now?" I re-plaited my hair, the motion as soothing as the rattle of the coach was jarring. Zech's gaze followed the motion of my hands while I worked the braid, and he blushed much like he had when he'd apologized to me for interrupting my sleep, asking me to dress quickly. My fingers no longer shook like they had while buttoning my periwinkle blouse over my pleated wool, knee-length skirt, worn over thick ranger's leggings and tall boots.

"The royal cabinet, the attendants..." Zech shrugged, still downcast, gazing out of the window. "A few."

Matthias cleared his throat and ran his fingers through his messy hair. "Basically everyone at court knows you're the princess now, his illegitimate but only heir."

Zech swung around and glared at Matthias, ever so serious. "I was trying to break it gently."

The backs of my boots hit my seat, clunking, and the coach wheels creaked. "No, I have to know the truth."

Matthias rolled his eyes at Zech and dragged his hand through his curls again. "She could be different than the King, Matthias."

The burn started in my chest and spread through my veins. My face heated, indignant. "Of *course* I can be different. I'd never lie and cheat my people the way he has."

"So you'll accept the crown, then?" Matthias leaned forward in his seat. It was the most attentive and least fidgety I'd seen him yet.

"How can I? I was hidden away across the Mists. I received no formal training for this."

"Ah, but you are angry. And bold." He winked. "These are the ingredients of a courageous leader."

The coach jolted as we hit a pothole, and each of us flailed our arms, trying not to slide or fall. Across from me, Zech gripped the edge of his seat. "Do you prize the truth?"

The world seemed to slow. I stilled my body as much as I could while we continued to bumble about. "I hold it in the highest regard."

"*That*," Zech said to Matthias, "is the light we need."

The coach settled again, less bumpy, but still careening a bit madly, and we leaned back in our seats. Three days ago, I'd have believed all soldiers of the crown to be rude, dishonest scoundrels, but Matthias and Zech had proven me wrong. They served with dignity. They served to save the crown as it died, quite literally.

"Layla, the crown hasn't known honesty in my lifetime, nor yours, but in this moment, the truth rests on a scale, and you have the power to hold that scale. One side is light, and the other, darkness." Zech lifted a hand, reaching for me, before retracting it quickly. "I—I will do whatever it takes to prevent war."

"War?" I swallowed hard.

Matthias nodded. "The king's greedy nephews are at a stalemate, arguing over the crown and threatening its integrity. I've no doubt they're about to stir about war against one another, and I'd not like to see either one of the scheming fools win. It will tear the kingdom to pieces."

Zech hissed at Matthias. "Don't say such things out loud."

Matthias ignored him as he leaned in, eyes shining in hopefulness. "But, if his only child came forward, even if she is half-royal, both would have to give in. We could push out the mists and unite the kingdom once again."

I'd leaned back in the coach, and now I was riveted by the scenery outside the window. The cobbled streets lit by moonlight and dim lanterns, the shifting light and shadows. Secrets in alleyways. Secrets daylight would reveal in a few hours. For all my talk of change and justice before the king had called me to see him, I'd never expected to become such a coward the moment I was handed real power.

The stones became more even as we neared the palace, the lanterns brighter and taller. Royal servants had been waiting for us. The gates opened before we approached, allowing the horses to canter through at an unbroken pace. *Haste, haste. The lying king is dying.*

The coach came to a stop, and Matthias launched himself from the coach ahead of me. Though in a hurry, he managed to straighten his blue jacket and fluff his curls. Then, he held out an arm for me. A bit superfluous, since my skirt was neither long nor frilled, best suited for a lady of business and not at all for a princess.

Behind me, Zech touched my elbow and whispered, "The court watches. They expect a princess. Better take his arm if you want to win them over."

His touch, so light, made my stomach do that similar flutter like that in the coach...except different. I thought it was just anxiety before, but now that I was facing him I realized it felt like something...other. *I can't name it...it's foreign to me.* "Why didn't you tell me back in the mists, when we first met, that we are at the edge of war?"

"Because it should not be the only reason you accept the crown. You must be ready." For the first time since we'd left the inn, his hazel eyes truly met mine. They were green and brown like the earth, slightly bloodshot, and shadowed from lack of sleep. Something ate at him, something tore him up inside, and he was close to breaking. He was hiding secrets and pain.

"You want me to accept, though. What does this mean to you?"

He swallowed deeply. "If war begins, my little brother will be drafted." Zech blinked slowly, visibly pushing away any escaping emotion. "Let's go."

Whether I accepted the crown or not, I had a role to play for however many hours the king lived. I took his arm. Zech walked close behind, watchful, guarding, as Matthias led me through the palace entrance. We fast-walked up the grand stairs beneath a sparkling chandelier and into the grandest, most bejeweled and yet ugliest bedroom I had ever seen.

I hoped never to lose the memory of this moment. The king was even more pale than he had been that morning, his lips so painfully grey. When I entered the room, the attendants and guards at his bedside bowed quickly and fled. There was no reason to protect their king any longer. Zech and Matthias fell away, my back suddenly cold without their steadfast presence.

"Wait," I spun around in the doorway, shaking. "I don't want to be alone. Zech?"

Zech nodded, and he and Matthias followed me, one soldier at each arm.

"Layla?" The faint whisper floated to my ears, ghostly. The king's weakened, shriveled hand fluttered in the air, searching, and flopped uselessly back at his side. "We would have had time."

I didn't understand what he meant, so I took another three steps closer. His chest rose and fell heavily. I was afraid of the touch, afraid to move, afraid to say anything. Suddenly all our rush to get here stopped. Time stopped, abruptly.

"W-would have?" I finally stood close enough to the bed to memorize the wrinkles around his eyes, the way his skin hung from wrists and bones, loose.

"If I had told the truth."

Something hot and wet slipped down my cheek and landed on the back of his hand. I pressed a hand to my mouth stifling my voice, shoving my heart back in its place. *Stay there.*

"I...am sorry." He gasped. "I should have told the truth."

Dawn breaks with the sweet notes of birdsong, and unfiltered light I have never before witnessed. I sit with both arms resting on the sill of a grand bay window. It is open wide like arms aching for comfort. One leg is bent beneath me, the toes of my other foot barely touching the ground.

In Foxfield, my cottage bedroom faces east, too, but east from the cottage looks straight into the band of Misty land. Morning light is always hazy there, reclusive, unsure. It holds back. Today, I see the bold sunrise from the other side of the Mist, and welcome in the first day of a new, different life. I should feel despair at the loss I suffered, or anxiety at the impossible choice I have to make. Yes, there is some of that, but there also is hope, rising in my chest with each inch the sun gains in the orange sky.

My fingers run across the facets of the diamonds and circle the smooth opals set into the iron crown in my lap. A heavy circlet, a symbol of the weight royalty must bear. With each stroke of my thumb across the center diamond, I revisit the memories of the past week, but especially these last hours, with Zech and Matthias escorting me back to the palace, and my tears falling onto the king's hand.

My father's hand. And his request for forgiveness.

I gave it, but perhaps for selfish reasons. I didn't want to carry that burden, especially not knowing then what would lay ahead. I still don't know what is ahead, though I know what this kingdom needs. Renewed light, renewed hope, and truth.

A knock interrupts my thoughts, and I know it is time. With a fortifying breath of air, I lift the crown and set it gently atop my pale, unbrushed hair. "Come in."

Not surprisingly, it is Zech who opens the door, and his serious, hazel eyes widen. He gasps at the sight of the crown on my head. "Your Majesty. You have accepted then." It's like the worry melts from his frame as his shoulders lift and relief erases the lines from his forehead.

"I have. And furthermore, if I hear you call me 'Your Majesty' even just once more, I'll have you sent to guard the Mists again." Unfolding my leg, I push away from the window seat.

His lips turn up in an amused smile and he coughs into his hand. "Right. Sorry, won't happen again."

"In the spirit of honesty, I confess I have never run a country before. I am inexperienced, and probably naïve. But you and Matthias stood by me all this way, and believed in me. I don't know what role to give you, but I know I need help."

Zech's cheek twitches. "We can work that out." He dips his head. "In the meantime, I came to ask if you would like breakfast here, in your room."

I am hungry, but it seems inconsequential in light of all that is about to change. Nodding, I start to turn back to the window, but then I stop, and call out for Zech just before he exits the bedroom swathed in ridiculous luscious velvets and drapery. He is the only sensible thing in the middle of it, and I don't want him to leave.

"Yes?" He turns on his heel.

"Thank you for reminding me, back in the coach, what is really important. I wouldn't have had the courage otherwise."

He nods slowly. "You're welcome."

"And, I'd like to hear about those ideas of yours and Matthias's, about improving the kingdom."

The spark in his eyes lights up his whole face. "Of course, my lady."

I watch him retreat, and sink back into the windowsill, framed in golden, welcome light. I lived in shadow only a few days ago, the child of deception. Now, the light will bring redemption and truth.

DANISH CROWN

Sarah Harmon

This is part of the Danish crown jewels in Rosenborg Castle, Copenhagen, Denmark.

CROWN JEWELS

Hope Bolinger

A crown helps a jewel thief steal it from its museum display case.

CROWN JEWELS

HOPE BOLINGER

IF YOU ASK ME...I much prefer this glass display case over a smelly head. Yup, you've seen me, whether on a Google image or in person. You've gawked at the emeralds crusted in gold, as you made plans to head to the gift shop after. I adorned the head of some royal in the past who had both a regicide problem and a thing for his cousin. Not to mention, dandruff issues.

Shudder.

And yes, I'm a sentient crown. It's a lot to take in. Take a deep breath, and don't think about it too much.

Oh, you don't seem to care about the fact that I'm sentient. Okay, then.

You don't care about me because I'm just another item for you to guard. So your eyes shift to the shady guy in the corner of the room. You know the look. Backpack looped around his shoulders—he's the kind of man who retail workers keep an eye on, because they fear he'll shoplift the heck out of a jewelry section at a retail store.

This time, he hasn't gone for anything with zirconium. His gaze beelines to me. And perhaps my imagination has decided to play tricks on me...whatnot being hundreds of years old and such and a fading memory...but the red light on the security camera has flickered off. Nice, the jewel thief has more experience than most in the past.

I'll give him that.

The usual guard has left for a tea break, or coffee break. I don't try to keep track of security's drinking habits.

The soon-to-be thief loops his thumbs into his book bag straps and approaches the display case. Fog from his breath blurs one of the glass corners.

Shakiness fills the fingertips of the jewel thief. Big brown eyes blink at me, once, twice. "You don't know me," he whispers. "But I know you. I'm one of the last descendants of his—the man the king killed." He sucks in a breath, frustration or sadness furrowing his face. "You know the one."

To be honest, I don't. My royal had a tendency to wipe out people like ornate dishes on a medieval dinner spread. Pity stirs somewhere within me, though. This man—this scared but determined fellow—deserves justice, as so many others do.

Jewel thief eyes you—the only thing keeping watch on him now. He has minutes, seconds even, before the guard returns. Let's hope he has a getaway vehicle at the ready.

Light from the display case bouncing off one of my emeralds in my crown winks at the jewel thief. I refract the beam just enough to hit you in the eye and blind you. Glass smashes all over the floor as he takes the opportunity to break into the case and nab me. As security alarms blare, I hope he finds his peace.

Maybe someday, I will too.

QUEENING

Hailey Huntington

It's a high-stakes game when a princess claims her rightful throne.

QUEENING

HAILEY HUNTINGTON

PRINCESSES ARE PAWNS. Like in chess, we are seen as useful mainly for sacrifice. Our skills and talents are overlooked or ignored. But if we defy the odds and accomplish the almost impossible...

The world will see who we truly are.

There's a soft knock, and the door to my chamber gently swings open as Miriam, my maid, comes in. I rise from my seat by the window, crossing the tower room. "Is everything ready?" I ask, tension knotting my shoulders.

"Yes, m'lady. The ministers are hosting the public audience in an hour. Everyone will be there." She nods, bouncing the grey curls that escaped from her bun.

I run my hands across the skirt of my dress. "And the letters were all delivered?"

"The couriers personally handed them off. They're ready." Miriam is silent for a moment. Her voice softens with motherly care as she asks, "Are you ready, Aileen?"

I roll back my shoulders and lift my chin. "I have to be."

Today is the tenth anniversary of my parents' deaths.

How tragic, the king and queen suddenly gone in a carriage accident one night, they said. *At least the princess was spared,* they said.

Yes, I was spared from death that night. But fate wasn't done with me.

Father's ministers had been hungrily eyeing his throne. Even at only twelve years old, I could plainly see their desire. Father saw it too. When my parents died, the ministers were quick to claim their places as my regents until I came of age, vowing to oversee the kingdom and my education until I took my place as queen.

All those promises were empty lies. I should have been crowned last year. Instead, I've stayed locked up in my tower wing, released only for public events when the ministers have to save face. Even then, they keep me on a short leash.

But girls can be more resourceful than they realize. Princesses are more than empty-headed, pretty baubles.

Miriam grabs my empty hand and squeezes. The wrinkles around her eyes crinkle as she smiles. "They'd be so proud of you." Ever loyal, Miriam has served me from the very beginning, originally my nursemaid and now as a handmaid. In truth though, she's the closest thing to a friend and a mother I've had since the regents upended my life.

"I hope so." I've often wondered what it would be like if my parents hadn't died, what they would think of me. Father and Mother had always seemed in favor of my strong interests in academics and politics over needlework and pianoforte. It's almost like they knew which skills I'd need in the future.

Brushing away my thoughts, I turn, walk over to the small vanity in the corner, and pick up the glittering tiara. Despite being hidden in a box under my floorboards for years, it shows no signs of wear.

I've pulled it out and admired it in the past—the strength and beauty of the intricate silver work and jewels. But I'd never put it on. It was my mother's tiara—a queen's tiara. The time wasn't right.

It is now.

Coming up behind me, Miriam rests a hand on my shoulder. "Let's get you ready."

The ministers are assembled in the great hall for their annual public audience. Their voices drift into the corridor through the closed oak doors. *They've already started. Good.*

I hold my chin high as I near the guards flanking the doors. Mother's tiara is heavier than I'd expected, but its weight provides me with a certain strength. I was born for this. I was raised for this.

For the past years, I've spent nearly every minute preparing for this day. Now, it's time to finally see the fruits of my labor.

The guards drop into a bow. I incline my head toward them, commanding, "Open the doors." Rising, they each grasp a handle and the doors to the great hall swing inward silently.

My heeled shoes tap against the floor as I walk inside. Gasps and murmurs ripple through the crowd of commoners as they part, creating a path for me. They gape, eyes wide. I move past them, my gaze fixed on the ministers seated on the platform at the other end of the hall.

For a moment, the regents keep pontificating about the new taxation laws. Slowly, however, they each take notice of me cutting through the room and stop. The room is silent when I reach the platform.

I turn and face the crowd. "Men and women gathered here today—I am Princess Aileen Evenfall. I am here to reclaim my rightful crown and throne from these men who murdered to have it."

The room breaks into chaos. "This is an outrage!" one of the ministers exclaims. The commoners turn to each other, faces animated.

"What's happening?"

"Did she say murder?"

"The queen?"

I glance over my shoulder to see Minister Herbert leaping to his feet, pointing a quivering finger at me. "Outright slander! This is a matter to be resolved in private. Guards!"

None of the soldiers around the platform move. "I think you'll find that the soldiers answer to me now, as they rightfully should," I reply coolly. General Grayson was one of the first to suspect that my parents' deaths might have been purposeful, and he supported and guided me as we waited for the right moment. The soldiers follow him over the regents, and he follows me.

The general steps out of the crowd. It's a wonder how the ministers didn't notice him, though it shouldn't surprise me. They've failed to see everything that was happening under their noses.

I turn to him. "Please escort these men to the dungeon."

Minister Terrance splutters. "On what charges? What proof?"

"Murder and treason evidenced by correspondences plotting the assassination attempt of King Martin and Queen Harriet." Ice fills my voice. "The carriage was no accident. Nor was your disregard for my rights these past ten years. I have suffered your wrongs. Now the time has come for you to pay."

The general snaps his fingers and soldiers descend upon the platform, arresting the regents. I don't break eye contact with them. "Don't think that you'll be able to arrange for 'help.' I've met with all the ambassadors of our neighboring kingdoms. You should have paid closer attention to my visitors and mail. Our neighbors all completely support my rightful ascension to the throne. You have no allies."

Still stumbling over objections and veiled threats, the ministers disappear from the room, led away by the guards.

How does a pawn become a queen? Through distraction and redirected attention. Through long, careful planning. Through silence and stealth.

Through secret letters, underground meetings, and loyal friends.

General Grayson touches my arm. I realize that the room has once again gone quiet. When I turn to look at him, he drops into a bow. Behind him, everyone else bows and curtsies, heads lowered in respect.

"Your Majesty."

Checkmate.

CHECKMATE

Megan Miles

When his family's castle is overrun and his father struck down, Tristan is left to face his enemy with the one skill his father trained him in: chess.

CHECKMATE

MEGAN MILES

THE WAILS OF MOTHER'S PROTESTS echoed behind me as two guards dragged me down the dark corridors of the dungeon. As her cries faded away, the hammering of my heart roared in my ears, and my feet seemed to trip over every crack in the stone floors.

Despite the trembling in my core, I pulled my shoulders straight as the guards brought me into the daylight. I kept my gaze above the red-stained cobbles.

Half the battle is the fear you show. If they can't see your fear, they hold no power over you.

Father's words surfaced in my memory, strengthening my legs to keep pace with the guards. We entered my family's castle through a door guarded by two more soldiers in colors not our own.

The guards ushered me through empty hallways until we came to the library. The familiar scent of leather and ink further strengthened my wavering courage, and when my gaze fell to the pock-faced man reclining in my father's chair, my blood boiled.

"Tristan, thank you for joining me." A smile spread across his smug face.

I set my jaw as the guards stopped me before him.

"I don't believe we've been properly introduced. You may call me Lord Crewe."

"You a-ar..." I closed my eyes and jerked my head, a tick that helped reset my mind to form the words. "You aren't the lord of this castle."

His smile turned into amusement as he chuckled. "So it's true that Montford's son can barely say his words. I'm sure it's also true he can't wield a sword."

I clenched my fists. "You k-k...killed my father."

Instead of replying, he picked up a marble chess piece from the table beside him. "Can't wield a sword, but can beat anyone at chess, isn't that so? Show me."

I eyed the board. "What?"

"Sit. Play chess with me." His voice filled with a mocking warmth as he flourished his hand toward the chair across the table from him.

His guards shoved me from behind to ensure obedience, and I swallowed my anger and fear as I sank into the leather cushion molded to fit my body over years of use.

"I want to go first." He spun the board to place the black pieces in front of me. "Tell me, Tristan. Why chess?" He eyed his pieces before moving a pawn.

"I enjoy it," I stated as I made my first move, without hesitation, yet my fingers shook as I released the piece.

"Yes, but why would a lord let his firstborn waste his time on something like chess when there are more important things to learn?"

"He said that a-all I needed to learn about leading w...was in chess."

The mocking humor returned to his dark gaze. "Oh really? How so?"

"The p-pill... The pillars of what make a strong k-kingdom are found on the chessboard."

Crewe raised a dark brow as he used his index finger to slide another pawn forward, and I slid my own to meet it. "P-pawns are the peasants. Most lords think of them as disposable, but my father taught me that they are our first line of defense. No kingdom can stand w-without loyal subjects."

Even as he chuckled at my words, I continued, "Next, you have the rooks or the c-castle. It must be strong and unbreakable, but a castle c...cannot defend itself on its own. That's why you have the knights standing behind your castles. Knights are w-well-trained and skilled at what they do. Like the pawns, they are w-willing to fight to the last of them."

"I think your father should have spent less time teaching you about chess and more time training his loyal knights," Crewe sneered.

I forced myself to remain focused on the board. "Following behind the knights are your b-bishops. To p-put it simply, my father always said that even the man who isn't afraid of the sword is afraid of wh...what comes after. History is riddled with the evidence of what happens when man invokes God in their wars."

"And what about the queen and king?" he challenged. "Why is the queen so much more powerful than her king?"

"My father a-always called my mother his strength." I picked up the queen and ran my thumb over her crown. "She was his level head in times of crisis. She was the b-b-back... She was the backbone of his reign. You may have taken my father away, b-but you have not taken away her strength or the p-people's love and devotion to her."

Crewe's eyes hardened as he rested his elbows on the arms of the chair. "I killed your king. That means checkmate. Unless you believe some ill-conceived idea that you're the king now."

I pressed my lips together, staring at the black king standing in its original place. "The k-k...king appears weak, limited in his c-capacity for action. His strength isn't in his physical c-ca-pabilities but in his a-abilities as a leader to garner the loyalty of his people. For a good k-king, people will obey and serve, but for a great king, they'll do anything."

Crewe's knuckles turned white as he gripped his last-standing rook to knock my final pawn off the table. I answered with my ready knight, taking his piece and preventing further advancement onto my side of the board.

"Chess shows that taking down a k-k...kingdom takes more than striking down one man." I slid a rook to fall into rank with my knight. "Where one falls, more will rise to defend."

Crewe narrowed his eyes on me, moving one of his pieces in vain, but the clamor of metal on metal followed by shouts in the courtyard drew everyone's attention to the windows.

"Wha—?" Crewe started to rise from the chair. His gaze dropped to the board as I picked up my queen.

With my eyes locked on his, I moved it into position. "Checkmate."

THE PRINCESS IS BUYING STABBY THINGS

Yakira Goldsberry

An assassin is appointed by the king for a dangerous mission. His quest? Stalk the realm's princess, find out where she keeps disappearing to each afternoon, and pray it's nothing too deadly.

THE PRINCESS IS BUYING STABBY THINGS

YAKIRA GOLDSBERRY

BEING SUMMONED BY THE KING is always something that strikes fear into the dark heart of a lowly assassin. Or at least, if they *had* a dark heart. Rebault wasn't sure if he fit that category, unfortunately. He tried his best, though.

Rebault stood before the king, hands hidden beneath his flowing black cape, jaw set, and brows furrowed into an exceptionally serious expression. He hoped the king would see just how serious he was, and His Majesty would *not* deign to see Rebault's head roll just because the king thought he wasn't taking things seriously. Indeed, he was so serious he was sure he would have won top award at the Most Serious Expression competition.

The king—none other than His Majesty King Farald himself—sat upon his throne in a rigid, upright manner, looking as if someone had just spat on his shoes. His mouth twisted to the side and his thick black brows crinkled toward his wide nose. The golden crown resting on his head glinted in the colored lights of the stained-glass windows.

"Master Vivian tells me that before you joined the—*ahem*—assassins, you were a tracker. Is that correct?"

Rebault bowed low. "Yes, Your Majesty."

"She has also told me that you are more inclined to tracking than assassinry. Is that true as well?"

Sweat beaded on Rebault's temples, and he swallowed. "I am afraid so, Your Majesty."

"Excellent."

Rebault froze at that. *Just what was the king planning to do?* He watched as the king oh so carefully lifted one finger. The guards came to life, shuffling out the throne room doors, leaving only General Zala and the Royal Scribe, who sat on her stool at the foot of the dais, scribbling away in the silence, her large, hooded blue robes nearly swallowing her whole.

"What I am about to say does not leave this room, understand?"

Now Rebault was really sweating. "Yes, Your Majesty."

"This concerns my daughter, Princess Dahlia."

Oh dear. What has she done now? Renault couldn't help but imagine the princess out in the city terrorizing the populace.

"It seems for the past three months, she has been sneaking from the castle. Where she is going, even my best trackers do not know. They have all tried and failed to find the princess's destination point."

So...could *be terrorizing the populace.* Rebault's mouth grew dry. "Not to question Your Majesty, but...if your trackers have failed, then...why me?"

The king looked at Rebault like the answer should have been obvious. "Because you are an assassin. If anyone gets in your way, you can simply kill them. Or torture them for answers."

Rebault held back the high-pitched laugh bubbling in his chest. "Of course, Your Majesty," he squeaked instead.

That presented a very large problem. Ever since Rebault had joined the Royal League of Assassins, not once had he ever been put on a mission involving...well, pointy things. Instead, they'd all been using him as their own personal scout. Seasoned assassins wouldn't wait ages for normal procedures like putting in a request for scouts, waiting for it to be approved, giving the scout instructions, waiting for them to get back, etc...

Not to mention the problem of Princess Dahlia herself. She was... Well, she and Rebault had a...delicate relationship. One the king very well knew about, but was conveniently *forgetting*.

"When do you wish me to start, Your Majesty?" Rebault asked in as calm a voice as he could muster.

"She usually gives her guards and maids the slip around just after luncheon. The moment she steps outside her room, follow her."

Rebault bowed once more. "I am at your service, Your Majesty."

This is going to be a disaster. He began to back away toward the doors when the king spoke. "Oh, and Rebault."

"Yes, Your Majesty?"

"If you fail to discover the princess's destination, your head will decorate the city walls."

Rebault swallowed and resisted the urge to touch his neck. "As you wish, Your Majesty."

With the king's warning sitting uncomfortably in the back of his mind, Rebault made his way outside the castle to watch for the princess's grand exit. After questioning her guards, he concluded the young woman was either climbing out her window or departing via a secret passage inside her room. But departing via secret passage would equal still having to exit within the castle, so outside it was. Sitting in the branches of a tall, old maple, he watched the balcony, feeling very much akin to the vultures that hung about the guillotine, and peered in through the sheer curtains at the princess. She seemed to be packing things into what looked like a picnic basket. This whole affair felt very criminal; the stalking, the loitering, the hopefully soon kidnapping of her back to her own royal rooms. But Rebault tried his best to remember that this was all approved by the king.

Not that it made him feel any better. After all, if this were any other moment, his head would have rolled for daring to peep into the princess's chambers. Rebault flapped his shirt. It seemed the sun had suddenly grown hotter.

Please come out soon, Princess, before I resign. Or have a heart attack. Or send myself off to the mines and end up having to do paperwork for the rest of my life. That last option sounded almost tantalizing compared to the rest.

After packing the basket, the princess walked further into her room, disappearing for a moment. After what felt like ages she reappeared, now dressed in what looked like a maid's outfit. No doubt her maid was in on her shenanigans and was sworn to secrecy. He wouldn't put it past Mildred, the sneaky, cunning woman.

Princess Dahlia walked out onto her balcony. Sunlight glinted off her dark hair. Instinctively, Rebault hunkered down further in the tree, feeling even more vulturous than before. Hopefully she wouldn't see him sitting here like a fool. He could just imagine all the things she'd come up with to tease him for it.

Lifting her hand, the princess stood staring down at the ground for several seconds. Rebault stiffened and watched as vines curled up from the ground to form a stairway, down which the princess trotted as if they were the carpet-lined stairs of the castle foyer.

Rebault nearly dropped his spyglass. *She's doing magic in broad daylight?* How had no one witnessed this before and told the king? Surely, they knew she had plant magic. Unless they *did* know and didn't think she'd apply it in such a salacious manner.

Before he could react further, the princess had already descended to the ground and was waltzing across the castle grounds. Rebault hurried to climb down—more like fall down, but who was looking?—and followed at a reasonable distance as Princess Dahlia made her way through the castle gates amid a handful of maids. The guards didn't even bother to check and see if the princess was among them. They just tipped their heads to the ladies, calling for them to be careful on their outings. Rebault shook his head. They certainly weren't doing their jobs correctly. He'd have to report this to the head of the guard.

Once outside the gates, Rebault did his best to stick close to Dahlia without alerting her. She wove through the crowd with practiced ease. Rebault wondered just how many times the princess had snuck from the castle. To him, it seemed she must have been doing this for more than a year. And the king had only just now caught on?

Smiling, Rebault shook his head. *Clever girl.* Whatever she was up to, she obviously knew how to evade detection. Rebault slipped through the crowds just as easily, however. Maybe even easier. She wouldn't be getting away from him.

It was one thing he could pride himself on, his ability to blend in. Today's espionage look was that of a low-level merchant much too full of themselves. He wore a bright red frock coat with a silver vest beneath and straight-legged, pressed trousers. His boots had a nice shine, and he walked with a swagger that spoke of arrogance and greed. Most in the crowd steered away from him, allowing Rebault a perfect view of the princess.

After making it to the center of the market square, the princess turned sharply and entered a small shop. Rebault sidled up to the window and peered inside. Small cubbies lined the walls, each filled with stacks of what looked like balls of colored string. A display at the counter held pairs of long and short objects in varying thickness made from both wood and steel. He narrowed his eyes. They looked suspiciously like witch's wands. Why would the princess need so many wands? In fact, why would anyone?

After chatting with the man behind the counter, the princess pulled a similar object from her picnic basket. It was so thin Rebault thought it a toothpick at first, especially since both ends were pointed. But upon closer inspection, it was just ever so slightly thicker, and longer.

They spoke some more, then the man behind the counter pulled out a small box, which he opened. Inside lay a set of long, thin steel objects with pointed ends. Rebault swallowed. Those looked like they could kill a man. The sight quickly made him change his opinion.

The princess was not buying wands. She was buying terrifying weapons.

The princess exclaimed over the stabby things, holding them up to the light. Rebault found himself sweating. He wasn't sure if

Princess Dahlia having possession of weapons was a good thing. She would most likely become even more of a menace than she already was, which didn't bode well for himself *or* his mission.

All previous trackers had faced a rather nasty and untimely end, either beheaded or—Rebault shuddered to think—forced to do endless paperwork. He swallowed and touched his neck. He'd rather not face either. The princess shifted, turning toward the window and Rebault ducked, cursing himself. He should have worn a hat.

When Rebault returned to the window, he watched as the princess placed money in the man's hand, then tucked the box into her basket. She called a farewell and Rebault slipped away from the window. He slid into the narrow space between the suspicious building and a tailor shop and watched as Dahlia exited.

This time, instead of trying to evade detection, she marched boldly across the square toward a café. Rebault followed at a distance, keeping his gaze on her bobbing black curls. Along the way he snagged a scarf from an open-air booth and wrapped it around his neck, covering the bottom half of his face. Yes, it was sweltering outside, but at least this way she'd be less likely to recognize him.

Dahlia entered the café to the sound of a ringing bell. Rebault hurried his steps and peered into the window. Instead of sitting at one of the tables, she called to the woman behind the counter, then trotted up a set of stairs in the back of the spacious room.

Rebault's stomach turned. *A clandestine meeting on the second floor of a café, eh?* What in the world was the princess up to, hiding in cafés and buying dangerous weapons?

Slipping inside the café, Rebault waited until the woman behind the counter had turned away before hurrying up the stairs. He winced as the top step creaked under his weight. Up here on the second floor, there was an open space that let him see a narrow hall running parallel to the stairs, leading to the back of the café. Next to him was a wall with a single door, a heavy lock warning away any unwanted visitors. Down the hall, there were at least four rooms, all left open to reveal unoccupied sleeping quarters. At the opposite end stood a set of glass doors that led out onto a balcony. White curtains fluttered in the fresh air that poured through the cracked entrance.

Women's voices and laughter trickled from the balcony. It sounded like a tea party, or a club meeting was going on. Rebault made his way silently down the hall, heart pounding. He could imagine all sorts of horrible situations that involved Princess Dahlia wielding her sharp weapons on poor, unsuspecting women in garden dresses.

He shuddered. What would he tell the king, then? That his dear, sweet daughter was really a bloodthirsty killer?

The king might just have his head for suggesting such a thing. Swallowing, Rebault stopped outside the doors. He chanced a look through the glass, heart in his throat.

What he saw left him utterly perplexed.

A group of five young women sat around a table with baskets at their feet. While the trappings on the table suggested a tea party—pristine pink and white china, a pastry tower filled with tiny delicacies, and a vase of pink lilies—what the ladies were doing themselves was... Well, Rebault couldn't figure out what on earth it was.

Strings snaked from their baskets and to their hands, where they all clutched those long, needle-like weapons. Their hands moved in strange patterns as from the needles hung woven items. It was mindboggling. *So…no wielding weapons on poor unsuspecting women?* Rebault had to rethink his entire theory. It seemed maybe more like they were in league. Hiding their weapons in string in order to disguise their plans of…stabbery.

Am I overthinking this? At this point, he wasn't sure what exactly he could tell the king other than his daughter was doing something he couldn't understand.

In a way, it reminded him of crochet. His mother had made him hats and mittens and scarves when he was a boy, but that had always been with a single hook. This looked far more complicated. Still, the women laughed and moved their hands as if what they were doing didn't look like witchcraft.

Princess Dahlia sat across the table so that she faced the door. The sun backlit her hair, making it look like a poofy crown around her head, her face alight with a smile. She looked perfectly content to be sitting there with those weapons of destruction tangled in thread.

Her gaze turned toward the doors and Rebault stiffened. He knew he shouldn't have anything to worry about—his form was hidden by the curtains—but the princess seemed to notice something amiss. She stood and made her way toward the doors. Rebault quickly backed away, dashing into one of the empty rooms on silent feet.

Her footsteps stopped. Then, she called out, "Rebault, is that you?"

Rebault's skin grew cold. *How on earth…?*

Her shoes shuffled across the floor, then stopped once more. "I know you're there. I knew you were following me from the beginning. Sulking in a tree? Parading around in a giant red coat and scarf like some peacock? You can do much better than that."

Rebault held his breath. Maybe if he stood still long enough, she'd give up and walk away.

"I heard my father talking to you. He doesn't know this, but there's a hidden passage behind the dais. I like to listen in on all his secret conferences. But don't tell him that I said that!" She added a little laugh.

Rebault stood stone still. How had this assignment unraveled so completely? Not a sound came from the other side of the open doorway. He held his breath, not daring to move. Wood creaked, and the pattering of feet signaled her approach. Before Rebault could take another breath, Princess Dahlia had snatched his wrist and dragged him from behind the door.

"Y-Your Highness—!"

"Come meet my friends!" Princess Dahlia said cheerily as she hauled him along.

Rebault wasn't sure what to do about this development. On the one hand, it proved to be advantageous, since he would be finding out exactly what the princess was doing with little effort. On the other, he felt his abilities as a tracker were being proven...less than ideal. He sighed. There was a reason he had been kicked out of the scout's guild. Perhaps he should have been an accountant like his father wanted.

Emerging onto the balcony, Princess Dahlia paused before the table. She lifted her hands toward Rebault.

"Ladies, this is Rebault. He's a childhood friend-turned-royal-assassin. What do you say we all show him our projects?"

Rebault stiffened at the introduction and looked at Princess Dahlia with wide eyes. *You can't just announce that someone is an assassin!* he wished to shout, but held his tongue. He'd learned from a lifetime of being Princess Dahlia's playmate—a terrifying but true fact—that saying anything would inevitably lead to *more* of her trickery, and Rebault being kicked off the playing board. She was a clever one. Rebault couldn't say the same for himself.

His parents had been royal spies and close friends of King Farald, which had earned Rebault the coveted position of the princess's playmate. They'd expected much of him but in the end he'd proved to be a failure. Rebault looked out at the castle in the distance. *Mother, Father, I'm sorry for being absolutely terrible at my job. I hope you'll be there when my head rolls so I can give my last goodbyes.*

You haven't finished your job yet. Rebault imagined he could hear his father's voice. That was right. He wasn't finished yet. He refused to let Dahlia win this round. And so he watched, appalled, as a group of well-to-do ladies stood with weapons in their hands and thick threads hanging off them. Well, he just had to bite the bullet and ask the question. "...What is it?"

Princess Dahlia's eyebrows raised, and a slight smile twitched across her lips. "Are you saying you've never seen knitting before?"

"Knitting? What is that? Some kind of secret martial art?"

At this, Princess Dahlia burst into laughter, doubling over with an expression akin to pain with tears in her devious eyes. The other ladies twittered delicately behind their handkerchiefs. Rebault's cheeks flamed, but he remained resolute.

Princess Dahlia held up a pair of those long, wicked weapons. "I guess I can see why you thought these weapons, Rue," she said, clutching them in her small hands. "But they're knitting needles.

You thread yarn onto them and make things like scarves, gloves, hats, sweaters...anything really." Dahlia crouched a little and held them as if she were in a fencing duel. "Though, now that you mention it, these *could* be handy if you were in a real pinch..."

Rebault's head spun. He stood, sagging and staring, flabbergasted. So...the weapons weren't really weapons but rather for crafting things, like crochet, but they could still be used as weapons if needed? He shook his head. He needed to sit.

"Here, let's show him how it works." Princess Dahlia grabbed Rebault's hand and dragged him to the table, where she forced him to sit in her empty chair. The other ladies crowded around as Princess Dahlia shoved the 'needles' into his hands. They were thin wooden ones, their size reminding him of the pair of *sai* his mother had been gifted by an Eastern assassin—a small weapon with a long, rounded blade, perfect for stabbing.

Princess Dahlia used her small, delicate hands to adjust his grip on the weapons—or, needles—and began to explain to him how to 'cast on' stitches, and how to 'knit' and 'purl', weaving together a pattern into a strip of what he began to see was the beginnings of a scarf. It was difficult at first, but once he caught on to the rhythmic movements, he discovered that this whole knitting business was actually quite *fun*. The ladies all clapped as Princess Dahlia took her hands away and Rebault went on happily knitting alone.

Sitting next to him, Dahlia perched her elbows on the table in a very un-ladylike fashion and grinned. "So? What will you tell my father? Must I petition to save your neck?"

Ah. Rebault paused, then placed the needles on the table. "I would be appreciative if you would, Your Highness. What you're doing surely isn't *illegal*, however I don't understand why you can't tell him what you're doing yourself and allay his worries."

Dahlia reached down into the basket at Rebault's feet and pulled out a giant, bulky item. She held it up and it unfurled into what looked like a half-finished sweater in a handsome forest green. "I'm making a present for Father for his birthday. I want it to be a complete surprise, so you're not allowed to tell."

"I can't even tell him that you've picked up the sport of knitting?"

"Of course not. I said I want it to be a complete surprise. Which means, he can't know what I'm doing."

Sighing, Rebault sat back and stared at the table with its teacups and cakes. The ladies all stared at him, as if they, too, were waiting for his answer. The one across from him, dressed in a white garden party gown, snapped open her fan and hid the lower half of her face in what looked like a rather bold flirtatious move. Rebault looked up at the sky. No doubt she was trying to keep him silent. Women tended to be more wily than most men gave them credit. He wouldn't put it past any one of them to pierce a purse-snatcher.

"I suppose," he began, thinking through his answer, "I could tell your father you've joined a local ladies' society that meets for tea and gossip. Save my neck, keep your secret. How does that sound?" He looked at Princess Dahlia, who wrinkled her nose.

"But that makes me sound so airheaded!"

"Would you rather I say that Princess Dahlia was meeting with a group of local women engaged in the highly dangerous sport of knitting, which involved needles primed for killing?"

Princess Dahlia seemed to put some thought into that. "That would sound rather mysterious and cunning..." She sighed. "But no. I can't let my father catch on. Or worry that I might turn into an assassin or something." She said this last bit with a wink in his direction. Standing, she folded her hands before her. "All right. Tell Father what you've suggested. But only on one condition."

Rebault stood and bowed, relief flooding his limbs. Thank goodness he wouldn't have to make his parents watch his head roll. "Whatever you command, Your Highness."

"From now on, you will accompany me here. After all, you've yet to finish your scarf."

Rebault looked up in surprise. "Are you sure about that, Your Highness?"

"You said *anything*, didn't you?" Princess Dahlia planted her hands on her hips.

"I did, regrettably."

"Rebault!"

"Forgive me, Your Highness."

"Then agree."

Smiling, Rebault straightened. Who knew? This could actually turn out fun. And when he was done, he could gift the scarf to his mother. "*All right*. I agree. I shall accompany you to your clandestine meetings of swiftness and stabbery."

Princess Dahlia laughed. "I like the sound of that!"

With that settled, Rebault excused himself and left the ladies to their meeting. He walked down the street, a spring in his step. The day had ended quite successfully. Rebault would get to keep his head, he would please his mother, and by accompanying Dahlia, he could keep the princess from becoming the criminal that simmered beneath her innocent smile.

All in all, it had turned out to be a good day.

ELVEN PRINCESS

Ruth Lumpkin

A freehand digital drawing.

ROYALLY IMPERFECT

J.M. Hackman

Princess Charlise isn't a perfect princess, but her mother hopes refresher decorum courses at The Institute will change that. Charlise never expected to meet someone like shapeshifter Finn, who likes her as she is—but her upcoming arranged marriage to a stranger may leave them both with broken hearts.

ROYALLY IMPERFECT

J.M. HACKMAN

IF MY FIANCÉ HEARD ABOUT THE SOUP INCIDENT, he'd call off our engagement. Not that it was my fault.

My mother had seated me next to the ambassador from Stabrea at our annual Western Kingdom Alliance Dinner last week. I'd conversed eloquently, asked after his family, and complimented his professional achievements when a fiery bite of Spiced Pepper Bread took me by surprise. When I reached for my water glass, my fingers flipped my soup spoon. Crimson borscht arced through the air and spattered the ambassador's all-white uniform. The media my father had invited gasped in unison as their camera shutters clicked.

I feigned a sudden illness and retreated to my bedroom with a dozen chocolate chip cookies.

My mother found me two hours later. "Palladia is looking for a princess, not a slapstick routine. Prince Mansfield could cancel the engagement. After tonight, I wouldn't blame him."

"I'm doing the best I can." I truly was, but I wasn't suited to be a cardboard cutout royal.

"A weeklong crash course at The Institute will soften your edges, Charlise."

I shot up from my prone position in my bed, scattering cookie crumbs across the lavender duvet. "What? Why?"

"We love you, but we must present you to Prince Claymore in the best light."

Before he comes to his senses and backs out. The unsaid words hung in the room as she left. Why in all of Cerith had Prince Mansfield Claymore agreed to the engagement in the first place? He should've picked some perfectly polished princess to stand by his side while he ruled.

Prince Mansfield was a year older than me, but that's all I knew of him. Unlike Cerith, Palladia hid their royals, tucking them away at elite boarding schools until their coronation or wedding. My fear had created its own version of the prince: an arrogant bully, a spoiled baby, or an unfeeling robot. I'd accepted my future a long time ago—an arranged marriage with the shadowy Prince Mansfield would secure our fledgling alliance with Palladia.

I arrived at Travel Unlimited via a private car, declining the royal jet that could skim over the fertile farmland with ease. The grey steel building sunned itself on the open plain. Nearby, the forbidding Mahib Canyon interrupted the vast stretch of oat grass. Acid coated my stomach as I eyed the sharp cliff sides of the canyon.

A handsome man approached, interrupting my scrutiny. His silver hair glistened in the sunlight, and his tanned skin set off his white shirt perfectly. Pointed ears indicated his fae heritage.

"Welcome to Travel Unlimited. May I help you?" He winked and pushed his silver hair back from his face.

I didn't react. Fae were notorious scoundrels. I was probably the two hundred forty-seventh person he'd flirted with today. "Hi, I'm Princess Charlise Rothchester. I need to go to The Institute."

"Right this way." He ushered me toward a long strip of asphalt next to a steel warehouse. Twenty feet away, the striped tan and red canyon walls plunged into the gorge. Despite my awe at its beauty, I swallowed hard against lunch's return.

With a handheld electronic device, the fairy gestured to the other side of the canyon, a smudge in the distance. "Travel Unlimited offers a direct, nonstop flight to The Institute. Our airborne chariot is available for your use. Leave your bags here. We will deliver them later."

Flight? Airborne chariot? A cold sweat broke out on the back of my neck.

An immense, yoked bird pulled a simple cart out from the shed. The cart's wheels creaked as it settled into place. The bird ruffled its reddish-gold feathers, thick ropes trailing from its harness.

I squinted at the scarlet bird. "Is that—?"

"A phoenix? But of course." Mr. Flirty gave me another glittering smile. "Despite his youth, Finn's prone to ignition. But he's a strong flier."

As though he understood, the phoenix gave the fairy a dark stare before flames shot from his wingtips. I moved back a few steps. "Can't I just take a taxi or a rideshare?"

"The taxi drivers are on strike. The other transportation companies are busy servicing the businesses on the south side. You'll need to wear this parachute." A brown bundle materialized in his hand, and he helped me strap it to my back. "The cord is on your right."

A parachute? My stomach dipped. I should go home. But if I didn't check into The Institute, the following conversation with my mother wouldn't go well. I climbed into the cart, my hands trembling as I tightened the parachute straps.

On the device, the male fairy pulled up a screen with tiny text. "Fingerprint here, here, and here."

"Why? I'm terrified of heights. What am I authorizing?"

He leaned closer, his gorgeous eyes hypnotic. "It's merely an agreement conveying your trust in us to ferry you across the canyon. You have nothing to fear here, Princess. We wouldn't be in business long if it was unsafe."

I fingerprinted the correct places then clenched my hands together, nerves roaring through me.

He slid the device into the back pocket of his tight black pants. "It also states you're legally unable to sue if you have to eject. Thank you for using Travel Unlimited."

"Wha—?" The chariot lurched forward with a groan. Finn flapped his massive wings, smoke drifting from the tips. The cart rolled toward the canyon's edge, and my breath stalled in my throat. At the last minute, canvas wings popped out from the cart's sides. The contraption lifted, clearing the yawning chasm by inches.

As the phoenix continued flapping, my stomach twisted. Large sparks as big as golf balls shot from his wings. The air currents swirled the flares around the cart. Several blew back toward the rope harness and settled into the fibers. In moments, the embers lit.

"No, no, no!" Leaning forward, I tried blowing on them. Finn picked up speed, the wind tangling my hair around my face.

The Institute came into focus across the chasm. From the entrance rose four towering embellished golden spires. They shone like beacons in the bright sunlight. Smaller white spires ran along each side of the extensive building. A garden maze lay behind the stone structure.

A cleared area as big as a football field became visible. As we drew closer, I eyed the smoldering ropes, muttering prayers under my breath. The rope edges curled and crisped black. "Finn, fly faster!"

Twenty yards from the field, the ropes snapped. The chariot plummeted toward the canyon's rocky bottom. I fumbled for the parachute cord, gripped it, and yanked. Despite several more desperate yanks, the canyon floor raced to meet me.

I won't recover from this. Squeezing my eyes shut, I concentrated on the memory of my parents' smiles. A wrenching yank snatched the air from my lungs.

I glanced up. My head brushed the underside of Finn's abdomen, his talons gripping the back of my shirt. I clutched his thick claws as we soared toward The Institute. When we reached the cleared field, he lowered me. I crumpled into a graceless heap. He landed, his dark eyes studying me.

Releasing a shuddering breath, I threw my arms around his neck, tears of relief soaking his feathers. "Finn, I think I love you."

As my tears slowed, I dipped my head into the feathered curve of his chest. The scent of wood smoke, pine, and oak surrounded me, and I nestled into the warmth. A faint rustle of feathers stirred the air before human arms pulled me closer into a firm, muscular chest.

"I usually wait until a few dates in before I say I love you." The teasing voice entered my consciousness. I wasn't snuggling a phoenix but a man.

Cheeks heating, I backed away. A red T-shirt and jeans covered a frame slightly taller than mine. Broad shoulders, slim hips, and a very nice set of biceps. I swallowed. I wasn't shallow, but well-toned arms were a weakness of mine. Strawberry blond curls, artfully mussed, competed with his square jaw and a playful smirk.

I pulled my gaze from his muscles. "Who are you? Where's Finn?"

He bowed. "At your service, milady."

"I'm not your lady, and you're not a phoenix."

He gave an exaggerated wince. "You wound me, you really do. You just proclaimed your love for me."

I ordered my lips not to smile. "I said I *thought* I loved you. I've since reconsidered."

"And after I saved your life, too."

"So you say. I distinctly remember a bird."

His chocolate eyes gleamed as he returned my stare. I blinked, and a phoenix shimmered into existence where the man had stood. My mouth fell open.

After a second blink, the man sparkled back into place. In his hand, he held out a phoenix feather. "For you. Now, do you believe me?"

I took it, twirling it in my hand. It flashed crimson and metallic gold. I shook my head and looked at him. "You're a phoenix shifter."

"That's right." Finn frowned. "I'm sorry about the chariot. I told them they needed to replace the ropes."

"You saved my life." Another brilliant statement. Maybe The Institute offered a course on conversation tips.

"Which wouldn't have happened if I'd refused to fly until they fixed the ropes."

"I appreciate you saving me." I briefly touched his arm, and electricity raced through my fingers at the light contact.

His eyebrows shot up and held. "That was a brave thing to do, taking that ride, even though you're afraid of heights."

"I fear my mother more than heights. If I hadn't checked in—well, I don't want to even imagine that conversation."

"That scary?"

I pulled a mock horrified face. "You have no idea."

His chuckle was the best sound ever. I enjoyed his brilliant smile before I asked, "So, Finn, do you know where I'm supposed to go now?"

He gestured to the double doors gleaming in the sun. "Right through there. They'll take care of you. And I'll make sure you have your luggage by tonight."

"Thanks again." I pulled my gaze from his smile, my feet slow to leave.

As I stepped away, he captured the edge of my sleeve. "I never caught your name."

"It's Charlise."

His eyes lit up. "Princess Charlise Rothchester?"

I hid a wince. "Apparently, my reputation precedes me."

"No. Just clarifying, Princess."

"No title. Charlise is fine."

"It was a pleasure, Charlise. I'll see you around." With a wink, he shifted and was airborne.

I twirled the feather once more before entering The Institute.

Decorum Basics 101R was the most boring refresher course I'd ever had the misfortune of attending. I'd been at The Institute for four days, each one more mind-numbing than the last. So far, we had covered how to sit properly, introduce meaningless conversational openers, and pick the appropriate utensil for each course in a seven-course meal—all things I'd learned years ago. So, so much fun.

The sun streamed through the classroom windows, highlighting the dust motes dancing in the air. Yesterday, the instructor, Miss Kyoshi, had lined us up, handed out books, and instructed us to balance them on our heads. Today, we added walking. While Miss Kyoshi demonstrated it perfectly, the thud of falling books echoed in the large, wood-paneled room.

Duchess Brea, an angelic-looking blonde on my left, muttered colorful curses under her breath every time her book fell. Princess Amiah, a friendly redhead from the south, had mastered the skill, as long as she held her arms straight out at her sides. Tamsyn, on my right, was a billionaire's daughter, and one of the most encouraging people I'd ever met. As my book tumbled to the floor for the millionth time, she shot me a reassuring smile.

The classroom door opened, and the headmistress popped her head in. "Excuse me. I need Charlise for her Community Service assignment."

The instructor gave a little bow. "Of course. Charlise, you're excused for today."

Hurrying from the classroom, I joined Mistress Osana in the hallway. She gave me a warm smile. "You signed up for the environmental and wildlife protection assignment, yes?"

I nodded. Anything was better than being stuck inside.

She continued. "Your assignment runs later than most. You'll finish past curfew, but we'll let the guard know to expect you later."

"What's the assignment?"

She stopped where two hallways intersected. "I'll allow the organizer of the trip to fill you in. See you both late this evening."

As she left, someone tapped me on the shoulder. I turned to find Finn smiling behind me. "Princess Charlise, you look beautiful."

Heat filled my cheeks at his appreciative gaze. "Thanks." I'd caught glimpses of him in the past few days, but always at a distance, and never long enough to talk. I assumed either The Institute or Travel Unlimited was his employer. He looked gorgeous, as always, in rugged canvas pants and a black T-shirt. He'd strapped a leather backpack to his back.

"Ready to head into the canyon?" he asked.

My heart gave a little jump. "You're coming with me?"

He chuckled. "I have to. I'm your guide."

"Oh, right. Of course." This assignment just kept getting better and better. Except for the canyon. "Did you say *into* the canyon?"

"Unless you'd rather hand out information pamphlets at the library."

"Ugh. No thanks."

"Pack a bag with some essentials and a large water bottle. I've got everything else we'll need in here," he said, gesturing to his backpack. "I'll meet you outside."

I rushed to my room to pack before the opportunity vanished. The Institute allowed students outside for only an hour in the afternoon, where we walked sedately through the garden. We weren't even permitted to go through the maze at the back.

Outside, I met Finn at the bottom of The Institute's steps. His strawberry blond curls shone in the bright sunlight.

We strolled toward the canyon. "I'll need to shift to get into the canyon," he said.

My stomach cramped. "How am I supposed to get there? Please tell me I don't have to climb down."

"No, you can ride in on me."

He meant flying. That nuance made all the difference. My hands shook, my mind offering up a horrific image of a fully engulfed, blazing phoenix streaking into the canyon. "Uh, I distinctly remember flames last time."

"Sparks. And they ended up behind my wings and tail," he said, glancing at me.

My face must have relayed my fear, because his expression softened. "Charlise, I've got you. I won't let anything bad happen, okay?"

I swallowed hard and nodded. Riding a phoenix I trusted was better than trusting myself to rappel over a cliff.

"Oh, you'll need to set up a perimeter with the Quantum Field Shield." He handed me a metallic blue gun.

The gun felt ice-cold in my grip. "How?"

"I'll fly in a low, wide circle," he said as we reached the canyon's edge. "When I tip my wings, fire a bolt into the ground every ten feet. They'll create a force field to contain the creatures."

"Creatures?" What exactly was in the canyon?

He winked. "You'll see. Climb on my back in front of my wings."

Finn flickered into a phoenix, and I climbed onto his feathery neck. With a running jump, he leaped into the canyon. I swallowed a yelp as the wind streamed through my hair. Finn flew to the bottom of the canyon. As he leveled out, he tipped his wings.

The nerves jittering in my stomach settled. With a careful aim, I followed his instructions. The bolts created a faint glowing barrier as we flew away.

After landing, Finn allowed me to dismount in a small clearing covered with yellow oat grass before he shifted.

I adjusted my pack. "Where do your clothes and your bag go when you shift?" My eyes widened as the words slipped from my lips. What was wrong with me? That question was way too personal.

He grinned as if he could hear my thoughts. "Because I'm a mythical shifter, my magic takes care of it. As long as I'm thinking about it when I shift. After a while, it's second nature."

We followed a small path worn through the grass. As we walked, he offered more information about the assignment. "I'm a member of PAW. Do you know about them?"

"Just what their name stands for; 'Protecting Animals in the Wild'."

"Right. Recently, we discovered a dead vixen, who left behind a leash of kits."

I blinked. "You just said words, but I have no idea what they meant. Except dead. That one's familiar."

Furrowing his brow, he shook his head. "Too bad. I'll have to take you back to The Institute then."

"What?"

"Just kidding," he said with a smirk. "Vixens are female foxes, a leash or a skulk is a group of foxes, and kits are baby foxes."

"I thought killing foxes was illegal."

A muscle jumped in his jaw. "It is. All we found was the dead fox with a gunshot wound. We don't know who committed the crime."

"Um, are we going to search for the poacher?" A shiver rippled through me.

"Nothing that dangerous. Instead, we contained the kits with the barrier, and we'll watch over them until help can come. Our contact's a couple continents away, and she won't be able to arrive until tomorrow. But you won't have to stay in the canyon overnight. I'll take you back tonight and then return to wait for her."

"I've never seen a baby fox, er, a kit before," I said with a smile. This was more fun than balancing a book on my head. The fact I was with Finn was beside the point.

A few yards away from the blue circle, we settled near the base of a rocky hill. Scrubby brush and sand surrounded us. The sky was a cloudless pale turquoise, the sun a relentless, fiery ball. Drops of sweat dribbled down my spine, dampening my shirt.

Finn pointed to a hole at the base of a large dune. "That's their den. We'll watch them come out to hunt or play, and we'll keep predators away." He shrugged. "It can get pretty boring, if it's not something that interests you."

"I enjoyed camping out with my brother when we were younger." Before being a proper princess had sucked all the fun out of life. "Believe me, this is better than learning how to sit. I thought I already knew how to do that."

He chuckled. "Later on, you can practice sitting near a fire. It can get cold at night."

I bit my lip, noting his muscles straining against his tee shirt. Maybe we could cuddle instead. My toes curled, and I looked away.

As he pulled the folded tent out of the bag, I stood. "Do you need me to gather some firewood?"

"Sure, but just small branches to start a fire. I brought an infinity log for warmth. Watch out for snakes and other critters."

I wandered, my thoughts returning to my arranged marriage. I'd never liked the idea, but meeting Finn had brought a sad realization. Finding someone I really liked didn't matter, because I couldn't do anything about it.

After I gathered a small armful of branches, I returned. Finn had set the tent up but sat on the ground, his face pale as he cradled his arm. Hurrying over, I dropped the wood next to our site. "What happened?"

He grimaced. "I think I sprained my wrist. I was setting up the tent when I tripped. I put out an arm to stop my fall, and well..." He trailed off and frowned at the offending wrist.

"I'll bandage it for you." I pulled the first aid kit from his bag.

"I was going to put an ice pack on it."

I nodded. "The ice pack's a good idea, too. I'll get it for you."

After a quick search, I found the pack, activated it, and handed it over.

"How do you know how to stabilize sprains?" Finn asked, then groaned as he adjusted the ice pack.

"My brother is accident prone." Hoping it would distract him from the pain, I continued to share camping stories as I put together a support with gauze and padding.

While he iced his wrist, I started a fire, then laid out a blanket to sit on. I turned to him with a smile. "It's a good thing you brought me."

He matched my grin. "Absolutely. The company's amazing."

I smiled, my chest lightening. "The feeling's mutual."

"There's just one problem."

I raised my eyebrows and waited.

"I can't fly until our contact, Emina shows up. She can heal my wrist. But you're stuck here until then. Sorry. I'll contact The Institute to notify them of what happened."

He rummaged in his bag with his free hand and handed me an energy bar. "This will tide you over until later tonight. I'll heat something up for supper."

"I can do that. You rest your wrist." I opened his chocolate and almond energy bar then mine.

Finn propped his good arm across his bent knees. "So what happens when you leave The Institute?"

I shrugged. "My mother will be deliriously happy, and she'll begin planning my wedding."

"You have a boyfriend?"

"No, I have an arrangement." I air-quoted the word. "Our parents arranged the wedding to connect our kingdoms." Bitterness tainted my words.

He frowned. "And you don't agree?"

"I've never met my fiancé. For all I know, he could be hairy, covered in warts, and call me 'Missy.'"

He choked back a laugh. "Or he could be a nice guy."

"Maybe. But I wanted to fall in love and marry someone who loved me for me. Instead, I have to become a perfect princess and marry a stranger for my kingdom."

What was it about Finn that made me spill my secrets? I took another big bite of the energy bar. With a full mouth, I couldn't say anything.

After a moment, Finn flicked a dark-eyed gaze at me. "What if you learned to love him?"

"You sound like you've talked to my parents. I suppose it's possible. But I'm looking for a purpose, too. I want to be more than just a married princess connecting two kingdoms."

"That's understandable. Any organization would be happy to have your support."

"Thank you." But it wouldn't matter much if Prince Mansfield decided he didn't want my perfectly imperfect self.

Twilight arrived, the sky turning pink and purple with the orange sun sinking to the horizon. After feeding the fire, I warmed up a can of stew we both shared.

The first sign of the kits came as we finished our simple meal. A small sandy-colored head popped out of the den. "Oh, he's so cute. I expected them to be darker," I whispered.

"Most of the desert foxes have that coloring for camouflage."

As soon as one fox climbed out, another two tumbled out behind him. Their tails were round balls of black-tipped fur. "Why is his tail so bushy?"

A smile rested in Finn's voice. "His tail is exactly as it should be."

Before I could speak, the bushiness separated into three tails. "Wait, he has more than one?"

"The kits are kitsunes, mythical animals with multiple tails. They can shapeshift, but without their mother, they would never learn how. Emina will help them with that."

"I'm glad there's someone who can help." We watched them play in front of the den. Our quiet conversation drifted to books, movies, music, and favorite hobbies. A small glow grew in my chest—we had a lot in common. It promptly dimmed when I remembered he wasn't mine. As darkness fell, the stars came out, and the kitsunes slipped off to hunt.

Finn took a drink of water. "This is a small leash. There are only three. So we just have to keep watch. The barrier will keep out most predators."

Silence fell, and a cool wind blew. Shivering, I dug my jacket out of my bag and draped a blanket around Finn.

I tilted my head up, looking above the canyon wall for familiar stars. There were so many glittering points of light against the navy background of the sky. I let my thoughts float for a moment. "How did you get involved with protecting kitsunes?"

"I'm involved with the magical branch of PAW. We protect all mythical individuals—phoenixes, griffins, unicorns, kitsune, and others. Because many are viciously hunted for their magic, they need protection, just like endangered animals do."

"That's wonderful you found what you want to do with your life."

"Unfortunately, I won't be able to do it forever. My father wants me to follow in his footsteps. But I'll do this as long as I'm able."

"What's your father do?"

"He's like a corporate manager. In charge of everything." Finn gave a one-shouldered shrug. "It is what it is."

"But you wouldn't choose it?"

His glittering gaze caught mine in the dark, his shoulder warm and solid against mine. "I'd do it differently. My life looks a lot like yours, Charlise. My profession's been chosen for me, and my parents arranged a marriage for me, as well."

"I'm sorry. I didn't know. And here I am, moaning about my problems, when you've got the same ones."

"It's fine, I can relate. But I don't think you'll have to worry about your soon-to-be husband falling in love with you. He'd have to be blind, deaf, and dumb not to."

The air grew heavy, expectation carrying its own weight. He was going to kiss me. And I wanted it more than anything. Anticipation fluttered in my stomach.

He leaned closer, his uninjured hand stroking my jaw. His breath skimmed my cheek, and his lips brushed mine once before returning. His hand tunneled into the hair at my nape, the caress sending a shiver down my spine.

The kiss grew, the world narrowing down to the two of us as he easily ruined me for anyone else's kisses. I pulled away with a gasp.

My heart pounded, and I sucked in a breath. "That was a mistake."

Finn's face shuttered. "My apologies, Charlise. It won't happen again."

I squeezed my eyes closed, so I couldn't see Finn's impassive expression. We both had arranged marriages waiting for us—I couldn't forget that. While part of me wished he hadn't kissed me, the other part of me tucked the memory away in my heart. I'd never forget this moment under the stars.

The night passed with us taking alternate watches. As dawn broke, I climbed out of the tent and stretched.

Finn's back was to me, and he didn't turn. "Emina will be here soon."

"And all three kits are safe in their den."

"Here." He handed me another energy bar, this one banana flavored with a chocolate coating.

By the time I finished, a reddish fox loped into view and approached our camp. With a shimmer, the fox morphed into a slender woman in a tank top and cut-off shorts.

"Emina!" Finn greeted her.

"G'morning, Finn." Brushing aside her auburn bangs, she gave him a flirtatious grin before air kissing both of his cheeks. I ignored the sudden twist in my stomach at the familiarity between them. Perhaps this was his fiancée.

He gave her one of his stunning grins. "Emina, this is Charlise. She helped me keep the kits safe. Unfortunately, I didn't fare as well. I sprained my wrist."

"Finn, you need a keeper. As always, I'm available." She winked, her almond-shaped eyes gleaming.

My heart cramped.

Closing her eyes, Emina cradled Finn's wrist with one hand, her other on his chest.

I reminded myself she was healing him. But her words and the predatory glint in her eye rankled.

When she pulled away, he rotated his wrist experimentally. "Thanks. It's as good as new. Let's go get those kits."

Even though I wanted to go too, I also wanted to avoid the awkwardness between me and Finn. After they left, I cleaned up the campsite. Finn could fold the tent himself.

They returned minutes later, laughing and talking as Emina carried a sling full of kits. They made a beautiful couple, and I ignored the jealousy winding through me. He deserved happiness.

"Thanks again," Emina said. "We'll get these little ones to a wonderful home."

Forcing a smile, I waved goodbye. She tightened the sling around her, shifted, and scampered off into the brush.

After he packed everything into his bag, he turned to me. "I'll collect the boundary markers, then we can leave."

"Can I help? Or at least walk with you?"

He blinked. "Sure."

It was another cloudless, sunny day with a slight breeze. I followed him to the first marker, a faintly glowing blue pole of energy. Finn pointed the gun, and instead of pulling the trigger, he pushed a button. With a sharp crackle, the pole of energy collapsed and disappeared into the gun barrel.

"What's your schedule for the last day at The Institute?" Finn gathered two more markers then scanned the landscape for the next one.

I wrinkled my nose. "I'll probably play catch-up. Tomorrow evening is the big dance."

His eyes flicked to my lips. "You don't like dances?"

"I like pretty dresses as much as the next girl. But I end up feeling self-conscious around others."

"I overheard some instructors talking. They said they might have some royal guests stop by so the students won't have to dance with each other."

I groaned. "That makes it worse. I have no social skills. I'm too opinionated, too clumsy, too..." I sighed.

"That's a load of garbage."

"What?"

His brown eyes glittered with a fierce light. "I never want to hear you criticize yourself like that again. *You* are what made this trip enjoyable."

The words buried inside burst forth. "Yeah, it looked like it, until it *didn't*. After our kiss, you wouldn't even look at me."

"I'm glad you were here." I scoffed, but he kept going, his voice hoarse. "I'm trying to respect your wishes. If I don't look at you, it's because I'm trying to forget your scent, the way you tasted, and how perfect you felt in my arms. You, Charlise Rothchester, are pure temptation."

My mouth went dry at the look in his eyes, and I shook my head. "No, my hair's a mess, and my outfit's dirty, and—"

"Your hair and your clothes don't matter."

Of course, *Finn* thought so. Prince Mansfield would expect much, much more, all wrapped in a flawless, refined package.

Finn collected another marker before he spoke again, his voice quiet. "I was hoping you'd sign up for this project. I wanted to see if my intuition was right."

"About what?"

"About you. That you were different. I wasn't interested in a shallow princess who only wanted to discuss the weather or the newest gossip. You're curious, determined, refreshing. I could talk with you for hours."

His low voice sent goosebumps skittering up my arms, even though there was no relief from the scorching heat. His words seemed to echo in my head. *He* wasn't interested in a proper princess who only discussed the weather or shallow gossip. Was it possible every negative my mother noted was actually a point in my favor? That not everyone was as embarrassed by her daughter as she was? While my thoughts spun, I followed Finn as he collected the perimeter markers.

Suddenly, I froze. "But your parents arranged a marriage for you. Were you going to break the engagement if you found someone else?"

"If I fell in love, yes. My parents want the arranged marriage to go through, but only if my fiancée and I weren't in love with someone else." He picked up the last marker and slipped the gun into his bag.

"So is she?"

Stopping, he gave me his full attention. "I don't know. Are you?"

"Am I what?"

"In love with someone else?"

My stomach bottomed out before surging back up to my throat. "That doesn't matter. We're talking about *your* fiancée."

He gave me a crooked, hesitant smile. "Princess Charlise Rothchester, I'm Prince Mansfield Finnley Claymore. It's a genuine pleasure to meet you."

My mouth fell open. The buzzing in my ears drowned out the chirping insects and birdsong. Spots filled my vision, went fuzzy, then I blacked out.

"Charlise?" A gentle fingertip stroked my cheek. "Lise, angel, wake up for me."

I kept my eyes closed. Finn was kneeling next to me, blocking the too bright sun, calling me angel. *Why was I lying down?*

His hand brushed back my bangs. "Should've kept your mouth shut, you sap," he muttered under his breath.

His comment helped me remember. That's right—he was Prince Mansfield, my fiancé. All this time, and he hadn't told me. Why?

When I opened my eyes, Finn's worried face filled my vision. With a relieved breath, he leaned back. "You're awake. You have a slight bump where you hit your head."

Frowning, I tried to sit up. My temple pounded, and I sank back with a groan.

He laid an ice pack on my temple. "Relax. Do you want some medicine for the pain?"

"Please."

I studied him as he rummaged in his pack for the pain reliever. Maybe, despite his words, he was realizing the real Princess Charlise wasn't proper princess material. I squinted, my headache a dull ache compared to the pain growing in my chest.

He handed me a capsule and a new water bottle. "Here. Once the pain eases, I can fly us back to The Institute. They can treat you there."

Was he happy to be rid of me? Upset? I wanted to fix this situation, go back when attraction was the only thing between us. I swallowed the medicine with some water before turning to him. "One question. Why?"

"Why what?"

"Why didn't you tell me the truth? Not at first, but later?" A kernel of hope rested inside—Finn was my fiancé. He wasn't a bully or a spoiled brat, but a sweetheart, full of fun and adventure. Still, I couldn't figure out why he'd withheld vital information.

He settled next to me. "You were everything I hoped for—brave, smart, interesting. But after hearing how unhappy you were about the arranged marriage, I worried you wouldn't be excited about *me* being your fiancé. Especially after you said the kiss was a mistake."

I tried to sit up, and he pulled me close so I rested against his chest. I gave him a quick side glance. "We both had a spouse waiting for us."

"Which was you," he said pointedly.

"But *I* didn't know that. I thought you and Emina were a couple. She's very flirty."

"She's like that with everybody." A slow grin bloomed on his face. "Were you jealous?"

I ignored his question, disliking his satisfied smirk. "I wish you had told me who you were, especially after we kissed. It matters."

He stiffened. "Why? Would you still have considered it a mistake?"

I cupped his jaw, the whiskers prickling my fingertips. "No. I'd have demanded a replay."

The tendons in his throat shifted as he swallowed. "How about now?"

"Better late than never."

Without hesitating, his lips met mine with passion and tenderness. By the time he pulled away, my swollen lips tingled, and my headache was gone.

I leaned my head against his shoulder. "We should probably head back to The Institute before they wonder where we are."

"I have one request," Finn said, helping me stand. He linked his hands together at the small of my back. "Skip the dance. Instead, I'll invite you and your parents to Palladia. It's time my parents met my fiancée."

"You never asked me to marry you." My question was subdued, but it was something I'd imagined before the arranged marriage had demolished my romantic dreams.

With a heart-stopping smile, he grasped my hands and dropped to one knee. "I don't have a ring with me. But I can give you my heart right now. Charlise Rothchester, would you marry me, love me, help me protect magical animals, and eventually help rule Palladia?"

My grin was instantaneous. "Yes, to all of it."

I leaned into his kiss. It was some time before we returned to The Institute.

ONCE AND FUTURE

Abigail Falanga

Two freedom fighters seek a legendary magical weapon in a seemingly ordinary mall. Local lore holds that the artifact will empower a future monarch, but what they encounter is not at all expected...

ONCE AND FUTURE

ABIGAIL FALANGA

THE MALL WAS STILL AND EMPTY, but if she listened carefully, Kira could almost hear ghostly keening from deep within. She ducked under the entrance and nestled her device against the lock. Beyond the glass, the interior was dark except for isolated lights.

Click.

"Done." Kira readied her bow.

"Expecting trouble?" Eymann smiled, though he'd checked his swords a second before.

"Always," she whispered gruffly as she slid inside. She made herself not glance back toward him. He was tall, handsome, fighting-fit—and after tonight, they likely wouldn't encounter each other again.

Mall security made half-hourly rounds, and the spell-bots she'd inserted should disrupt the cameras for at least the next hour. Kira spread a map inscribed with the mall blueprint, and the fiber optics woven into the parchment began glowing.

Eymann exhaled a soft whistle. "You were right. There *is* a portal here."

Kira grinned. "I told you! There were always stories around here about a magical treasure behind a hidden door. I never thought there was anything to it until meeting the Resistance."

"It matches the prophecy: A great monarch will come through the line of a local family and will be empowered by a soulsphere—the kind of 'treasure' that would enter urban legend."

"Monarch?" Kira raised an eyebrow.

"Monarch or not, a soulsphere will give the Resistance the edge we need." Eymann tapped a glowing magenta spot on the blueprint. "That's the likeliest place for the portal."

Kira's ears caught something. She looked around, not daring to use her flashlight. *Movement down the hall, just behind a store display. A cart with... Are those mops and brooms?*

Kira swore and ducked behind a decorative pot, motioning Eymann down beside her. The cart rolled past, propelled by an older gentleman she recognized—looking the same as ever, except with more grey in his mustache.

Eymann's sword glinted in the half-light.

"No!" Kira hissed. "That's just Mr. Myrick."

Eymann scowled at her but sheathed the sword. "You know him?"

"He's just the janitor—used to keep an eye out for us kids. Must be working late."

"As long as he doesn't get in our way. Come on."

They ran silently down the escalator. Downstairs, the mall was even eerier—not least because of a keening just beyond the range of ordinary hearing. Kira's perceptions had sharpened since discovering the reality of magic, but this sound was unfamiliar. And dangerous.

They made a methodical search, reaching the furniture store at the back of the mall.

Eymann's silhouette hesitated. "The keyhole must be here somewhere."

"What about that pillar?" Kira suggested. "It's load-bearing, so it must be part of the structure."

"More than that—it's ancient." Eymann sheathed his swords and unbuttoned his right sleeve. "Keep a lookout—I'll open it."

Eymann was himself a Key and could open any portal with his innate magic. Already, the pillar responded to his presence, lines rising along it where there had been nothing before. He raised his forearm and matched the intricate arrow tattooed from elbow to wrist to a corresponding section of the concrete. Instantly, the outline of a door shimmered into existence a few feet away.

Kira stifled a cry of triumph.

A strong flashlight beam swept over them. "What's going on over here?"

Eymann swore, blades hissing out. Kira raised her bow too—but toward the portal. Because now the keening was deafening: Something was coming through.

"Get down, Mr. Myrick!" She dove for cover as something dark swooped from the opening, aware of Eymann, who was in a sharp tussle with another creature to her right.

They were strong, foul, ravenous. Kira released an arrow, heard the impact, then dropped her bow and pulled a knife as she charged toward the portal. She had to get the soulsphere and close the door—they didn't stand a chance otherwise. It was the only way...

The only way to prove yourself to the Resistance.

Time slowed. She stared into the portal, at nothing but a glimmer of golden light—and sweet promise. *Kira, winning the soulsphere. Destroying an incursion of monsters. Winning the respect of all fey. Eymann, steadfast at her side, pledging love...*

A future envisioned in a flash. Kira reached toward the orb of light that seemed to manifest from her desire—

A huge mouth bore down on her.

THUNK! The monster was gone before she had time to shriek.

Mr. Myrick followed up with a couple more solid whacks from his mop. Then, he drew a sword from the handle and turned to face the monsters. He attacked them in a flurry of blows.

Then, all was still. The monsters were gone.

Kira gaped at Mr. Myrick. The orb circled him, making him appear grand, mighty. Regal.

He lifted the hand not holding his sword and the orb rested a moment over it. He smiled, shook his head, and waved the orb back beyond the portal, which closed. The mall fell again into semi-darkness.

"Phew!" Mr. Myrick bent and put his hands on his knees. "I'm getting too old for this."

Eymann slipped down so that he sat with his back against the pillar. "It's you. You're the prophesied scion."

"One of them." Mr. Myrick chuckled.

"But—" Eymann shook his head. "You could have taken the soulsphere."

"Kira could have, too."

"I almost did." Kira stumbled, found her voice, "It would have destroyed me, though, wouldn't it?"

"Taken in selfishness, it would have devoured you," Mr. Myrick said sadly. "It has many others."

"But not you. You could have been the king!"

"That's not my place." He cleaned his sword with a dirty rag. "That's for some grandson or great-great-granddaughter of mine. I am content with what I am."

"A *janitor*?" Kira couldn't help scoffing.

Mr. Myrick pulled a broom from his cart. "Do you know what the word 'janitor' means? It means a guard at a door." He winked at her. "For now, that's a far more important task than being a king."

A COLLISION OF FATE

Sara Anderson

The poem *A Collision of Fate* is a play of sensory words, memories, and emotions depicting the traditional fight of a knight defeating a dragon for his lady love.

A COLLISION OF FATE

Sara Anderson

Sulfur and stone, fire and ash
  Feet leaden, stiff, soul-honed longing
  A memory keeps him going
  Of whispered words and swaying grass
  While forging through searing heat and flame
  Her song echoing, a wisp in the mist
  Deft fingers stringing flowers in her hair
  Swinging steel to win her name
  Wings and wind, fear and rage
  An inferno bright, heart surging—then
  Crimson paints the night
  Bold strokes on a shadowed page
  Her laughter woven from rays of sun
  An embrace, a collision of fate
  Words woven on silken strands
  That bind their hearts as one

MOSAIC

Ava Lauren Grayson

The two quarreling daughters of a fairytale researcher split up and journey to find the prince of an unpublished Grimms' fairytale, in order to prove or disprove his existence.

MOSAIC

Ava Lauren Grayson

WE BOTH GET TO THE PRINCE at the exact same moment.

Months ago, when our mother died, the world lost its most ground-breaking fairytale researcher. I wanted my sister and myself to continue her work.

Arellia said fairytales aren't real. I said fairytales are the truth.

So, we made a bet. We took Mother's copy of unfinished fairytales, containing a map she devised to *The Trapped Prince*—the story Grimm never finished. A map she didn't get the chance to follow. Arellia and I each set out separately to find the prince—to prove whether he exists or is simply rubbish.

Three weeks later, we stand face-to-face before a mosaic of a medieval prince amongst the ancient ruins of a castle.

"Well?" I cross my arms. "Did I not prove that fairytales are real?"

"I don't see a prince anywhere." Arellia cackles and extends her arms in gesture. "This is a wall of stone, Misty."

I open my mouth but stop. She's right. Our long searches have led to this moment, and the prince *is* real...but not alive. Glancing down at the map, I notice a symbol just barely sketched in beside the last marked location. The inked marking of fae language. My muscles tense.

I cannot read fae.

I can speak, read, and write nearly ten mythical languages, but fae is one I struggled with in my studies. I scold myself for not being able to translate this.

But there is someone who can.

And I really do not want to ask for her help.

"Do you remember when we were ten and both took a liking to Mother's summer apprentice?" I force myself to ask Arellia.

She snorts and crosses her arms. "What does that have to do with anything?"

I smirk. "You learned fae to impress him so that you could speak to each other in a language I couldn't understand."

She lightens at the childish memory. "Yeah, I remember."

"Good." I thrust the map out at her. "Translate this."

Arellia hesitates before snatching the map and reading the symbol. She huffs and chuckles at the same time.

"What does it say?"

"Mother wrote 'centaur,'" she translates.

My heart leaps as I figure out the riddle. I beam.

"What?" Arellia questions with irritation. "Mother wrote a lot of nonsense, and this just proves it."

"No." I shake my head. "This just proves she was right. Centaurs have two hearts. Two hearts to unlock one."

Breaking the distance between us, I take Arellia's reluctant hand and place it on the heart of the prince. I do the same with mine.

And we wait.

"See?" Arellia snaps. "The prince—"

Just then, the mosaic cracks in half and golden light bursts from within. Arellia and I shield our eyes. When we look back, the wall containing the mosaic no longer exists. Instead, a prince stands in its place, and my sister and I stand speechless.

"Hi." The prince throws a handsome smolder our way. "My name's—"

Neither Arellia nor I care about the fairytale prince before us. We embrace one another tightly.

"I'm sorry we fought," I cry.

"No, I'm sorry," Arellia exclaims. "I should have believed you and Mother." After a moment, she smiles. "Does your offer still stand? To continue Mother's research?"

I smirk. "Yes. *If*...you admit fairytales are real."

Arellia's lips twist like taffy before she rolls her eyes. "Yes, fairytales are real."

I giggle and squeeze Arellia's hand. "Of course. Let's go home."

Hand in hand, the two of us turn away from the ruins of the past and head toward tomorrow.

"Um..." the prince calls behind us. "So, I take it you don't want a prince?"

THE WEIGHT OF WORLDS

Abby Johansen

Tae's life would be perfect if not for her odd little ability to cross realities. Since stumbling upon a portal to the fantasy world of Elessia, she's been forced to leave her comfortable modern life every time she feels the tugging in her heart—and time is running out to secure her happiness in either reality.

THE WEIGHT OF WORLDS

ABBY ELISSA JOHANSEN

I DIDN'T OPEN MY EYES. Not until I could be sure which world I was in.

I ran my hand across the bed. *Walmart-grade sheets.* Listened for any tell-tale sounds. *Alex's low snore.* This was the real world. At least, the one I claimed as real.

I opened my eyes, only to wince at far too much sunlight streaming through the thin curtains. "Ugg." A glance at my phone confirmed my suspicions. *7:43.*

I thumbed through to the alarm app, ignoring the half-dozen notifications. I hated this phone. Being in Elessia had proved a Gen-Zer like me could live perfectly fine without electronics. Especially ones that malfunctioned so badly that a simple alarm wouldn't—

Never mind. The six-thirty alarm glared at me, still resting contentedly in the off position. Now that I thought about it, I hadn't turned it on last night...

I flopped backwards and slammed my pillow over my face. The puppy had probably peed in his crate. The chickens had probably let themselves out of their hen house. And—the repairman. He'd be here at eight to fix the dryer.

I turned and shook my husband awake. Good grief, he was a hard sleeper. "Alex. Wake up. Wake up!"

He moaned and rolled toward me. "What?"

"We overslept. The dryer repairman is coming in seventeen minutes."

"What about your alarm?"

"I forgot to turn it on last night." I grinned sheepishly.

He sighed, then leaned up enough to kiss me. "I love you, even if you are a hot mess."

"Love you too. Now, we've got to hurry."

He swung out of bed and half-stumbled into the bathroom.

I reached for my phone—I still hated it, even if the alarm ordeal was all my fault—and scrolled through the notifications.

Arina.

I blinked, dream-like memories from Elessia crowding my mind. *Lady Arina, Alexandran, the war...*

Nope. I blinked again, and the name morphed into *Arianna.* My sister. I answered the text from her and tried to shove the cloudy thoughts from my head.

"Tae?"

I looked up at my husband. He'd dressed already, his short hair combed and any traces of sleepiness gone. How long had I spent staring at my phone?

"You planning to meet Milo wearing Mickey Mouse pajamas? Your call, but..."

I glanced down at my black-and-red nightshirt and shorts. *Bad idea.* "Yeah, I need to change—wait, his name is Milo?"

"It's eight minutes til he's supposed to be here." Man, he looked so much like Alexandran. Slightly longer hair, add a few scars, and you had the man that haunted my nightmares even here. Why did fate have to be this cruel?

"Alex?"

"Hmm."

"Have you ever thought about growing your hair out, just a bit?" I didn't know why I'd asked. Maybe I just needed to see that Alex *would* actually look different than the man I'd married in Elessia.

"Not really." He glanced at me, still sitting in bed in my cartoon PJs. "Are you going to get up?"

I swung my bare feet to the cold floor, then pushed past Alex to the chest of drawers.

"You laid your outfit out last night." He handed me jeans and a t-shirt from the wingback chair in the corner.

"Right. Right."

He smiled and shook his head. Goodness, even without the long hair and scars, he was *hot*. How had I ended up so lucky?

It took me one minute to change, another one to fix my hair. I'd made it halfway through brushing my teeth when Alex called, "He's here!"

I leaned out of the bathroom to glance at the clock on the wall. "Four minutes early!" I yelled around a mouthful of toothpaste.

"Is that illegal?" he shot back.

I spat into the sink, deciding my molars would survive without a thorough brushing this morning. "Should be."

I followed Alex to the door, where a man who looked exactly what I would expect from a 'Milo' stood. He was tall, pale, and scrawny, with long blond curls that were almost dreads. Acne scars pitted his face, and tattoos traced his jawline and ran all the way down his neck and under his work shirt. Eyes that said he would rather be anywhere but here flashed in my direction.

I'm not sure exactly why he fit the description of a Milo, but he did. It was either him or a tabby cat with a pug for a best friend.

Alex led him to the dryer, guiding him expertly around three days worth of laundry strung on a clothesline around the kitchen. I really should have done laundry *before* the rainstorm.

I let my husband explain the dryer problems while I let the puppy out, cleaned up his pee, fed both dogs, and made coffee. Then I slipped back into the crowded mudroom, which certainly lived up to its name with all the dirty shoes and puppy paw prints. "What's the good news on the dryer?"

Milo looked up at me—and then down. More of a leer.

I shifted closer to Alex, who, of course, was oblivious as he looked at the inner workings of the dryer as if he had a clue what went on in there.

"Milo?" I asked.

He cleared his throat, but didn't look away from me. "Shouldn't take but half an hour to fix. I have the parts in the van."

"Good." My skin crawled even after he turned away. The dream-like memories crowded in again. They hovered above consciousness, too vague to explain, but somehow I knew. This had happened before. Something bad had happened. The air in the mudroom thickened, my heartbeat pounded heavier inside me. I nudged Alex. "I'm going for a walk. I—I'll feed the chickens on the way out."

He nodded toward Milo. "He bothering you?"

So maybe he *was* a little more observant than I thought. My pulse slowed a little as Alex ran his hand up and down my arm. "It's okay. Just let him finish with the dryer and leave."

He nodded, even though I knew he didn't like it. He'd been a pro football player for two years—he could take scrawny little Milo any day of the week.

But I really needed my dryer fixed.

I slipped out the back door, sucking in the sultry air. It warmed my skin as the humidity made my shirt cling to my body. I let the hens, who, wondrously, hadn't escaped, out into their run. Now that the panic I'd felt coming on in the mudroom had settled, the woods were tugging at me. I fought the pull, hard. I didn't want to go. I liked my life here, where the world made sense and I had Alex and my biggest responsibility was showing up to work on time. Days like this I wished so badly that I'd never found that portal fourteen years ago. I could have lived my life just fine without Elessia.

But it'd been a week since I'd been to Elessia. I needed to go back. See what damage I'd been able to inflict in seven days.

I tossed our three hens their chicken scratch and started on the well-worn path. A quarter mile in, the path stopped in a tiny little clearing no bigger than our kitchen. I walked to the oak tree with the big knot, placed my hand inside the hole, and whispered, "I'll be back soon."

Then I was falling. I closed my eyes to quell the nausea and the spinning. Soon the sensations of being dropped and tossed through realities became all I could feel, all I could think, all I knew...

Then the memories slipped in place, and I was home.

I arrived in Elessia smoothly, as always, and landed into a normal breakfast scene inside my chambers. I sank right back into my life, memories flooding through me as if I'd never left—except for the knowledge that, while I'd been gone, my life in Elessia had deteriorated.

I picked at my tray of food, suddenly not hungry. The memories of my complacency swirled through my mind like so many leaves down a raging river. I'd been in the other world for a full week, and my life here had continued down a predictable, safe track while I'd been away. It was always that way when I crossed realities–my consciousness crossed, leaving all my habits and instincts to pass the time in the other world... Which meant I'd been quite the horrible queen over the past week. Those memories were clearer than the vague thoughts of my other life that kept trying to surface.

"My queen, you need to eat," Carryn said gently.

I smiled at my adviser and closest—no, only—friend in Elessia Castle. "I don't feel well."

She brushed her auburn mane over her shoulder and lifted the tray off my lap. "You'd best recover your strength soon. Lady Arina requests your presence for luncheon."

I grimaced at Carryn. My mother-in-law's voice already pounded in my head. I knew the speech she would give me. *You're the queen now, Tayerna. You must act like it. I picked you for a reason, and my son needs you by his side. I don't regret choosing you, dearest. But I need you to be the queen Elessia needs.*

I had never asked to be queen. I'd never asked to enter a loveless marriage with Alexandran. I'd never asked for any of this. Gracious, I'd never even asked to be able to cross realities. Was it so wrong of me to live most of my conscious life in the other world? The one where I was happy and life was easy?

I stood and crossed to the split door that led to the balcony. Carryn had opened the top panel, letting the breeze from the sea flit into my room. I ran a finger along the vine that twisted across the stone in the doorway.

"I don't wish to dine with her," I whispered, hoping the words were low enough that Carryn wouldn't hear.

But Carryn had spent a lifetime eavesdropping—she hadn't missed my comment. "You may be a queen, but only because Lady Arina made you one." She stepped between me and the door, her barely-taller frame still managing to tower over me. "You have no choice."

"I know." I still toyed with the idea of leaving here forever. But the tugs on my heart always turned into physical pain if I waited too long to visit the other world. And, as much as I hated being queen, I had a duty here. If I never came back, the complacent Tayerna that took over would live here forever. I would never be the strong queen Lady Arina chose to rule with her son. Not even on the few days I returned.

Carryn and I both turned at a knock on my door. I started toward it, but my adviser waved me off. The door blocked any view of my visitor, but I heard Carryn's curt, "My king," and held back a groan.

"May I speak privately with the queen?"

"Of course." Carryn led him in, gave a tiny bend at the waist—enough to show respect, but no more considering she was essentially a part of the royal family—and backed out the room with one last sympathetic glance at me. When the door clicked shut, I was alone with my husband. The fear and anger became so palpable that my chest began to ache.

I turned my back to him, looking out over Elessia. The country's beauty peaked in early summer, when the spring blossoms still bloomed bright but the days stayed warm enough you never needed a cloak.

"Tayerna."

A shiver ran up my spine. I loved the way he said my name. Perhaps only because he reminded me so much of Alex. I blinked, forcing the dreamy memories back into their box and locking them away. If I was going to survive a few days in Elessia, I couldn't spend the time longing for my other life.

"I have nothing to say to you, Alexandran."

"I'm going to meet with Milo—I mean, Miko—in an hour." He frowned. "I'd like to discuss our defensive strategy with you first."

Milo. The name toyed with my memories, dragging some out of the little black box I'd tried to lock them in. *Milo. Blond hair, pale skin, leering eyes.* I'd met him today, hadn't I? I held back a shudder. The vague images from his name collided with the all-too-real memories of another man with the same look in his eyes. I closed my eyes, counted to ten. Still the panic threatened to choke me. I counted to ten in Farthian, the harsher tongue of the people south of Elessia.

Finally, I opened my eyes. As my thoughts calmed, one settled at the forefront of my mind. Why had Alexandran said 'Milo'?

General Miko was one of his closest confidants. He would never forget his name. My chest tightened again, the tendrils of pain racing through my blood. The room dissolved into spots of color. But my mind was aflame with an idea so potent that the discomfort didn't matter.

What if Alex can cross realities, too?

The idea haunted me, stronger now. Oh, how I wanted it to be true.

But, no. There was no way we had somehow met and married in two completely unique realities. Fate was too cruel. Instead, I was destined to be taunted with a husband who looked like my Alex but spoke more harshly, always carried a sword, and never touched me.

And that was not my Alex. No matter they looked like twins. No matter their names were similar. No matter... Anything. Some things were just impossibilities.

"Tayerna," he said again. Annoyance crept into the deep timbre of his voice. "War is coming. If we build a strong defense, we can hold off Rynwood for at least a month while we prepare an offense. This is important."

"Miko knows more about this than me. Why not ask him? I'm not a general."

"Your father is, as is your brother." He shifted his weight from his left to his right foot, the only sign of impatience such a king would show. "You know more about war than nearly any man I know. It's one of the reasons my advisors favored you for marriage. I would value your input on our strategy."

I rubbed my temple against the headache beginning to form. "Very well. Perhaps then your mother won't be as harsh in her reprimands if I can tell her I helped plot a war this morning." He never did seem amused with my sarcasm. At his silence, I glanced his way.

He'd tensed, as if bothered by the mention of Lady Arina. "We've been married scarcely two weeks. Prior to that, you'd never met me or even set foot in Elessia Castle," he reminded me. "Surely she understands."

"I don't believe so." I snapped. "Your mother is more insufferable than *you*."

He sighed, then pulled out a chair for me at my small table. "This will only take a moment."

Two days later, I awoke to my Walmart sheets and a blaring alarm.

At least I'd set the alarm this time. The past two mornings had been nightmares, considering I'd somehow managed to leave the alarm off again. I grabbed my phone and tapped until the sound stopped. 6:30. Perfect.

The bed shifted as Alex sat up beside me. "Finally remember your alarm?"

"Yeah." I slid out of bed, only to almost step on Timber. The big dog jumped out of the way. "Sorry, pup," I said.

Alex walked around the bed and pulled me into a tight hug. I relaxed inside his arms, even as the nightmarish memories swirled in the edges of my mind. They soon floated away, leaving nothing but a few tendrils, like the bad dreams they were.

But, no, nothing would ruin this. When he let go, I laced my hands behind his neck and pulled him down until I could kiss him.

I finally stepped away, and he smiled. "Well, good morning to you too."

"It's Monday," I said. "No work for you, and I'm remoting in all day. I say we make nachos and plan on binging Disney movies as soon as I can finish work."

"Sounds good."

But he didn't sound good. "What's wrong?"

"I just hate to see those trees go, that's all."

Memories from yesterday—from this world—smacked me like a train. I hated when they did that, but an unpredictable memory was my punishment for switching realities so late at night. Not only did I not remember anything but the barest traces of my other reality, but, at times like this, memories from my current reality would come back too slowly.

The Davidsons, who actually owned most of the woods behind our house, were cutting down some of the trees to sell for lumber. Including the oak tree.

Nausea hit me and I stumbled to the bathroom, just in case. I leaned on the sink and waited for the wave to pass. Life had just given me the out I'd been begging for, hadn't it? If the oak tree disappeared, surely the pull I felt to it would go away, too. Then I could live my life here with Alex without ever worrying about Elessia again. There wouldn't be a thing I could do about it—the complacent, passive version of Tayerna would just have to be queen forever. Because without the oak tree, I could never cross realities again.

Alex's hands rubbed my shoulders. "You okay?"

"Yeah. Yeah, I'm fine."

"Really?"

I turned to him. So much sorrow on his handsome face. Why did this hurt him so much? It was only a few acres of trees. The woods behind our house were huge—most of them would still be fully intact. The only important thing was the oak tree.

Maybe Alex can cross realities, too.

The thought came again, but I remembered it from a different life. While I'd been talking with Alexandran. My gut swirled violently. I had to ask him. Had to bring it up, somehow. Maybe...maybe it wasn't all just cruelty. Maybe it wasn't all just that whatever controlled this reality-crossing hated me.

"Alex?"

"Hmm." He kept rubbing my shoulders, even though I faced him now.

"Do you... When you go for walks in the woods." Half a sob tried to choke me, but I pushed past it. "On the Davidsons' property. Does anything...odd ever happen?"

"What do you mean?" His eyes lit up. Some spark of recognition. Something that propelled me to keep pushing.

"Like...like suddenly you're in another world." I picked every word carefully. If I was wrong, he'd think I was crazy. When I'd been eight years old and discovered the oak tree, I'd never told another soul out of fear. I'd kept the facade of normalcy for fourteen years. I couldn't blow it now.

His eyes softened, the creases in his tanned face relaxed. "Near the oak tree," he finally whispered.

The butterflies in my gut kicked it up a few more gears. *He knows. He knows.* Timber nudged between us, and I heard the puppy whining from the living room. "I...I better let the dogs out," I said, never breaking eye contact. *He knows.*

"I'll start breakfast."

As soon as I stepped outside, the already warm air knocked the sense back into me. How could this be happening? One impossibility was quite enough for a lifetime, thank you very much.

Maybe he meant something different. Alex had always been an outdoorsy person. Maybe he just had some super special connection to a random oak tree. Or maybe there was something just a little beautiful in all of this. I stopped halfway to the chicken coop, hand over my heart. The tugging to the woods was strong, which made no sense. I'd come back late last night—surely I didn't have to go back now.

The tug turned to pain the further I went, until I finally dropped the chicken scratch to clutch my chest with both hands. I grunted, partially in pain and partially in disgust, and just let the chickens out to forage the yard. Then I dashed off into the woods. Mental note: Put the chickens back up before the puppy chews their heads off. Hopefully complacent Tae would remember it. I slowed my pace as my aching heart pounded too fast. As far as I could tell, my life here stayed simple enough that there was rarely an issue when I left. Except maybe forgetting to turn alarms back on.

The pain in my chest dulled when I reached the oak tree, but I knew it wouldn't last long. I had to hurry. I placed my hand in the tree and willed myself to remember one thing clearly:

Alex just might be waiting for me.

I paced my chambers again, a glance at the sun confirming at least two hours had passed since I'd settled back in this world.

If Alex is real, he'll come for you.

Of course Alex was real—I had enough faint memories of my other reality to know that much. But when I'd arrived here near sunrise, the only thought left from my other life was "Alex is real." Which, hopefully, meant my suspicions were correct. Perhaps Alex was a reality crosser, just as I was. And perhaps, somehow, he and Alexandran were one and the same.

At the knock on my door, I whirled and nearly ran to answer. King Alexandran stood on the other side. My heart pounded nearly out of my chest. "My king," I said, adjusting the small circlet that rested on the back of my head. My voice held the same chill as usual, but even I could hear the hope hiding underneath. "Please, come in."

He held my gaze captive with his smoky grey eyes. "Tayerna, I...I need to know."

Oak tree.

If this was real, if this was Alex...he would know about the oak tree. I couldn't even explain what an oak tree looked like, considering we had no such tree in Elessia. But I knew, to the farthest corners of the mind, that an oak tree was the key to everything.

"Oak tree," I whispered. The words left my mouth before I could control them. My face heated, and I stepped away from Alexandran. What if I was wrong? What if—?

But I'd only said two words. He couldn't call me mad just for that.

"The oak tree," he whispered back. Then, even softer, so I barely heard it, "Tae?"

My heart dropped to the floor, my palms began to sweat. I retained enough presence of mind to close the door before I stepped closer to Alexandran. “You...you’re real. Alex. Real.”

He touched my face with rough, calloused, war-scarred hands. I jumped back, the contact strange from the man I’d grown to loathe.

But somehow the touch was gentle. Almost familiar. A tear rolled down my cheek. “Make me understand.”

“All this time, I never knew you lived in both worlds,” he said. “I kept it a secret. I would be stripped of my crown if anyone knew. And... I don’t know. I can’t remember anything about the other life.”

“But we knew each other for much longer,” I said. “And we could never say.”

He pulled me toward him, and, for the first time in this reality, my husband embraced me. My body froze, hating the touch, until the warmth rushed through me. Alex. The word echoed in my mind. Alex. I wrapped both arms cautiously around him.

“When my mother introduced us,” he said softly. “I could scarcely breathe. You looked so much like the woman that I dreamed of at night. That I knew was mine in another world. I waited a few weeks, but you never once slipped and said anything. So I tried to convince myself it was only a coincidence.”

“Or a cruel trick of fate.” I settled deeper into his arms, suddenly so safe with the man I’d despised. “Two weeks of marriage, yet we spent our days avoiding each other.”

“If it wasn’t you... I couldn’t be unfaithful. I didn’t care that it was another reality entirely. So I pushed you away.”

My Alex. "How did I end up married to such a good man in two different lives?"

"I'm not the same, Tayerna. I'm sure whoever I am in the other world is...cleaner. I've fought for Elessia. I've done whatever I needed to do to keep her safe. I have blood on my hands."

I knew all of that. "I think I can love this side of you, too."

His lips pressed against the top of my head, then the weight of his chin settled there. I stay tucked against him, afraid that, if I moved, this dream would evaporate.

Then he spoke, and my perfect little dream did begin to vanish. "I can't keep crossing over like this," he said. "Elessia needs me."

"I need you. I need you in the other life."

"We're both here. Isn't that enough?"

"I...I..."

He held me away from him, just far enough he could tip my chin up and meet my eyes. "What is it?"

"I never wanted to be a queen. I never asked to find Elessia. I never even wanted to be here."

The hard edges of his face softened. "Then why were you put here?"

"I found it as a child. That's all I remember." I searched his face, and the gravity written there told me everything. The weight crushed my chest. "This is where you started, isn't it? It's your home."

He nodded. "I didn't even begin to visit the other reality until I was nearly ten." Then he sighed. "I need to stay here as long as possible. With the war looming, Elessia needs a strong king. Perhaps it's selfish, but I want you here with me." He brushed a tear off my cheek. "All of you."

My insides clenched. "I don't want to be queen."

"Perhaps that's the entire reason you found Elessia." His eyes lit up. So full of purpose. "So you could one day lead her."

I shook my head, blinking back tears. "No. It can't be. I want to go back. I—I know everything is simpler on the other side. Easier."

"And easier is better?"

"I didn't say that. Not always."

"Tayerna, I can't stay there. This is where I was meant to be. My duty is to lead my country."

"I know." And my desire was to be safe in my other life. But it would never be the same, knowing Alex's heart was somewhere else. Knowing he'd almost never be fully there with me.

Alex jerked his head up. "Do you feel it?"

After a moment, my heart started pulsing harder, tugging me downwards. Toward the portal tucked in the gardens three levels below us. "Yes."

He met my eyes. "I don't know what. But I know something in the other life is going to change things."

I nodded, the vague memory tugging at my mind as well. Oak tree.

He picked up my pale, dainty hand. "I want to face it with you."

I slid easily back into my life inside the quiet, old little farmhouse. I'd spent the morning doing my usual routine, plus rounding the chickens back up into their pen. Now I was knee-deep into edits on a marketing proposal for my less-than-exciting, but very safe, day job.

Alex set my second mug of coffee down beside me. He'd fixed it perfectly—enough milk to turn it blonde. He hesitated as he pulled his hand away, though.

Then the hazy, dream-like memory surfaced—Alexandran had come back with me. He was my Alex. For certain. None of the doubts that usually plagued my crossing memories followed this thought.

I caught Alex's hand. "You're back," I whispered. As if there were anyone but a petting zoo's worth of animals to hear us.

He leaned down and kissed me until I lost my breath. When he pulled away, the desperation in his eyes scared me.

I set my computer aside and stood up so I was slightly closer to his height. I wrapped my arms around his waist. "Alex..."

"They're cutting down the oak tree," he said, resting his forehead against mine. "And... I can't stay here, Tae. I have to go back."

"I know." But the thought of leaving this reality behind forever... Of pledging to stay in Elessia, to rule as queen, until my dying breath... It terrified me.

"I love you more than I've ever loved anything in this life or the other," Alex said. "I can't imagine what would have happened if I'd never found the portal in the garden all those years ago. You are the most beautiful thing to ever walk into my life."

I took a deep, steadying breath, trying but failing to ignore the tears slipping down my cheeks. "But Elessia is your duty. You have to go back."

"And you feel nothing for the other reality?"

"I'm scared to death."

The silence stretched on, neither of us moving as we stood together, foreheads braced against each other, eyes closed. Finally, Alex said, "Which life are you called to?"

Another deep breath. "I'll need time to think on that one."

He kissed my forehead. "They're cutting down the oak tree tomorrow."

The next twenty-four hours passed almost in a dream—or maybe a nightmare. Alex's words haunted my every step. *Which life are you called to?*

And I only feared the question because I knew the answer.

I rinsed off the last of the dishes as Alex stuck his head around the corner of the kitchen. "I just saw the trucks going down toward the woods." His eyes begged me to answer the question.

I dried my hands slowly, savoring every last moment in the little home we'd built for ourselves. I laid the towel back on the counter, spun around the kitchen to capture every detail. Praying I could remember even the tiniest nugget.

Then I held my hand out to Alex. "Let's take a walk out there. One last time."

He met my eyes, and I fought back the tears. One spilled out anyway, and he caught it with a swipe of his thumb. "Together?"

"Together."

A heavy sense of loss followed me into my reality in Elessia. But overshadowing it remained an elation, a thrill that raced through me every time I remembered Alexandran.

My husband met me in the halls of Elessia Castle on the way to luncheon. He brushed his calloused hand against my dainty one. And I remembered. I remembered different hands joined—his with less scars, mine tanned from days spent in the sun. And I knew we could never go back.

"The portal is gone, isn't it?" I asked.

He nodded. "I just tried the one in the garden, to be certain. It does nothing. As if it never existed."

"Someone destroyed the oak tree."

"Yes."

"But we're together."

"Thank you," he said. "For staying with me. For being Queen of Elessia."

I forced a smile. "You were right. It's where I belong."

"I talked to Miko before I found you. Rynwood's men are getting closer, and we don't have as much time as we'd first thought. We'll have to use most of our resources for an offensive move if we want to win this war quickly."

"I'll do whatever I can."

We continued toward Lady Arina's chambers, where she'd requested we join her for luncheon. I expected another reprimand from her today, but never again. I had no choice in the matter now—I would be fully present here for the rest of my days. Passive, complacent Tayerna was no more.

"Don't let my mother treat you badly," Alex said, as if reading my mind.

"I'll do my best. I feel I deserve some of it, though."

"You're here now. That will have to be enough for her."

I'm here. Forever. I closed my eyes, trusting my feet to guide me, and tried to calm my racing thoughts. This was my only reality now. "Alex, I—"

"It'll be all right." He stopped in the middle of the hall and ran a thumb down my cheek. "I'll be right here beside you."

He tugged me into an alcove tucked nearly out of sight. I leaned into him, drawing from his strength until I knew I could face whatever the day held. When I pulled away, his eyes held me to the spot like they had so many times before. Only now, I knew this was truly the man I loved.

"Just think," I said. "We managed to marry each other in not one, but two lives."

"I would love you in every life, Tayerna. No matter what world we find ourselves in."

I reached up and adjusted the circlet on his head. "But it might as well be a world where we can be king and queen."

He grinned, and he looked so much like the Alex from another life that it almost hurt. "Might as well."

THROUGH THE LOOKING GLASS

Shannon Alldredge

Through the Looking Glass, from the "Mirror Mirror" creative shoot, shows a royal contemplating the weight of the crown, debating whether to forge ahead or run away from it all.

HEAVY IS THE HEAD

AJ Skelly

When the young king breaks all tradition and asks the princess to marry him ahead of schedule, what is a girl in a poofy Alexander McQueen ball gown to do?

HEAVY IS THE HEAD

AJ SKELLY

HEAVY IS THE HEAD that wears the crown.

That's what my mother has always said, and as the sole ruling monarch of Montico, she should know. I repress a shiver. Soon it will be my turn. Because, as of this bombastic evening, on the very anniversary of my parents' coronation, I am to be publicly engaged to the young king of Aierland.

But...the unexpected has happened.

My belly clenches, churning the tea and toast I put in it earlier. Dread and something akin to panic fizz along my backbone, pressing against the cinched waist of the Alexander McQueen ball gown of eggshell blue that Mother had specifically done up for my engagement.

My nice, predictable, orderly life has shattered with the utterance of a few words.

I blink stupidly at the sizable diamond glittering on the fourth finger of my left hand, and I cannot quite process what has just happened. Shock cements my tongue to the roof of my mouth.

Callumn's hand still ghosts against my wrist. His skin is cold. Is he as unsettled as I am?

"Say something, Charlotte Grace," Callumn whispers, his voice strained as his wide eyes search mine.

I swallow on a dry throat. "I, I don't know what to say," I admit. Words fail me. Utterly. What does one say when the prince you've been promised to since birth suddenly becomes king and ten minutes ago, threw all tradition out the window and proposed ahead of schedule in a dark alcove off the grand ballroom where several hundred of Her Majesty's subjects are dancing? Paparazzi and their expensive cameras line the room like sharks trolling chum, all expecting to witness the grand proposal of the young king of Aierland to the Crown Princess of Montico.

His voice is low, deep, and trembling. "We are meant to marry, Charlotte Grace. But I would have you come to me willingly. Not because of a betrothal made when we were babes, not because the kingdoms expect it. Not because it's what your mother wants." He pauses and draws a shaky breath, his fingers tightening slightly against my hand. I rip my gaze from the sparkling gem on my finger and meet Callumn's anguished, vulnerable gaze. My heart trips into my throat.

His gaze darts to my lips, then back to my eyes. "Heavy is the head that wears the crown, Charlotte Grace." His words echo my mother's. "A burden unlike any other—a joyful burden that removes many personal choices." He swallows and when he speaks, there is a rasp to his voice. "I'd have us take this one small measure of freedom back. I'd have you marry me because I'm your choice; as you are mine." Strains of the orchestra rise and float from the ballroom, cocooning us in this moment together. "I wish to marry you, Charlotte Grace, because I need you. Not just as a figurehead beside me. I cannot rule alone. The weight is too much. Somewhere over the years of social functions, forced outings, all the dances and jaunts set for the public eye, I fell in love with you.

Your courage, your grace, your poise, your gentleness. Even your stubborn streak." He smiles, though his gaze is still nervous.

Warmth unfurls in my belly as his words wash over me. He's never said these sorts of things to me before. Not in all the years we've known each other. Perhaps his eyes tried to convey them once or twice, but Callumn has always been my steadfast friend.

Has he become more?

Time stands still as I study the man before me. Though only a year older than I, he's grown tall and broad, jacket sleeves tight over the muscles of his arms. His eyes are earnest. He means what he's said.

"Can you love me, Charlotte Grace? Someday?" His whisper cuts into my thoughts and I realize he's waiting desperately for me to speak—to say something—anything. The next words from my lips will change the course of my future.

I swallow. I always knew I would marry Crown Prince—King Callumn of Aierland. That we'd marry and combine our kingdoms. That was never in question. But as the pages of my life flip back and show me the time spent with him, I see the little ways he's cared for me. Doing more than duty required, his easy smile, the dimple in his left cheek, the small touches, the way he held my hand when my parakeet died, his compassion and tenderness, his fierce determination.

With a sudden start, I realize that despite the expectations put upon me, I *do* want to marry Callumn. How could I desire to marry anyone else? Rushing fills my ears.

"Yes." The single syllable fills the space around us, filling it until my heart may burst with its ringing.

"Yes?" The air rushes from him as he staggers back a step.

A smile tips my lips.

Without waiting for him to recover, I take a half step nearer him so that the gold and crimson braid swathed across his chest bumps against the blue satin of my bodice. Going up on tiptoe, I kiss him.

For a full three seconds, he freezes, then he jolts back to life. His arms wend carefully around my waist, drawing me flush against him as his head slants and his lips move over mine. It's more than I was expecting, this first kiss of ours. His mouth molds against mine, teasing me, dragging me under in a delicious wave of sparkles, girlish longing, and a soul-deep love for this man who is to be mine.

At last we break apart. He stares unabashedly at my face, his own wreathed in smiles and splendor.

Somewhere in the ballroom, an archaic trumpet sounds, signaling that it's our time.

He grins my favorite crooked smile, his dimple appearing in his left cheek. "Shall we go get engaged, Charlotte Grace?"

A silvery giggle bursts from my throat.

His features relax. "Heavy may be the head that wears the crown, but light is the soul that shares the burden."

Callumn leans over and places a soft kiss against my forehead.

Yes. We will bear it. Together.

KNOTS AND TANGLES

S.M. Jake

A royal marriage is never about love. Yet, the romantic ramblings of Ozanne's sewing circle ladies have pressed her patience and tangled both her embroidery magic and the feelings she normally keeps well in hand.

KNOTS AND TANGLES

S.M. JAKE

A ROYAL MARRIAGE WAS NEVER ABOUT LOVE.

To think that it could be was childish ignorance at best and masochistic stupidity at worst.

Ozanne's needle plunged downward at her mental command, driving through the white muslin with far more force than required, blue thread dragging viciously behind. Her fingers flexed, flipping the needle and bringing it back up with a flick.

She was not stupid. She had known exactly how many political considerations had gone into the decision, which treaties and trade agreements it had pushed through, even the gossip strategically squashed by their marriage four years ago. It hadn't been her decision to make, but she had agreed with the choice.

The needle jerked to a stop, the thread clustered in a knot. She huffed, reaching in to stop the needle's fight, switching from mental to physical guidance as she glanced at the clock hands that had barely crept an hour, the others still prattling on about frivolous romance. Evidently, the masochist part was still up in the air.

"Oh, to find a love such as yours, Highness," Iona sighed wistfully.

"His Majesty is not in love with me," Ozanne said firmly, scowling down at the bright, half-finished flower, a snarl in its center.

Lady Brina barely shook her silver head as she watched her needle dance gracefully up and down, smirking like an old grandmother who knew when a child was lying but chose to keep their secret.

"But, the way he held you during that dance at the midwinter ball last month!" Iona insisted, holding a hand gingerly aloft as she stared at imaginings with glassy eyes, pastel threads drifting in the air about her rather than working. "And how he held your hand in a tender moment at its end."

Ozanne rolled her eyes. The girl was nearing marriageable age, but still saw the world through dream-fogged glasses.

"It was a *dance*. People traditionally hold hands while dancing." Ozanne picked at the knot, tipping her work to catch the grey afternoon light coming through the diamond-paned window.

"Then what about the smile he gave you upon returning from his trip last week?" Iona clutched her embroidery to her chest, eyes bright. "If ever a look could speak of love..."

Ozanne sighed. "'A look' in front of half the court and a hundred subjects is not love. It's performance."

Iona gasped. "How could you say such a thing? Those fleeting glances are what betray a man's true feelings!"

"Silk and string, girl." Ozanne yanked harder at the knot's tail, frustration tangling her insides. "How many leaflet romances have you been consuming?"

"But, to call it *performance*!"

"...is nothing more than the truth," Ozanne insisted. "Ren and I are aligned in political and personal convictions. Even so, a bit of affection does much to assure the people there is stability behind the crown."

Iona shook her head, embroidery forgotten as she leaned forward. "But, don't you love him? And don't you hope for love in return?"

"Iona!" Ozanne slammed her needlework into her lap, a pair of thread scissors jumping into the air beside her, her cheeks and neck growing warm. "I am not a wistful maiden who falls apart at a man's passing smile, or swoons upon brushing hands or"—she snatched the scissors in a tight fist—"goes aflutter at sly glances! If that is love, then I'm glad I don't need to bother with it!"

Iona opened her mouth to start again, but closed it under Ozanne's glare.

"Indeed," Lady Brina said softly, "none of that is love."

"Thank you," Ozanne huffed, replacing the scissors and picking up her needle again.

"Oh, I'm not saying he doesn't love you, child," she stated flatly. "It's obvious he does."

Ozanne's needle hovered mid-air as she stared at the woman.

"Did he not ask for your opinion on the trade proposal from Norten?" Lady Brina didn't look up from her work, the smile still fixed in place.

"He needed to talk through it. That was all." Ozanne fought to maintain a respectful tone with the woman. This was getting out of hand.

"He has advisors for that." Lady Brina's eyes turned up, boring into Ozanne even as her thread spun into a delicate four-legged knot. "And he brought you back those yards of silk."

"It was considerate, yes. But general kindness is not the same thing—"

"In your favorite shade of green?"

"It's not as if my favorite color is a state secret."

"Then perhaps we should consider the way he excused himself from the ball that Iona spoke of, when your headache set in."

"That was not—" Ozanne's jaw squeezed tight as she fought back the heat building in her chest, her needle growing warm in her grip. "You cannot call every small kindness or consideration love. If that were the case, then one could claim I am in love with the Beranithian Ambassador!"

"No," Lady Brina's smile deepened. "No, I suppose you're right. Love is not just general kindness."

Ozanne's face burned. "Your words agree, and yet your tone says otherwise."

Lady Brina gave the slightest of shrugs. "So, if love isn't warm looks and holding hands, yet it is also not simply kindnesses, nor special consideration...what is it?"

Ozanne focused on her embroidery to avoid eye contact, lifting her hands into the proper position to restart her needle, though a pinky twitched. *It's not as if he's ever said it.* But love wasn't just words, either.

"Don't tell me you think love is only within the bed."

Pain speared into Ozanne's thumb. She jolted up from the chair, work flying into the wall, face flaming. "Obviously not! Physical intimacy is—" No, she did not want to go there. "Producing an heir is part of..."

Lady Brina's brow arched.

A most unqueenly growl rumbled in the back of Ozanne's throat. She spun for the door.

"Highness?" Iona called.

"I need air."

Ozanne stomped out into the arched hallway, fanning her face with one hand as she scowled at the prick of red growing on her thumb. A fountain bubbled in the courtyard below, its chipper splashing doing nothing to soothe her tangled nerves. Scraps of thread that had clung to her clothes lifted free and floated around her.

She and Ren had a solid marriage, one that made complete sense, that was good for the country. Never had she questioned his motives or thought twice over his actions. He was considerate, kind even. But that wasn't—

"Ozanne?"

She jumped, spinning. "Don't sneak up on me like that!"

A pair of aides and an advisor hovered in various states of shock, though she realized none of them had spoken. Ren stood at their center, watching her, his circlet half covered by dark curls that had crept out of place, per usual.

Her snarled insides pulled taut. "Apologies," she stammered.

"It's fine." He smiled, same as he always did, and something fluttered within her. "Are you all right?"

"Yes." She squeezed her thumb harder, internally stomping out the flutters. She was no leaflet romance heroine. "Fine."

"Are you sure?"

"I said I was fine!"

His brow flickered, smile dimming. She forced out a breath. "Apologies. Again. I didn't mean... It's not you."

But it was. And now, she could see it.

All the moments he'd taken from his over-full schedule to check in with her. The places where he had been a buffer with some politician, or brought her a small gift he thought she would like.

She'd held his arm a hundred-thousand times, and yet now she saw all the places where he wouldn't have been required to offer it. The unspoken signals they had developed without realizing. The late-night conversations. The quiet jokes.

He was a good king, and treated his queen with respect and care.

Yet, underneath that were a thousand moments he had chosen to go farther, to do more than what was simply expected or right.

"Really. I just needed some air. I'm fine." Warmth of another kind slipped into her cheeks, weaving yet another complexity to her emotions. She knotted her fingers together.

"All right. See you this evening." He turned, his entourage sweeping back alongside him.

Her heart jerked. "Do you love me?" she blurted out, the shaky words reverberating down the hall.

Ren froze.

What are you thinking! her mind screamed; chest, neck, face, and all burning with embarrassment.

"Give us a moment," Ren commanded softly, his back still to her as the aides nodded. They hurried off down the hall, and she stared at the back of Ren's head so she wouldn't see the pity in their eyes.

He slowly rotated to face her, calm, though his perfect composure was frayed at the edges by the way his hand flexed in and out. Was he angry? Surely, he was. She was acting the fool, here in the middle of the palace, for all to see. What was she thinking? What had she just done?

"May I ask," his voice was tight as he took a cautious step toward her, "why you are asking?"

"I..." She should tell him it was a mistake. She was being emotional, getting wound up by the words of others. An egregious mistake and one that was unacceptable as queen. She'd do better! But, those words wouldn't come.

"You just... You've never said." She swallowed. Did he need to? He spoke easily with her about other things. *Why not this?*

A gentle wind slipped up from the courtyard below, tossing his curls and tugging her sleeves. He stepped back to her, not stopping until their toes nearly touched, his closeness nearly overwhelming.

He took her hand, tracing his thumb across her fingers, leaning even closer. "Forgive me. I never meant to let you wonder."

Her breath hitched, and she cleared her throat. "I didn't think... I mean, that isn't what..."

His eyes narrowed, confused.

A huff of irritation slipped out of her and a scrap of tangled blue jumped free, floating beside them. She squeezed his hand tight.

"I didn't wonder. Not really." The tangles in her middle finally pulled loose, a thread of giddiness tugging at her cheek. "But, please...say it anyway?"

He smiled, plucking the blue thread from the air, the strand immediately smoothing. He looped it around her finger, tying a perfect square knot, and placed a whisper of a kiss upon it. "So you never forget, I love you."

THE CROWNMAKER'S CURSE: PART ONE

Cassandra Hamm

As the royal crownmaker, Azucena devotes her life to caring for the magical gems she imbues into her crowns. When the future king comes to her shop the night before the coronation, she must choose between her heart and her crownmaker's vow—before a dangerous plot overthrows the king's rule before it even starts.

THE CROWNMAKER'S CURSE: PART ONE

CASSANDRA HAMM

AZUCENA FROWNED DOWN AT THE UNFINISHED crown gleaming on her workbench. The gold had long since cooled, twisting in elegant curves and regal points. But the setting sat hollow and empty, devoid of the gem that would change the crown from a normal piece of jewelry to something...*more*.

She cracked open the shop door and peered at the moonlit pathway. Imposing, vine-snarled trees lined the empty road to her shop. If Isidro didn't deliver his decision within the next hour, she'd have to choose a gem for him. Scandalous. Unheard of. *Weak*.

She could almost hear the court whispering now—"The *príncipe* couldn't even choose a gem for his crown. How can he rule Terrajoya?"

A flicker of movement caught her eye. A shadow shifting. A branch snapping. She squinted. A man materialized from the trees. Tall and slender, strong shoulders tapering down to narrow hips. Clutched against his chest was a handful of red carnations. Not even the bland servants' clothing he wore could hide his royal blood.

Not a messenger. The príncipe himself.

Her mouth went dry. He hadn't come here since...since...

Manners, Azucena! She dropped into a deep curtsy, holding the position. "To what do I owe the honor, Su Alteza?" Once, she would've called him Isidro, no titles necessary. But now...

With his free hand, Isidro took her elbow and gently raised her to her feet. Her breath caught at the tenderness in his warm brown eyes. He thrust the flowers at her. "Here. I know they're your favorite." His words came out rushed, as though he'd been waiting to say them.

"Oh." She stared stupidly at the flowers. This was so very inappropriate—not just the flowers but him being here at all. *You could've just sent your answer and been done with it.*

She stepped back, withdrawing from his hold. His hands fell to his sides, limp and unsure, the flowers a vivid stain against his tan clothing.

"You'd better come in," she said.

He squeezed past. The familiar scents of pine and sweat sent her mind to stolen kisses and whispered promises. Blinking hard, she shut the door. His broad shoulders filled her tiny workshop, making it impossible to put enough space between them, but she tried anyway.

"You weren't followed, were you?" The last thing Isidro needed on the eve of his coronation was rumors of an illicit tryst—particularly not with his crownmaker. *At midnight, no less!*

"Of course not. I'm in disguise."

She held in a snort. "*That's* your disguise? Isi—" She coughed, clearing her throat. "You're still wearing your crown, Su Alteza."

He touched the circlet atop his head—fine, filigree silver in a braided pattern, sans jewels. Azahar had crafted that one long before she took Azucena on as an apprentice.

"Oh," he said in a small, embarrassed voice.

She hid a smile. *Oh, Isidro.* His eyes held hers and softened, and she leaned forward, just slightly.

"*A crownmaker's heart is with her gems.*" Azahar's rasp filled her head, sharper in memory. "*Loyal to the gems above all, always protecting them from those who would use them for harm.*"

Wincing, she hurried toward the workbench. "A messenger could have delivered your response just as easily, Su Alteza, but since you're here..."

"Dios mío!" Isidro rushed to the workbench. Setting the flowers down, he lifted the crown, tracing his fingers along the spun gold and delicate arches. "It's stunning, Azucena. The craftsmanship. The detailing!"

"Gracias, Su Alteza." It was her first crown, and though she knew objectively that it was beautiful, hearing the words from Isidro's lips brought a pleased flush to her cheeks.

"Dare I say it's even better than Azahar's finest work?" he said.

Azucena stiffened.

Isidro's lips parted, then closed. Something flashed across his face—a stab of pain, a twist of regret. "I'm sorry, Azucena." He set the crown back onto its cloth. "I know she meant a great deal to you."

White roses gilding a wooden coffin. Wails and moans as they carried the crownmaker's limp body through the streets. A small, nearly-empty room where Azucena spoke the words that would forever alter her life—the vow of a crownmaker.

Azucena swallowed the lump in her throat. "Gracias, Su Alteza."

He started to reach for her hand, then pulled away. She pushed away the sting, reminding herself that this was right. This was what she had to do.

But his father! Dios, how could he think about her mentor when his father had just passed less than a week ago? "And I'm so sorry about the *rey's* passing," she blurted. "He was too young."

It's because of his gem, her mind whispered. Rey Damián chose aquamarine—courage—and a well-aimed arrow had ended his brazen life.

Now a grieving young ruler was forced to take on his father's throne. No time to process the hole rey Damián had left behind. No time to grieve the loss of his freedom. But such was the way of things.

What if the gem she gave Isidro would result in his death, just as the aquamarine had resulted in rey Damián's?

"Gracias, Azucena," Isidro said, his voice thick.

Do you fear the same fate? she wanted to ask. His family's reign had been short and bloody, taking the throne by coup and then assassination after assassination. Poor Azahar had made many crowns in her brief life. Too many crowns. *Please choose peridot, Isidro.*

Because she'd seen the way his cousin Escarra looked at the throne, even when they were children. He'd never respected Isidro the way he should respect the príncipe, cousin or not. And with him next in line for the throne...

"You haven't answered my note." Azucena winced as the words came out of her mouth. *You're one to accuse him of not answering. How many of his letters have you ignored?*

"Ah, sí." Isidro palmed the back of his neck. "The gem. I am…still deciding."

She groaned. "Your coronation is *tomorrow*, Your Highness. You must make a decision!"

"I'm sorry. I know I'm hindering your work. I just…" A muscle worked in his jaw.

Azucena stifled a sigh. She couldn't blame him for his indecisiveness, not when his reign's success rested on this one choice.

The crown jewels weren't just jewels. Something about the fusion of metal and gem amplified the magic, sent it through the wearer's skin, past marrow straight to dance with the soul. And only she, *the hacedora de coronas*, the crownmaker, could fuse it together.

"Topaz?" she prodded. "Intelligence is certainly an admirable quality. Or aquamarine like your father?"

His mouth tightened in a firm line. "Excessive courage is no blessing."

Azucena swallowed, remembering rey Damián's casket and the wails that followed it. "Then peridot for protection?"

"I won't hide behind my crown."

"That isn't…" She bit her lip hard. How could he be so careless when even now, a jealous conde—Escarra, perhaps—might be planning another coup? When a disgruntled nobleman might seek to have his head on a platter, as had happened to his grandfather?

"An amethyst, perhaps?" Mental clarity had always seemed odd amongst the rest of the gems—inconsequential, somehow *lesser*. Azahar hadn't used them in any of her crowns, nor had her mentor or her mentor's mentor. Azucena wasn't sure why they even kept the amethyst geodes in the gem vault. "Or you could have sunstone for good fortune—"

"Azucena." His soft voice halted hers. "Is it true that there is a cost to your magic?"

She stiffened, her eyes darting back to the crown. The empty setting haunted her, reminding her that for the first time, Azahar would not be the one to bear the curse.

"*You don't want to make more than a few crowns in your lifetime, girl.*" Azahar's words thundered in her mind.

"*Why not?*" She heard herself, young and foolish, drunk at the thought of all the power contained in these jewels.

"*Because each crown costs you.*"

"Oh, Azucena." Isidro moved closer to her—too close. Her traitorous gaze dropped to his lips just for a moment. "I can't ask you to do that. Not for me."

Was this why he hadn't chosen yet? Not because he was indecisive, but because he didn't want to hurt her, even after she'd shut him out?

Her eyes flicked to the carnations. Her favorite flower, as he'd so kindly remembered. Swallowing hard, she forced herself to put space between them. "You are my príncipe, soon to be my rey, Su Alteza. I will do as my position requires." *What my vow requires.*

Silence pulsed between them, thick and heavy. She found herself remembering his kindness—how even as a child, he'd given her his food when he heard her stomach growl or offered her his overcoat when she shivered. How he'd never viewed her as lesser, not even when they grew older and realized they were of different stations, peasant and príncipe.

But that same kindness made him a target among his court. She saw how they looked at him, like he was a calf ready for slaughter, a rey ready to be overthrown. Escarra and his lackey, Alatorre, among others...

Peridot, she thought. *If you won't protect yourself, I will protect you, just as you always protected me.*

"What is the cost, *querida*?"

She stiffened. *Please don't call me that*, she wanted to beg, but a traitorous part of her heart drank in the term of endearment. How could he still care for her when she'd ignored him for months and pretended he wasn't even there, when she'd hurt him so deeply?

"Azucena?"

"The surplus must be taken from somewhere." She stared down at the crown's empty setting. "In giving courage, I would lose some of my own. In giving beauty, I would become plainer. And so on."

He sucked in a breath.

It wasn't that the cost was a secret, exactly. But royalty rarely cared enough to ask—or considered the cost to their crownmaker a hindrance.

"Give me no gem at all, then," Isidro said.

Azucena huffed a laugh. As if the court would ever forgive her for making a mediocre crown. She was meant to bless his reign, not stunt it.

He sighed. "If you must give me a gem, give me the smallest you can find. I won't have a strong rule at the cost of your life."

"It won't cost me my *life*." Though in the end, it had worn Azahar down so greatly she'd withered away.

During her twenty years of service, she'd made four crowns. Premature wrinkles had dug into her skin. Her hair turned silver as moonlight. Her hands became stiff, barely able to fashion the soft gold into circlets. She'd lost courage, beauty, protection, and good fortune. But that was Azahar's vow as *hacedora de coronas*—to put the rey and reina ahead of her own happiness.

That, too, was Azucena's vow. A vow she now regretted.

"Azucena." Isidro stepped closer, almost hesitantly. So near, she could see the flecks of gold in his eyes, the faint stubble marking his chin. She could press a kiss against his scratchy jaw if she just leaned in—

Stop. Don't torture yourself.

But would it be so terrible to give in for one night? Tomorrow, he would be her rey, but tonight...perhaps tonight he could just be Isidro.

He took her hands in his. She tightened her grip involuntarily. His dark eyes were so soft, so desperate. A weakness he could not show in front of his bloodthirsty court.

"I thought it was your grief," he said softly. "I thought that was why you didn't return my letters. But it's because of your vow, isn't it?"

Her lips trembled as she nodded. "Impartiality, so as not to give unduly to one ruler over another. No romantic entanglements, especially not with royalty. Not using the gems for personal gain, whether for myself or the people I...love."

"Oh, *querida*." His hands shook in hers. "I should've thought about that. I'm so sorry. I...I should go."

"Please don't." Warmth pricked behind her eyes. "Not yet."

It was foolish, she knew. But for this one moment out of time, she wanted things to be like they used to be between her and Isidro, before she took her vow, before Azahar found out about their relationship.

"*I won't stop seeing him,*" Azucena had raged. "*We love each other—something you would never understand.*" The last words she'd spoken to her mentor.

She withdrew her hands from Isidro's only to cup his face. He inhaled sharply. His stubble pricked her fingers, and she brushed a stray eyelash away. Anything to forget her harsh words, the pain in Azahar's eyes.

"Azucena." His voice was hoarse. His hands hung limply at his sides instead of circling her waist. "Your vow..."

"*He will be your rey someday, Azucena,*" Azahar once said. "*If you give your heart to him, you might just give him the key to the gem vault. And then you will have doomed us all.*"

But Isidro—good, kind, sweet Isidro—would never misuse the gem vault. He wasn't interested in increasing his beauty or passion or intelligence. He wouldn't force her to use her magic any more than she had to. And it was too late for Azahar's warnings. Her heart had always belonged to Isidro, ever since the thirteen-year-old príncipe stood up to his mother when the reina had disparaged their friendship.

Isidro, in his ridiculous disguise, with his impassioned letters and sweet bouquet, his concern for the toll the magic would take on her—

My love, my only.

She closed the distance between their lips and kissed him. He responded eagerly, hands splayed against her back, deepening the kiss so that he was her oxygen, her anchor. His arms tightened around her, pulling her flush against him. Her hands tangled in his curls, knocking the crown free with a thump. His lips found her neck, and she arched against him, her fingers digging into his shoulders.

"Azucena," he gasped. "I thought...?"

She pressed a kiss to his jaw. His sharp inhale sent a delicious thrill through her veins. "Kiss me, Isidro," she said against his neck. "Just for tonight."

He found her mouth again. They fused together like gem to gold, giving instead of taking, a magic all of its own.

When he departed—it could have been a moment, an hour, a lifetime—he still had not told her what gem he wanted. She did not ask. He did not ask her to rescind her title. She did not ask him to rescind his.

Adjusting her rumpled dress, Azucena shivered. *Don't run after him,* she told herself. She still had a job to do. A crown to finish. There was no more time for kissing royalty. There would never again be time for kissing royalty.

As she touched a hand to her swollen lips, her breath hitched. A whimper. A tear slipping past her eyes' defenses. And then the flood, encompassing every conflicting feeling that swelled inside her chest, finally bursting free.

The night had been beautiful. The night had not been enough.

Once her tears had ceased, Azucena lowered the crown into her satchel. Though the empty setting disappeared beneath the cloth, its reminder throbbed behind her aching temples.

What gem?

It would be hard enough to choose a gem for a ruler she felt nothing for. But this was her beloved. All he'd said was, "You are the one who will bear the cost, so you should choose." She supposed there was a sort of honor to that, but how could he ask her to make this decision? One that would influence the rest of his reign?

She rubbed her swollen eyes, willing them not to leak any more. A glint of silver caught her attention—Isidro's gem-less crown, sitting on her workbench. Right, she'd taken it off while running her hands through his hair. Her face warmed as she tucked it into the satchel, metal clinking against metal. Not that Isidro would need it anymore, but maybe she could return it to him surreptitiously so no one realized it was gone.

Reaching for a clean cloth, she tied it around the back of her head, letting it drape across her mouth and nose. Protection from the gems. She touched the hidden pocket in her dress and felt the solid reassurance of the key to the gem vault.

With a fortifying breath, Azucena left her workshop. The chilly night air seeped underneath her cloth mask. The moon winked down at her, as though reminding her that it had witnessed their passion through her workshop windows.

Her mind whirled as she traversed the dirt path leading from her shop to the gem vault. Not garnet or ruby for Isidro—she couldn't imagine him choosing passion or beauty. No aquamarine either—she could understand why courage would turn his stomach. He hadn't been too keen on peridot, either, unfortunately. That left topaz, sunstone, and amethyst. Intelligence, good fortune, and mental clarity.

Peridot, cried her heart. *Give him protection.*

He hadn't said no to the yellow-green gem. Not in so many words. And if he wanted her to choose a gem for him, why couldn't she choose the one her heart pleaded for? He wouldn't die a horrible, sudden death like his father or grandfather. He'd be *safe*.

But he would never forgive her if she gave up her protection for him. She knew that as deeply as she knew the gems' magic.

"Crownmaker."

Two men in guards' uniforms materialized from the trees. Azucena flinched and hugged her satchel to her chest. Guards patrolling the palace at night? Except...weren't those the uniforms of vault soldiers? Why were they away from the vault?

Her eyes fixed on one guard in particular. That sloping nose. That long, straight hair. Those prominent cheekbones, so reminiscent of Isidro's.

She clutched the satchel tighter. "Escarra! What are you doing here?"

El conde de Escarra—Isidro's cousin—inclined his head to her. "Can't I come see my *hacedora de coronas*?"

The other man laughed, high and refined. El señor de Alatorre, Escarra's lackey. Two nobles dressed in guards' clothing, traversing the road leading to the gem vault on the eve of the coronation?

Peridot for protection, her mind screamed.

"On your way to the gem vault, I think?" Escarra gestured to her cloth covering with long, thin fingers.

"I don't see how that's any of your business." Azucena lowered her head. "Now, if you'll excuse me, I'll be on my way now."

She started to move past them, but Alatorre caught her arm. She recoiled, trying to pull free to no avail. Her pulse pounded in her throat. She'd heard stories about the young lord's penchant for finding women alone.

"I saw you had a visit from my cousin," Escarra drawled.

He'd been watching her cabin? Chills crept down her spine.

She'd never liked Jorge de Escarra. Even as a child, his disdain had settled over her like a stain, making her feel as though she didn't belong at the palace, no matter how many times Isidro told her he wanted her there. To the conde, she was just a charity case, temporary, unimportant, undeserving of the favor she received from the future rey.

When she and Isidro started their secret relationship, she'd felt Escarra's eyes on her, as though he suspected that their close bond as children would blossom into something more. Something forbidden. And he was just waiting for them to slip up and show it so he could take his cousin's crown.

Maybe he *had* known. They'd tried to be discreet, but Isidro, darling boy that he was, was never one for lies.

"The príncipe was simply informing me what gem he required for his crown." She tugged free from Alatorre's grip, able to breathe normally again now that his slimy hands weren't on her.

"Don't lie to me, crownmaker. I saw him leave your cabin. Those swollen lips of his were not the aftermath of 'just talking.'" Escarra's eyes, dark as pitch, lingered on her mask. "I expect you wear the evidence underneath that cloth as well."

Her cheeks darkened, and she turned her face away, suddenly ashamed. How could she have let her emotions get the better of her? This was about more than just her and Isidro. This was about the future of Terrajoya.

She shouldn't have kissed him. Shouldn't have let him in when he came calling. No, he never should've come to her cabin in the first place. He should've just sent a royal messenger and been done with it. They could have been rey and crownmaker, distant and formal. Their feelings would have faded in time.

How could I have been so stupid?

She forced herself to meet Escarra's gaze. "What do you want from me?"

His refined smile was somehow more terrifying than the unhinged visage of a madman. "You will let us into the gem vault, *hacedora de coronas*."

Her mouth fell open. *Of all the things...* "You can't seriously think I would betray my country like that."

"You've already broken your vow." Escarra's eyes flicked to her facial covering again. She flushed. "You can break it again."

"That is entirely different, and you know it." She clenched her jaw. "Isidro will receive a single gem for his crown, just as his predecessors have. I would never show him favoritism. Tonight was just—" Her voice wobbled. "It was a mistake, and it won't happen again."

"*Isidro,*" Escarra drawled. "So informal of you, crownmaker."

Her cheeks darkened further.

"I can't wait to tell the court about this." Alatorre grinned toothily, almost wolf-like. "Can you imagine?"

She'd certainly lose her position, might even face time in the dungeons. Would they execute her? Showing favoritism in her gem care was no light offense—she could enable tyrants and control the fate of regimes.

As for Isidro, his reign would end before it even began. His subjects already thought he was weak. If he was accused of romancing his crownmaker, they would think he'd taken extra gems. Public opinion would turn against him even more. Riots. Accusations. Maybe even a coup, as had happened to his grandfather.

And who would step in to take the throne? His cousin.

But the *gem vault*. It was the sacred place of the crownmaker—a place of deep magic, so much so that she covered her face to keep from ingesting too much. If Escarra and Alatorre controlled the gems inside...

"You want me to make crowns for you," she said.

Escarra shrugged. "Any gem-infused metal would do, but since you have a crown ready for the taking..." His eyes locked onto her satchel. "Let's see the one you've fashioned for Isidro."

"No." Azucena lifted her chin. "You cannot force me to open the vault. I won't do it."

"Not even to save your beloved from public humiliation and coup?" Alatorre stepped closer—too close. His complexion was lighter than Escarra's, more golden than brown, and his features were perfectly symmetrical. A god in human form. A god who took whatever he wanted.

"You would overthrow him no matter what I did," she said.

"*Chica lista,*" Alatorre said.

Then their plan was to overthrow Isidro. She'd been right to worry for his protection.

"If you help us, you can still be crownmaker." Escarra gestured to her satchel. "Doesn't that sound better than rotting in the dungeons?"

Because she was the only *hacedora de coronas*. She hadn't yet found an apprentice, not when Azahar had passed into paradise just six months ago. They needed her alive.

She set her jaw. "I will *never* help you."

Escarra smiled that refined smile again, and she took an involuntary step backward. "I was afraid you'd say that. Mateo, if you don't mind?"

Like a predator released from captivity, Alatorre stalked toward her. His chiseled features twisted into a grin. "Where's the key, crownmaker?"

Her heart slammed against her ribcage. She took another step back. The men matched it with steps forward. She was their crownmaker. They wouldn't dare touch her. Would they?

Dios, what had she gotten herself into?

"Mateo can search you, but I think you'd rather he not," Escarra said pleasantly. "Not that your reputation could fall any further."

She turned and ran. The satchel slammed against her thigh, mimicking the thumping feet behind her. Their gasping breaths grew nearer. A hand caught her arm and nearly dislocated her shoulder. Crying out, she stabilized herself against a tree trunk.

"Where is the key?" Escarra hissed, his face entirely too close to hers. Alatorre reached for her waist. Bile curdled in her stomach. His hand grazed her bodice—

"Wait!" she cried. "I'll show you the vault—if you'll unhand me."

Alatorre pulled his hand back with a disappointed huff.

Escarra smirked. "I thought you might see reason."

You would betray Azahar like this? Betray Terrajoya? But they were going to get the key anyway. They'd open the vault. They'd ruin both her and Isidro no matter what she did. Unless she tried to stop them. Because if there was one thing she knew, it was gems. And gems had power.

She'd already broken her vow. As the conde so aptly said, she might as well break it more.

CROWNS OF CONSEQUENCE

Brooke J. Katz

Crowns of Consequence is a poem that reflects on the consequences of relying on our own strength.

CROWNS OF CONSEQUENCE

BROOKE J. KATZ

A Stately Queen sits upon her throne of emeralds

Hearts filled with envy
Look upon her beauty and youth

Hearts wrapped around her finger
Know not of the truth

She rises they fall
Descending steps of marble

Echos of her foot falls
Fill the endless hall

Appearing before her
Mahogany doors open
What is held beyond
Only she can tell

Pedestals line three walls

On each, a heart that holds a crown

She comes to the heart of envy, taking the crown from upon her royal head; she lays it down
Ignoring the reflection in the mirror behind it.

Moving around the room she lightly brushes
The crown that sits on the heart of greed, briefly turning her finger green.

She stops at the rapidly beating heart of anger.
Placing its crown upon auburn curls

Her reflection morphing in the mirror reveals coal black eyes, fangs for teeth, her fingers bleed
Blood red dripping down the sides of her cheeks—

It's not the time

Placing it back upon its bed

She passes the heart of joy, laughter singing in her soul.

A heart of sorrow,
Its crown a hue of blue,
Her soul aches, her tears don't last.

She rushes past

A heart with a crown for each occasion,
Each one hides its own mask.

She settles in front of an empty heart barely beating

The mirror before her holds a reflection she no longer recognizes

Empty eyes, hollow cheeks, hair of string

A hag

She lost her crown, her crown of identity,
Relying on the crowns for their power.

Reaping their consequences.

THE CROWNMAKER'S CURSE: PART TWO

Cassandra Hamm

Crownmaker Azucena must rely on the power of the royal gems to save herself and Isidro's reign—even if it means going against everything she has sworn to uphold.

THE CROWNMAKER'S CURSE: PART TWO

CASSANDRA HAMM

"IT'S ALREADY THE END OF THE SHIFT?" A vault guard let out a low whistle. "Time sure does fly."

"It sure does," Escarra said in an imitation of a lowborn accent. It was still a bit too crisp, but the guards didn't seem to notice.

How had Escarra and Alatorre gotten guards' uniforms anyway? Bribery? It didn't appear they'd killed anyone for the uniforms since these two men were still alive and well, thank the heavens. But wouldn't the guards recognize these weren't men they'd trained with and fought with? Or were they just that tired?

One of the guards yawned, his eyes half-mast, much too tired to be on shift. Azucena would've yelled at him for his incompetence, but Alatorre had warned her that if she revealed herself to these guards, it would mean their deaths. She didn't doubt he meant the threat.

No need for innocent men to die tonight. Not when the vault was *her* territory.

Tree bark dug into her skin as she peered up at the seemingly-impenetrable fortress, far from the palace grounds. At least her aching shoulder was still functional—*curse you, Alatorre.* Her body hummed with anticipation of the magic inside those stone walls.

I'm sorry, Azahar.

"Oh, by the way, I expect the crownmaker will be stopping by tonight," the first guard said. "I heard the crown's not finished yet. So be on the lookout for her."

"I will," Escarra said.

The guards disappeared down the dirt path. They'd discover their mistake when they got back to the castle—she winced thinking of what the captain of the guard would do to them—but that was at least a twenty-minute walk.

"All right, crownmaker." Escarra turned toward her hiding place. "Time to come out. Please don't try to run. I'm sure Mateo would enjoy chasing you, but timing is of the essence."

For a moment, she thought about running, but the thought of Alatorre's hands on her made her want to retch. So she fished the key from her secret pocket and strode from the trees. She held her chin high even as her lungs threatened to fail her, ignoring Alatorre's hungry gaze.

She fit the key inside the lock and opened the door. The spicy scent of magic filled her nostrils as she stepped inside the dark room. Escarra and Alatorre followed too closely.

The door clicked shut, locking them inside.

Rows upon rows of jewels, organized by type and size, glittered on the shelves. Iridescent rubies, marbled sunstones, glittering aquamarine. Massive amethyst crystals, not yet formed into refined gems, swallowed one corner of the vault, probably because so few royals ever chose the gem.

Escarra muttered something reverent under his breath, while Alatorre stared slack jawed. They wore no cloth over their faces, no protection from the unfettered magic in the cavernous room.

"So this is what you've been hiding." Escarra's luminous gaze swept across the cavern. "So much power in one room."

Only if you know how to use it. She considered the piles. Peridot, definitely. Aquamarine could be helpful, so long as the courage didn't overwhelm her common sense. But after what happened to rey Damián...

The risk is worth it.

"Let's see that crown," Escarra said. "The one you made for the príncipe."

Reluctantly, she pulled the gold crown from the satchel.

The men gasped almost in unison. She thought of Isidro's reaction to the crown, how his words had made her feel, and clung to that instead of the shallow admiration of these slimy *gilipollas*.

"Isidro is not worthy of the crown you made for him," Escarra said reverently. "It is magnificent, crownmaker. When I wear it, Terrajoya will see that I am their true rey."

She wanted to spit on him.

Alatorre scowled at Escarra. "Hey, why don't I get the gold one?"

Escarra ignored his partner. "Begin your work, crownmaker."

"But you haven't told me which gem yet." Her mind whirred. Peridot might not work for her plan, actually. It would help her stay alive, but it wouldn't help her actually stop the nobles.

Escarra scoffed. "Why limit yourself to one?"

Her skin grew cold. He couldn't be saying...

Escarra's lip curled. "The royals haven't dared try more than one gem. They are fools."

She gaped at him. Combining gems just wasn't done. She was pretty sure there was a law against it, actually—not that Escarra or Alatorre cared about laws.

"One of each," Escarra said. "Only the best for my crown."

Her hands shook as she dropped the crown back into the satchel. The mask moved against her mouth with each breath, allowing bits of gem magic to seep through, but it couldn't be helped. "I can't do that."

"You will." Alatorre pulled a knife.

"I mean that I *can't*. Each fusion drains me more and more." No need to go into the details. "If you want a crownmaker, you'll have to keep me alive, won't you?"

Escarra stared at her. Perhaps he'd never considered the fact that crownmakers were rare for more than just the honor of the position.

"She's lying." Alatorre lifted the knife higher.

"No, I don't think so." Escarra scowled. "Fine. Three in one crown, then. Surely you can manage that."

Still such a great cost. "I..." Azucena cleared her throat. "I have never tried, señor. And the setting will only fit one gem."

He waved a hand dismissively. "You'll figure something out. Now, I'll have..." He pursed his lips, looking over each gem. His eyes skimmed over the amethyst pile but lingered on aquamarine.

Maybe if he chose extra courage, she could use it against him. Trick him into exposing himself and then destroy him. Because courage without common sense was just suicide.

Hmm...common sense...

Alatorre reached for a large teal aquamarine. With a yelp, she lurched forward and smacked his hand away. He growled, turning the knife on her.

"You can't touch them." She rubbed her shoulder, trying to ignore the way her heart pounded. *Please put down the knife.*

"Why not?" Alatorre sneered.

"Because gems in their raw form are dangerous." Why had she tried to protect him? He'd done nothing but hurt her.

"Liar." Alatorre lowered the knife and grabbed a handful of aquamarines. A screech tore from his throat. Jewels spilled across the floor like an ocean wave, ranging in shades from dark blue to almost-green. He cradled his hand to his chest, revealing a palm marked with swelling white blisters.

She winced. *Well, he certainly doesn't need any more aquamarine.* Her mind returned to the thought that had been niggling at her. *Courage and common sense combined...*

Escarra curled his lip at Alatorre. "*Gilipollas.*"

She looked around at the rainbow array of gems. *Common sense...*

Escarra's words pulled her from her thoughts. "I'll have sunstone, ruby, and peridot."

His choosing peridot would make things harder if she had to follow through with the crowns. She hoped it wouldn't come to that.

Alatorre's lips flattened. "And I'll have aquamarine, garnet, and—"

"You just get one," Escarra interrupted.

Alatorre's face flushed. "Why don't I get more?"

"Because we can't wear out the crownmaker."

Azucena's eyes flicked to the amethyst crystals, their geometric spikes and unused potential. *Mental clarity.* And then it came to her, the thought that had been eluding her. *Common sense. Amethyst.*

What if combining amethyst with aquamarine was enough to outweigh the dangers of unchecked courage?

"You think I'm not worth more gems?" Alatorre's voice pitched low and aggressive. "What, are you planning to get rid of me afterward?"

"Why would I do that?"

Azucena could hear the smile in Escarra's voice. Shivering, she started toward her workstation.

"What are you doing?" Alatorre snapped.

"Getting my equipment." She grabbed a pair of tongs. "So I won't burn myself like you did."

Alatorre's face turned almost ruby-red. Escarra barked out a laugh, then covered his mouth.

"Aquamarine, then." Alatorre sulked.

She walked over to the shelf lined with ocean-colored stones and searched for a smaller one. *I certainly will need courage to do what I'm about to do.* She reached out the tongs and closed them around a cerulean specimen.

"That's not big enough," Alatorre complained.

"You don't need more courage," Escarra said. "It'll addle your brain. Now that I think of it, maybe you should have topaz. You could use more intelligence."

Azucena coughed to hide her snort.

"How dare you?" Alatorre snarled.

Azucena dropped the aquamarine into her satchel, then glanced at the amethyst geode. Maybe they'd be too distracted to notice if she grabbed one—

Escarra turned back to her. "Do mine first. Peridot, if you please."

Her jaw clenched. She couldn't use the aquamarine yet. She hadn't grabbed any amethyst. Cursing her stupidity, she grabbed a medium-sized yellow-green gem.

"I want to see the fusion process." Escarra's grin turned feral. "Show it to me."

She should've used their distraction to grab what she needed. But one gem fusion wouldn't be a problem. She hoped. As long as the conde didn't actually wear the crown.

She settled down at her workstation and pulled out the golden crown. Isidro's crown. Swallowing hard, she used the tongs to lift the peridot and placed it in the empty setting. Though the gem was a little too small, it'd fit once she used her magic.

"Well?" Escarra stared at her expectantly.

Azucena set her hand on the crown, right around the setting. The peridot's magic throbbed just next to her fingertips, not quite close enough to burn. She closed her eyes.

Azahar's words filled her mind: "*Imagine the gem and metal becoming one. The gem will obey, though the metal will resist. The gem will always win.*"

She thought of that glaring, empty setting, sad and hollow. She thought of the jagged, uncut mass of yellow-green, like sun-dried grass. She thought of the gold and green combining into a beautiful, glistening surface.

Despite the gold's softness, she felt its reluctance. The metal pushed against her, but she pushed back, thinking, *Become one.* The gem filled the space of the setting like a liquid, settling into its new home. But the metal still kept itself separate.

Trust me, she thought to the gold. *I know change is scary, but this will make you whole.*

Slowly, the gold yielded. The peridot welded to its surface and seeped further inside—power whispering through the golden braids, filling every piece of it. Something tugged on her—the peridot, grabbing her strength and filling the gold with it. She gasped, sagging against the back of her chair. She couldn't pull her hand away. The peridot just wouldn't let go.

"Crownmaker?" Escarra's voice jerked her from her stupor.

She yanked her hand back. Immediately, the drain dissipated.

Shaking, Azucena cradled her hand to her chest. If Escarra hadn't interrupted, would the peridot have taken everything from her—every last bit of protection she had so the slightest hint of a threat would claim her life? *I have to be more careful.*

"Did it work?" Alatorre demanded.

Escarra ran his finger along the golden spikes with a low whistle. "It even feels stronger."

She resisted the urge to yank the crown away from his grasping hands. The center sparkled with a beautifully-faceted yellow-green gem. A perfect peridot.

She tottered to her shaking legs, steadying herself against the chair. She couldn't do any more fusions tonight. She'd have to get that amethyst no matter what it took.

"Let me try it on," Alatorre whined.

"No!" Escarra held the crown protectively to his chest.

Satchel still slung over her shoulder, Azucena crept across the room. Sunstone resided next to the amethyst geodes, so she hoped if they noticed her passage, they wouldn't realize what she was doing until it was too late.

The tongs! She'd forgotten them on her workbench. Swearing under her breath, she kept going.

She edged past the sunstone pile and reached toward the amethyst geode. She yanked on a protruding crystal. It burned white-hot against the pads of her fingers, and she couldn't help the yelp that escaped her lips. She hadn't felt that pain since she was a young, foolish apprentice, ignoring Azahar's warnings just as Alatorre had ignored hers.

"Crownmaker!"

Escarra's startled exclamation boomed in her ears. She noticed everything—the skittering of a roach's legs against the stone, the soft *drip drip drip* from the ceiling, Alatorre's grunt as he launched himself in her direction. Mental clarity at work. Then she reached into the satchel with her other hand and grasped the smooth aquamarine.

Fire scalded her palms, but she drank it in, letting the power seep into her skin, her very veins. The pain distilled throughout her body, like tiny sparks stinging her various limbs, pinpricks of danger. But she was ready for the danger.

Escarra said something, but she couldn't hear him. Blood rushed in her ears, amplifying her heartbeat crashing in her chest, her lungs pushing air in and out of her body.

She was the crownmaker. She didn't need metal to channel the gems' magic. She was a living conduit.

Silver flashed—Alatorre's knife. She darted to the side, easily avoiding his clumsy, left-handed strike. She heard the intake of breath from behind and lunged away from Escarra's tackle. Her fist—the one holding the amethyst—smashed into Alatorre's perfect nose, crunching bone. His mouth opened in a gaping wail. She felt her stinging fist distantly, like it belonged to someone else.

Scrape. A foot moving. She whipped around. Escarra lunged for her, shouting something. *No time to run.* She shifted her grip on the amethyst so she was holding it in her blistered fingers and shoved it at Escarra's face. The crystal connected with flesh and sizzled. Howling, he stumbled backward. But she lost her grip on the crystal, and it clattered to the stone floor.

The aquamarine took control of her mind. It crashed over her like a wave, fierce and compelling—a complete, utter lack of fear. How could anything touch her? She was in *her* domain among *her* gems. She was unstoppable.

No, she was missing something. Something that would help her win this battle. But how could she need anything but the aquamarine clutched in her fist?

Azucena scanned her foes. Alatorre held a hand to his nose and shouted garbled obscenities. Escarra stumbled toward the work-bench.

Threat.

She raced toward him, boots pounding the stone. The cloth fell away from her mouth. Gem dust filled her nostrils—let it come. She was the *crownmaker.* One thought repeated: *I will stop him if it is the last thing I do.*

Escarra lifted the crown to his head. It settled onto his silky dark hair. His eyes rolled back in his head as the magic seared through him, filling him with the strength she'd sacrificed.

Rage filled her, as hot as the pain in her hands. How dare he take her protection and use it for himself! Fists swinging, she threw herself at him, but he sidestepped and captured her arms from behind.

The aquamarine fell from her grasp. She gasped, her ears popping. The fierce, unstoppable feeling fell away.

She sucked in a breath. *That* was what she'd been missing. The mental clarity of amethyst. And now she'd lost.

Alatorre stalked toward them, blood smearing his mouth and jaw. "I'll kill her."

"Would you be quiet?" Escarra scowled.

"Jorge, you're wearing the crown!" Alatorre practically devoured the circlet with his greedy gaze. "Fine, I'll kill her *after* she puts aquamarine in my crown—"

"You don't need a crown," Escarra said slowly.

Alatorre's eyes bulged. "Is this you trying to cut me out of the deal? It's not going to work. I'll—"

"No, no." Escarra tightened his grip on Azucena's arms. She cried out as her shoulders bent in ways they weren't supposed to. "You weren't trying to save Mateo, were you, crownmaker? You were trying to stop him from wielding this power!"

She blinked hard, trying to think past the pain in her shoulders and her hands. What was he referring to? *When Alatorre burned himself.* "No, that's not—"

"All this time, we could wield gems, yet you reserved them for royalty?" Escarra spun her around to face him. His eyes blazed as he gripped her wrists like shackles. "You held them in your hands. You channeled their power."

"I—" How could she explain that only crownmakers could? That she'd had extensive training and exposure to the gems? She could resist them. She could wield them—at least, when she was masked and protected.

It was what I had to do. She didn't regret it. She only regretted failing. *I'm sorry, Isidro.*

"You're saying she held the gems?" Alatorre sputtered. "But—they burned me! Why didn't they burn her?"

"Oh, they did." Escarra twisted her hands so her palms flipped upward. The skin was red and raw, starting to blister. She whimpered. "But not like she'd have you believe. She's trying to keep it all for herself."

"I'm not—"

"You see those gems?" Escarra nodded at the walls. "Everything you see over there is a raw form of magic. The true magic. Not like this metal-mediated magic. This *farce.*"

"You can't hold the gems." Her voice pitched high. "Please, just let me explain—"

Alatorre's hand cracked against her cheek. She bit her tongue hard and gasped, tasting blood.

"We've had enough of your lies," Alatorre said.

Escarra shoved her to the ground. She caught herself on her hands and screamed as gravel scraped her palms. Tears filled her eyes.

"We don't need you, crownmaker," Escarra said. "We never did."

She looked up through tear-blurred vision as he walked toward the shelves and took a massive ruby in his palm. He grunted but otherwise showed no pain. A red glow slid across his skin, reworking it until only perfection remained.

She gazed up at him in wonder. He was too beautiful to be real—skin the warm golden brown of a sunset, eyes rich and deep as soft, loamy earth, hair spilling over his shoulders like a waterfall. She stared at him wonderingly.

A thought intruded—messy curls. A shy quirk of a smile. Soft hands taking hers. *Isidro.*

She blinked hard and looked at the ground. A tiny violet crystal winked up at her, forgotten, its magic nearly spent.

Her fingers closed around it. Her scattered mind whirred to a halt, the unimportant pieces falling away.

Escarra. The gems. The crown.

She pushed herself to her feet. As long as Escarra wore that crown, he'd be able to channel gems with little consequence. She couldn't let that happen. She had to get that crown.

She ran toward him, her boots pounding. He met her gaze with his dark, silken eyes, and she faltered, as though she were running through molasses. She blinked, and the illusion cracked, showing the real conde beneath—not superhumanly beautiful but ugly in spirit.

She knocked the crown from Escarra's head. It clattered against the stone floor with a *crack*.

Escarra screamed. A black stain spidered from his palm to his wrist, up his arm—the side effect of holding a gem too long for anyone who wasn't a crownmaker. Alatorre shouted something behind her, but she couldn't focus on anything except Escarra's desperate cries as he held onto the ruby that was slowly killing him.

A blade thrust through her side, pushing deeper, cutting through muscle. She cried out, dropping the amethyst. Alatorre's knife had found its mark.

Aquamarine for courage, she thought. But maybe she didn't need a gem for this.

She ripped the blade from her skin with a muffled scream and slashed out, catching Alatorre in the chest. He stumbled back, holding a hand against his skin. It didn't look like she'd cut him too deeply, but she hissed, holding the knife out.

Escarra let out one final scream and collapsed, his entire body mottled black, muscles shriveled. Magic burst from his body, liquefying the nearby crown, leaving only melted gold and a cracked peridot.

Alatorre let out a horrified screech and threw open the gem vault door. It clicked shut behind him.

Azucena blinked hard. The knife clattered to the ground with a dull *thud*. She sank to her knees, her blistered hand pressing to her side and coming away slick with blood.

Wait for me, she thought. *Don't leave me here. Not with...* Her unfocused eyes slid to Escarra. Her stomach twisted, and she dry heaved, her body wracked with pain.

She didn't know how long she lay on the stone floor, shivering. Through the fog, a pounding—*thumpthumpthumpthumpthump*, like her heartbeat but much faster. She barely opened her eyes. Shadows shifted and twisted around her. The gems throbbed in her vision, each color swimming together.

Wake up, she told herself. *Open the door.*

She tried to crawl, but her arms gave out. She shivered.

"Azucena?" The shout penetrated the heavy door just barely. It was a familiar voice, a beautiful voice, low and desperate. Isidro's voice.

Her limbs allowed one last burst of energy, and she reached the door on hands and knees. She grasped the handle and pulled herself up inch by inch. The door swung inward, knocking her backward, as though someone had been yanking on the handle and pushing forward while she was pulling the handle.

"I've got you, Azucena," Isidro said, scooping her into his arms. She blinked hard, his face swimming before her eyes. Then she knew no more.

Azucena awoke to a throbbing pain in her side.

She blinked hard, trying to process her surroundings. A tray by her bedside. Unfamiliar sheets. A small room, simply furnished but well-kept.

A woman in healer's garb gasped and rushed toward her. "You're awake, crownmaker!"

Azucena blinked groggily. She opened her mouth to speak but couldn't force words through her dry throat.

The healer offered her a cup of water from the table by Azucena's bedside. The lukewarm liquid slid down Azucena's eager throat, and she gulped it down like the sweetest juice.

"I'll let the príncipe know you're awake," the healer said.

Azucena barely had time to process that sentence before the healer bustled off. Azucena took another sip, trying to remember what had happened. *The gem vault. The nobles. The knife.*

She gasped, dropping the cup. It shattered, spilling leftover water onto the floor.

"Azucena!" Isidro ran toward her, kneeling by her bedside. Dark circles rimmed his haunted eyes. He was so much more beautiful than Escarra had ever been, even with the ruby. "Oh, *querida*, you're all right! I thought—"

"Isidro," she whispered.

He took her face in his gentle hands, despite the others in the room. "I should've been there. I should've—"

"You couldn't have known they'd target me to get to you." She shoved away the mental image of Escarra's blackened body. "Alatorre was part of it too—"

"I know. I saw him leaving the gem vault covered in blood," Isidro said. "Suspicious circumstances, to say the least. He's in the dungeons as we speak."

She exhaled. For now, at least, Isidro was safe. His attempted usurpers would answer for their crimes—though Escarra already had.

"How did you find me?" she asked.

"When the guards came back from the vault claiming dismissal, the captain alerted me. We came as quickly as we could." He shook his head. "I shouldn't have left you. Should've given you guards. Should've known someone would target you—"

"It's all right, Isidro," she said. "I'm all right."

He stroked her jaw as though trying to make sure she was real. She leaned into his touch.

"What happened, Azucena? Did they hurt you?"

"No," she said, though maybe that wasn't entirely true. "But Isidro…I had to use the gems." Blinking back tears, she showed him her palms.

He gasped, releasing her face to cradle the back of her hands in his. "Oh, Azucena."

"I felt that it was the only way to keep them from carrying out their plans." Her voice dropped to a whisper. "I know I have broken my vow in all its facets. Taking them into the vault, using the gems for my own power, being with you..."

His breath shuddered, as though he was trying not to fall apart. She bit her lip.

"You did it to save me," he said quietly.

She nodded. "And I know I must be held accountable for it."

He didn't speak for a long time. She could see the war raging in his eyes.

"I can no longer be your *hacedora de coronas*," she said, and those words were somehow both a stabbing pain and a burden lifted. "I've tasted the gems' magic. I'm no longer impartial."

"But..."

"I can't, Isidro." Not after she'd tasted that power and gone against everything Azahar had taught her. Not after she'd seen that ruby burn Escarra alive. "It's all right. I made my choice. Now the court will decide my fate."

"I wish..." His voice cracked. Her heart cracked with it. "I wish I could spare you from that."

Please don't. She'd done all this to ensure he would become rey. He couldn't throw that away now by abusing his power to help her. "I am happy to sacrifice for my country," she said. "For my rey." But how she would miss the gems.

"Will you train a new crownmaker?" Isidro asked.

"I will." She could think of several possible candidates. They'd be able to handle the pressure, probably much better than her. "They can make your new crown."

"I guess I'll just have to wear my old one for now." His smile was weak. "If you still have it."

She barked out a hoarse laugh. "Oh, yes. I think it's still in the satchel I left at the vault." She wished he wouldn't have to wait for his gem, but she supposed he hadn't even wanted a gem in the first place.

His gaze shifted to her mouth, then back to her eyes. She swallowed hard.

"The court will never accept us together," Azucena whispered.

"I'll find a way, *querida*." He pressed a feather-light kiss to the inside of her wrist, just past the burns. She shivered. "If they understood why you did what you did—"

"It won't work. I was your crownmaker."

"That doesn't mean I can't try." He held her gaze. "I won't stop fighting for us, Azucena. For you."

Blinking back tears, she reached up and pressed a kiss to his lips. "I know," she said.

Maybe she should feel regret. Loss. Despair. But she couldn't regret saving his reign.

"You will be a wonderful rey, Isidro," she said. "But when you do get your new crown..." She smiled through her tears. "Decide what gem you want *before* the night of your coronation."

He choked on a laugh. "I deserve that. But...if you were to choose my gem..." His eyes were soft, vulnerable. "What would you pick? Since you know the gems best."

She stared at him. Hours earlier, she would've said peridot. But now... "Amethyst."

He blinked. "*Amethyst?* But..."

"It's more useful than you'd realize," she said.

He gazed at her, as though trying to decipher all she wasn't saying. She'd tell him eventually, if she ever got to speak to him again after this. But for now, she drank in his presence, his kindness, his sweetness.

He kissed the back of her hand. “Amethyst it is.”

NEW LIFE IN OLD PLACES

Benjamin Cromey

Cherry blossoms sit in the foreground while Himeji Castle, one of Japan's finest surviving castles from the 1300's in Himeji, Japan, sits in the background. The photo was taken in the peak of cherry blossom season in April, 2019.

ABOUT THE AUTHORS

ABOUT THE EDITORS:

BRITTANY EDEN has the heart of a poet and sees the world through rose-tinted glasses. She loves a good K-drama, tea, and finds joy in the simplest of things. When not swooning over the romance in yet another fairy tale (BCC: "ARRG they're KISSING AGAIN"), she can be found hiding in the office under the stairs of her cold northern home with a giant mug of tea (love of teapots being one of the tenants of her loyal friendship with Brigitte), listening to Ludovico Einaudi, and crafting love stories of her own. You can find her @brittanyedenauthor or www.brittanyeden.com.

BRIGITTE CROMEY speaks fluent sarcasm, includes way too much action in her books, and is still baffled by romance. If she's not cuddling cacti or listening to scifantasy music (ie: video game soundtracks), she's cooking hobbit food while pretending not to love the characters in the shows Brittany forces her to watch. (Brit: "HaVe YoU SEeN AlcHeMY of SoULs YEt?!") Her pragmatism is the perfect balance to Brittany's starry-eyed poet's heart, yet she refuses to let a story end without hope. You can find her @yarrowleafauthor or www.wordsinmyblood.com.

ABOUT THE CONTRIBUTORS:

One of the first purely creative shoots SHANNON ALLDREDGE did after closing her business was a styled shoot entitled, "Mirror Mirror". Several images from that shoot got published in photography magazines. She couldn't believe the "success" she had in photography after quitting the industry in a professional capacity. Never underestimate God's plan for you, it's always going to turn out better than anything you thought of yourself! You can find her at www.artistsadesigns.wordpress.com.

SARA ANDERSON has a Bachelor's Degree in Elementary Education. She is a mother to four adorable kiddos and has a fierce love of stories. She's from Arizona, where they claim two seasons—boiling hot summers and mildly cold winters. Because of this, she and her husband love visiting places with bright fall colors. You can find her @authorsara_anderson.

C. ASH is a Graphic Designer/Illustrator who writes YA books with her remaining creative juices. She lives in Texas, where you can find her collecting vintage books, playing dramatic classical piano, and losing board games with her family. She survives mainly on Italian food and mochas. You can find her @imaginationcandy.

KRISTEN BAZEN is a recovering perfectionist who never outgrew her love for horses and is fascinated by all things Middle Eastern. She writes YA fantasy that focuses on themes of deep transformation, fierce hope, and beauty in the midst of brokenness. Her short stories are featured in anthologies *The Willow Tree Swing* and *Wither and Bloom*, and her poetry is published in *The Heights We'll Fly To* and *Masquerade*. When she's not wrestling words or running her photography business, Kristen dabbles in languages, trains in martial arts, and raises awareness on how ordinary people can fight human trafficking. You can find her @kristen_thewriteending or www.kristenbazen.com.

HOPE BOLINGER is an acquisitions editor and the author of 30 books. When she isn't accidentally writing a book in a week, she likes to do local theater and get lost in Ohio's hiking trails. You can find her @hopekbolinger or www.hopebolinger.com.

Arizona transplant KAITLYN CARTER BROWN decorates cakes by day, writes by night, and drinks plenty of coffee while tending her army of houseplants in between. When not crafting adventures for the undaunted and unafraid, she can be found seeking inspiration while camping and trekking through our National Parks. You can find her @mrscarter_theauthor or https://www.kaitlyncarterbrownauthor.com/.

Realm Award winner HANNAH CARTER wakes every day hoping to find that she's secretly a mermaid. Her debut YA fantasy novel, *Depths of Atlantis*, is out now through SnowRidge Press, and her short stories and flash fiction pieces have been published in various anthologies. In her spare time, she's probably cuddling her cats, drinking tea, listening to an absurd amount of Taylor Swift, or practicing for her imaginary Broadway debut. You can find her @mermaidhannahwrites.

ANNEE CLARK is a young aspiring author who enjoys all things fantasy. From reading and writing about fantastical creatures, heroes, and villains, to entertaining children's parties as their favorite fairytale characters, Annee enjoys immersing herself in the whimsical plane of imagination. She (very sheepishly and with slight embarrassment) posts her short stories to Tumblr @watercolorfreckles.

AMELIA E. CLAWFORD is a young adult writer with a passion for any genre that happens to strike her fancy at the moment. She writes to feel things, and to share those feelings with other people. As a Christian writer, she also hopes to bring glory to her Creator by using the talents He has given her. You can find her @amelia.procrastiwrites and @amelias.little.library.

BENJAMIN CROMEY likes photography and the science of how it works enough that he got a PhD in optical sciences/engineering. While he makes space telescope cameras professionally, he still enjoys terrestrial photography of exciting places and the people he cares about. He lives in Colorado with his wonderful wife and son, and enjoys escaping to the outdoors all around the world. You can find him at www.benjamincromey.wixsite.com/cromeyphotography.

SARAH HARMON is a writer, editor, photographer, and tutor. She splits her time between Washington, DC and Paris, France, but (like a real world version of Carmen Sandiego) may be spotted wearing a red hat and dress pretty much anywhere across Europe.

Her only child is a black cat named Evil, who loves books as much as her mama but hates almost all people. When she's not writing, Sarah is taking part in crazy adventures, such as ax throwing, dancing on the banks of the Seine, or getting horrendously sunburned at the Acropolis.

ABIGAIL FALANGA writes fantasy and science fiction (and is possibly some kind of fae creature), living in New Mexico with family, books, and wild ambitions. She's released many flash fictions, short stories, a novel, co-edits the Whitstead Anthologies, and plans to fill libraries with more writing. You can find her @abigailfalangaauthor.

KATIE FITZGERALD is a children's librarian turned stay-at-home, homeschooling mom. She lives in Maryland with her librarian husband, four daughters, and one son. Her short fiction has appeared online at Spark Flash Fiction and Havok Publishing and in print in *Wither and Bloom* (Twenty Hills Publishing, 2023) and *Of Ink and Paper* (Nightshade Publishing, 2023). When she's not writing humor or romance, she's usually listening to an audiobook at triple speed or buying used paperbacks to add to her to-be-read pile. You can find her @read.at.home.mom or www.katiefitzgeraldwrites.blogspot.com.

YAKIRA GOLDSBERRY started writing at the age of eight, when she first discovered the power of words. She has since then buried herself in the magical worlds of fiction—and has yet to return. She is the author of the *Tales of Faerie Land* series and has several short stories published in online magazines and anthologies. When not writing, she can be found feeding feral librarians, reading, or attempting to learn foreign languages. Her one mission in life—set the world afire with truth. You can find her @yakiragoldsberry or www.yakiragoldsberry.wordpress.com.

AVA LAUREN GRAYSON is a fairytale novelist, screenwriter, and director based in Los Angeles. With a portfolio of clean and faith-based fantasy and historical fiction YA books, screenplays, and short stories, Grayson has published four flash fiction stories with Havok Publishing and is a Junior Editor at Quill & Flame Publishing House. If Grayson is not writing, you can probably find her directing a film or rewatching *Lord of the Rings*. You can find her @avalaurengrayson or www.avalaurengrayson.com.

Award-winning author J. M. HACKMAN loves thunderstorms, bookstores, and happy endings. She's written *Spark*, *Flare*, and *Burn* (her YA fantasy series *The Firebrand Chronicles*) and has had her stories published in the anthologies *Encircled*, *Tales of Ever After*, *Mythical Doorways*, and *Realmscapes*. You can find her @jm_hackman_author or www.jmhackman.com.

CASSANDRA HAMM is an art collector, jigsaw puzzler, and cat lady who spends most of her time lost in another realm. Her award-winning work appears in various anthologies such as *Warriors Against the Storm* and *Fantasea*, and she served as editor-in-chief for the charity anthology *The Sun Still Rises.* A mental health advocate with a passion for social justice, she writes about shattered girls finding their way in the world. You can find her @cassandrahammwrites or www.cassandrahamm.com.

ANNE J. HILL is an author who enjoys writing fantasy for all ages. She runs Twenty Hills Publishing with the help of her circus performing best friend, Lara E. Madden. She spends her days dreaming up fantastical realms, researching ways to get away with murder (for writing!), arguing over commas at the kitchen table, talking out loud to the characters in her head, promising her housemate that she isn't, in fact, crazy, and rearranging her personal library—affectionately dubbed the "Book Dungeon." You can find her @anne.j.hill.editing or www.annejhill.com.

HAILEY HUNTINGTON is a speculative fiction author, penning tales of wonder, hope, and heroes, with a dash of wit. Her stories can be found online and in various print anthologies. You can find her @haileyhuntingtonauthor or www.haileyhuntington.com.

S. M. JAKE is a sinner saved by the mercy of Jesus. She draws writing inspiration from fairy tales and tall tales, taking every opportunity to add a dad-joke or sweet, awkward romance. Her other favorite things include her husband and two boys, singing at church, spotty gardening, and chaos sewing clothing on ridiculous deadlines. You can find her @s.m.jake or www.smjake.com.

ABBY JOHANSEN can usually be found obsessively studying, organizing, reading, writing, cleaning, and people-watching. As a first responder, psychology geek, slight conspiracy theorist, and all-around nerd, she powers her tales with pieces pulled from the broken world around her. And the best part of all? Beneath all the brokenness is a little bit of beauty, just waiting to be revealed. You can find her @abbyjohansenauthor.

BROOKE J. KATZ is a stay at home/homeschooling mom by day and aspiring author by night. She loves Jesus, homemade lattes, and Lyons tea. Her passions are writing, painting, and supporting and encouraging others in their creativity and life. She spends her free time reading, and always has a book on her. You can find her @Brookejkatz or www.brookejkatz.wixsite.com/brookejkatz.

AMBER KIRKPATRICK enjoys exploring different genres and writing styles. Her short stories can be found in various anthologies and occasionally she writes poetry. She released her debut kingdom fantasy, *Until the Rising*, in May 2023, and urban fantasy *Unleashed* (Quill & Flame Publishers) in November 2023. Amber lives in the Texas Hill Country, and when not writing, homeschools her three wildlings. You can find her @amber.kirkpatrick .writer or www.amberkirkpatrick.com.

LIZ KOETSIER is a Christian fantasy author who writes stories about fearful characters becoming brave, and finding freedom in imaginative worlds. The weirder the world, the better. She lives with her cat and plants in Michigan and loves that feeling of invincibility you get from long, golden-hour summer evenings. You can find her @ink.lizard or www.lizkoetsier.com.

RUTH LUMPKIN is a teen who created her digital art freehand based on the royal theme and submitted to this anthology at the encouragement of her creative writing teacher.

MARIE LYNCH is an avid reader, procrastinating writer, photography dabbler, and daily dreamer. She enjoys all things creative and nature related, and has been imagining fairytale lands as far back as she can remember. She tries to find joy in everything, and desires to find ways to use her creativity to bring glory to God. You can find her @galvanized_reading_potato.

MEGAN MILES began writing at nine years old, and it grew into an unstoppable habit that has filled her free time and her dreams ever since. While most of her works-in-progress are Christian historical novels, she enjoys dabbling in other genres and styles. Her first published work, *Gumbo to Die For*, was published by Spark Flash Fiction. When she isn't writing or working, she can be found reading, sewing, or playing with her dog. You can find her @mmiles.author.

ROBIN RAKKEBY grew up in the sand and surf of San Diego, California. When it became clear she could not, in fact, become a mermaid, she contented herself with exploring far off lands through books. She's particularly fond of exploring themes of healing, resilience, and what it means to find home. Robin currently lives in Georgia, where she works as a PhD Physiology student researching the neural mechanisms of prosthetics. You can find her @aspoonfuloflanguage.

DANIELLE ROBERTSON writes character-driven novels and short stories. Her work has appeared in the print anthology *The 12 Days of Book-Club-Mas* (Volume 4) for Once Upon a Book Club, as well as in online publications including Breadcrumbs Magazine and Storychord. She lives in New Jersey with her husband, her daughter, and many overstuffed bookshelves. You can find her @danjvrobertson or www.daniellerobertson.net.

AJ SKELLY is an author, reader, and lover of all things fantasy, medieval, and fairy-tale-romance. And werewolves. She has a serious soft spot for them. As an avid life-long reader and a former high school English teacher, she's always been fascinated with the written word. She lives with her husband, children, and many imaginary friends who often find their way into her stories. They all drink copious amounts of tea together and stay up reading far later than they should. You can find her @a.j.skelly or www.ajskelly.com.

Milton Keynes UK
Ingram Content Group UK Ltd.
UKHW012212221123
433098UK00011B/183/J

9 798868 968754